Tangle of Matter & Ghost

Leonard Cohen's Post-Secular Songbook of Mysticism(s) Jewish & Beyond

New Perspectives in Post-Rabbinic Judaism

Series Editor—SHAUL MAGID (Indiana University)

TANGLE OF MATTER & GHOST

Leonard Cohen's Post-Secular Songbook of Mysticism(s) Jewish & Beyond

Aubrey L. Glazer

Boston • 2017

Library of Congress Cataloging-in-Publication Data

Names: Glazer, Aubrey L.
Title: Tangle of matter & ghost : Leonard Cohen's post-secular songbook of mysticism(s) Jewish & beyond / Aubrey L. Glazer.
Description: Brighton, MA : Academic Studies Press, 2016. | Series: New perspectives in post-rabbinic Judaism | Includes bibliographical references and index.
Identifiers: LCCN 2016056308 (print) | LCCN 2016056861 (ebook) | ISBN 9781618115492 (hardcover) | ISBN 9781618115508 (e-book)
Subjects: LCSH: Cohen, Leonard, 1934-2016—Criticism and interpretation. | Cohen, Leonard, 1934-2016—Religion. | Popular music—Religious aspects—Judaism. | Mysticism—Judaism. | Mysticism in music. | Jews—Canada.
Classification: LCC ML410.C734 G53 2016 (print) | LCC ML410.C734 (ebook) | DDC 782.42164092--dc23
LC record available at https://lccn.loc.gov/2016056308

ISBN 9781618115492 (hardcover)
ISBN 9781618115508 (e-book)
ISBN 9781618115812 (paperback)

On the cover: CBS/Sony Inc.
Leonard Cohen with Ichigaya-Tamachi, Shinjuku-ku. Tokyo, Japan.
Courtesy of the Leonard Cohen Archives, University of Toronto.

Cover design by Ivan Grave

Published by Academic Studies Press in 2017
28 Montfern Avenue
Brighton, MA 02135, USA
press@academicstudiespress.com
www.academicstudiespress.com

Dedicated to:
Talya Sahara *(leBeit Nuriah)*

Keep dancing my gypsy girl
in your rags of light…

In memoriam:
Leonard Norman Cohen, CC GOQ
(September 21, 1934-November 7, 2016)

You heard that secret chord
That pleased the Lord
Our minor falls, you played into a major lift
Redeeming the lost princess of Hallelujah!

אליעזר בן ניסן הכהן ומאשא
(י"ד בכסלו, תרצ"ה—ו' במרחשון, תשע"ז)
ת.נ.צ.ב.ה.

Table of Contents

Acknowledgements

This book wrote itself—*almost.* The inspiration for this book came in waves. In truth, it started with an archaeology of self and coming to the realization that my early attraction to Leonard Cohen's song, "Who by Fire" changed the course of my path forever. Then through decades of *sprache-denken* with Elliot Wolfson—his deep listening, constant encouragement (including a generous invitation to deliver the first lecture from this book at his UC Santa Barbara Religious Studies Faculty colloquium) and his willingness to provide the postface of this book—I came to appreciate that my passion for Cohen's lyrics was worthy of analysis like the mystical texts we studied together. Finally, my gratitude to George Mordecai for two decades of friendship in song that he continues to bring to life on the path. Thanks to Zachary Braiterman and David Koffman for their insightful critiques that lead to a more cohesiveness throughout the book. And special thanks to Shaul Magid, who has always been there to listen, reflect, and work through the thicket of thinking together, especially in his willingness to be the "midwife to thinking" for this truly strange book, which features his helpful preface a debt of thanks to Marty Cohen, editor of Merarah Matrix for lighting a spark!

I am also grateful to Congregation Beth Sholom, San Francisco, my new communal homestead, for supporting my ritual artistry and understanding the need for balance between the synagogue as a laboratory and scholarship retreat. A few Canadian ex-pats around the homestead are always welcome, so my thanks to Angie Dalfen, as well as Jeremy and Ariella Toeman for keeping Montréal alive as one of my traveling homelands. The trilingual *Canadian Haggadah Canadienne* first came to my attention immediately after the Toeman family experimented with it on Passover 5775 (2015). Thanks to the Toeman family for rapidly lending me a family copy! Special thanks to Noa Storz-Andrews for lending her copy-editing skills to an early draft of this book as well as her insightful suggestions on structure and overall coherence of my argument as well.

Place and its *(dis)placement* have marked much of this book, so thanks to the following caring souls who nurtured me with the space and time of a writing retreat: Dara Nachmanoff and Glenn Chertan in Guerneville, California; David and Pauline Soffa in Napa, California; Albert and Ruth Lowenberg in Brichen, Ontario; Bruce and Esther Glazer in Toronto, Ontario.

Thanks to the following journals for permission to reprint previous articles published therein as chapters of this book:

"Leonard Cohen and the Tosher Rebbe: On Exile and Redemption in Canadian Jewish Mysticism." *Canadian Jewish Studies*, Volume 20 (2012): 149-189.

"A Priestly Blessing of Love & the Question of Pure Consciousness in Judaism." *Birkat Kohanim*: *Mesorah Matrix Series*, ed. Martin Cohen (New York: Mesorah Matrix Publications, 2016), 207-230.

"Never Mind this *Neuzeit*, here's *Kaddish*: Between the Nameless & the Name." *Kaddish*: *Mesorah Matrix Series*, ed. Martin Cohen (New York: Mesorah Matrix Publications, 2016), 419-430.

"Tangle of Matter and Ghost: Objective Spirit & Non-Dual Reality in the Prayerful Poetry of the Primordial Artist." In מיש לאין

From Something to Nothing: Jewish Mysticism in Contemporary Canadian Jewish Studies (*Reb Zalman Schacter-Shalomi Gedenkschrift*), ed. Harry Fox and Daniel Maoz (Cambridge: Cambridge University Press, *forthcoming*).

"Falling with Our Angels, So Human: Zoharic Afterglow in Leonard Cohen." *Future of Zohar in Honor of Daniel Matt's Completion of Pritzker* Translation of the *Zohar* (Berkeley: UC Berkeley, Easton Hall, 2016).

Special thanks to Jennifer Toews at the Leonard Cohen Archive, housed at the Thomas Fischer Rare Book Room, University of Toronto, and to Leonard Cohen for permission to consult the vast archive and cite the following sources:

"A longing beyond/flesh & loneliness." Hydra small notebook, Leonard Cohen Archive, MS 122: Box 8b, n.d.

"We need eman-/cipation from/desire & no-desire." Hydra small notebook, Leonard Cohen Archive, MS 122: Box 8b, n.d.

"Untitled poem." Hydra small notebook, Leonard Cohen Archive, MS 122: Box 8b, Strattford, CT, August 19, 1959.

Graphic #21, Leonard Cohen Archive, MS 500: Box 73, December 23, 2003.

Graphic, Leonard Cohen Archive, MS 500, Box 74, January 3, 2004.

Graphic #70, Leonard Cohen Archive, MS 500: Box 74, 2003-2005.

Graphic #3, Leonard Cohen Archive, MS 500: Box 73, 2003-2005.

Graphic #14, Leonard Cohen Archive, MS 500, Box 64, n.d.

Graphic #3, Leonard Cohen Archive, MS 500: Box 73, Montreal, 2003.

Graphic #39, Leonard Cohen Archive, MS 500, Box 73, January 1, 2004.

Graphic #50, Leonard Cohen Archive, MS 500, Box 64, n.d.

Graphic #54, Leonard Cohen Archive, MS 500, Box 73, January 11, 2004.

Graphic #28, Leonard Cohen Archive, MS 500, Box 73, ca. December 2003.

Letter from Neal Donner, Cimarron scholar-in-residence, to Leonard Cohen, Oct. 30, 1978, Leonard Cohen Archive, MS, 500: Box 64, 1-2.

Lotus Sutra (1-14), *Heart Sutra* (15-16), *Dharani of Removing Disaster, Dharani of the Great Compassionate One* (17-19), *Dai Segaki* (20-21), *National Teacher Kozen Daito* (22-23), *The Four Great Vows* (24), in *The Rinzai-Ji Daily Sutras* (n.d., n.p., included with *Mt. Baldy Zen Center Newsletter,* 1975), Leonard Cohen Archive, Box 64, n.d.

"Untitled poem." Written on three *Takanawa Prince Hotel Bar* napkins, Leonard Cohen Archive, MS 500, Box 64, March 20, 1996.

Letter from Kim Krull (Spokane, Washington) to *Buddhist America*, Leonard Cohen Archive, MS 500: Box 64, 1992-1994.

Mount Baldy Zen Center Newsletter, Issue 7, Leonard Cohen Archive, MS 500: Box 64, Winter 1997.

Last and most beloved, my gratitude to Elyssa, who continues to inspire and encourage me on this path, within and beyond every word of this book, dancing with the love of our life, Talya—*take this waltz, it's for you!*

Preface

Baby boomers like to opine about the "prophets" of their generation, the seers and mystics who bend the countercultural arc toward themselves and their peers, the people whose words embody the spirit of collective angst. Dylan is the preferred choice here, outshining all the others with his explosive bursts of subversive creativity and force of will coming from the Rust Belt of America to the East Village. The musician Steve Earle once said that his mentor, Townes Van Zandt, was as good a songwriter as Dylan, perhaps even better, and as a child of the Texas heartland who never left Texas (except for a short stint in Nashville), he better represents the true Americana of the postwar era. But Townes was no prophet. He was a tragic Texas story of only partially fulfilled genius. And then there is Leonard Cohen, the urban bard from north of the border. What do we make of a man who looks more like a tailor than a rock star or folk singer?

Dylan and Van Zandt were songwriters and not really poets—separating their words from their songs does not always yield good poetry. Leonard Cohen began his journey as a poet and only later found song as a way to disseminate his words. He did not help create the folk revival; the folk revival helped create Leonard Cohen.

Cohen is no prophet—the very thought would be antithetical to Cohen—but as Aubrey Glazer suggests in his *Tangle of Matter and Ghost*, he is better described as a "pop-saint." The difference between a saint and prophet merits a brief interlude. The prophet sees, the saint lives; the prophet is often angry, the saint is often melancholic. The prophet proclaims, the saint teaches. The prophet is a critic of society; the saint, a self-critic. The prophet wants to change the world; the saint wants to change himself, and as Tolstoy taught us, "everyone wants to change the world, but no one wants to change themselves." In our world, the prophet often takes acquired wealth and becomes the very thing prophesized against. Cohen retreats to a Buddhist monastery in Mt. Baldy, California, and maintains a modest home in Montreal, where he grew up. He loses his fortune to a corrupt manager. He starts with little and he goes back to zero. That might destroy a prophet, but not a saint.

Leonard Cohen starts out as a Jew and he remains a Jew. But what kind of Jew is he? Dylan runs as far from his Jewishness as he ran from Hibbing (who later finds his way back to Christianity and then somewhere in-between). Cohen never had a need to hide his Jewishness, to run from it. In fact, one could argue that Cohen's life-work is precisely to ask the question "What is it to be Jewish?" But not in any parochial way. It is for him the same question as "What is it to be human?" Or, what is it to be anything at all? What is it to be at all? Glazer's *Tangle of Matter and Ghost* takes us on a journey to find Leonard Cohen, to hear his voice anew, or perhaps to witness Leonard Cohen finding himself.

Along the way, Glazer takes us on numerous detours into the dense woodlands of the North Country. He asks us to consider the determinacy of place—of Montréal, of Canada, that country that gets swallowed up when we Americans say "North America" the same way Judaism is consumed when Christians say "Judeo-Christian tradition." But let us consider Canada. Really consider it. Does Canadian Judaism have its own spirit, its own mysticism? Can Leonard Cohen be juxtaposed to the Tosher Rebbe, the Hasidic rebbe from the northern suburbs of Montreal? This is not a trivial comparison but a more subtle juxtaposition. What does it mean to live "up there," to dwell in a bi- or trilingual society as opposed to the monolingual world in the U.S.? What is it like to live next door to the beast?

Like any saint, popular or classical, Cohen is a product of his time, a postwar, post-Holocaust "Jewish account" taking of the world. He just expresses it better than most.

To complete this task of finding Cohen or helping Cohen find himself, Glazer must deploy the arsenal of thinking about the fragility of the human condition, at this time, in this time: From the Zohar to the radical Hasidism of Mordecai Joseph Leiner, to Nietzsche, Adorno and *Žižek*, and of course, to the poets, Jew and Gentile, believers and heretics.

There is an inherent danger in such an enterprise. How does one avoid becoming dilettantish? How does one avoid the pitfalls of unsubstantiated comparison when one shatters the barriers that keep the scholar on the straight path? Glazer notes this in the beginning of his prelude. This book, he writes, will strike the reader as strange, maybe even *unheimlich*, that Freudian term that can indeed capture the travails of being Jewish, which Cohen certainly was, always. And of being human.

Glazer treats Cohen as a poet and reads him as a poet should be read. Glazer constructs an image, almost pictorial, through his verse. He explores his spiritual journey through the changing tenor of his poetic interests. This book is not a straight path, and in many ways, it contains no map or GPS. When you begin to read, you have begun the ride. In the end, I think Glazer finds Cohen's Jewishness, but not through Judaism; he finds it in the crevasses of Cohen's hope for the world that he shares with us through his words. Just as there is no Jewishness without the Jew, there is no poetry without a life. And Glazer situates Cohen's life—in postwar Montréal, in a Buddhist Monastery, on a Greek island, as an itinerant—as a life in which home is carried with him. Like Daniel Boyarin's claim about the Talmud in his book *A Travelling Homeland*, Cohen writes his home where he is. And therein lies his Jewishness!

Is Cohen a mystic? Not in any conventional sense. He was not an expert in any mystical tradition. His Buddhist practice was periodically monastic but seemingly quite normative for its time. He is a wholly (post) secular seeker, a troubadour who looks for more, not out there, but inside. Glazer shows us that his search for God is his search for love, that love of God can only be found in love itself, and that love itself, teaches Cohen, is broken. Thus God must also be broken, if God is to *be* at all. Not in the Dylanesque sense of "everything is broken" and not quite in the Kafkean sense of utter hopelessness. Kafka was once asked, "Is there any hope?" to which he responded, "There is infinite hope. Just not for us." One gets the sense that Cohen chooses otherwise. It seems that somewhere Cohen actually believes—it is just not quite clear in what. But maybe that does not matter. Maybe we mistakenly justify belief in its object rather than in the act of believing itself. If you don't believe in *this*, then you don't believe. So perhaps the very act of believing is a (post) secular mystical act. And here Cohen finds a place for himself and is a lighthouse for the many weary sailors in the night.

Tangle of Matter and Ghost is a truly original work by a scholar who is not afraid to write himself into his work, who is courageous enough to buck convention while retaining the discipline of scholarship. Cohen should be humbled that such an adept mind and spirit has taken him on as his subject. The portrait is complex, subtle, and imaginative. And *unheimlich*. As it should be.

Shaul Magid,
Jay and Jeanie Schottenstein,
Chair in Jewish Studies & Religious Studies,
Indiana University Bloomington

20th of Av, 5776

1

Prelude

New Skin for a Post-Secular *Circum/Fession*

To be a Jew and a philosopher in this post-secular moment is often portrayed as a process of thinking and writing in a manner attuned more to concealing than revealing the truth for fear of persecution.[1] But as Leonard Cohen—the bard behind this book—shows time again, navigating the *(dis)placement* of self requires a willingness to peel back the layers and expose the truth of one's own journey toward redemptive homecoming. It is, as Cohen puts it, a "going home/without the costume/that I wore."[2]

Through every movement of Cohen's life, his songbook reveals the exoskeletons of his spiritual evolution. Yet, Cohen's truth has an infectious rhythm of universal "truthiness" that dances us along on our own steps to self-discovery. That process of confronting the unraveling of meaning in the world is less alienating when embraced through song, and as I will argue, through the post-secular songbook of the bard in question—Leonard Cohen. Paradoxically, in the revelation of his truth we find ourselves.

Cohen's lyrics are a symphony of circumscribed confessions or *circum/fessions*,[3] a kind of self-justification that emerges during the process of writing and explaining ourselves. A *circum/fession* is both a confession and a circumcision. We cut a hole in our hearts as we spill our story onto the page. Yet, like the Jewish ritual of circumcision, which represents the covenant between the male child and God on the eighth day, so too, in his eightieth year, Cohen continues peeling away at the layers of self to justify a more expansive bond with the Divine.

Tracing a small cluster of "days" in Cohen's journey, from 1973 through 1977, we confront a series of courageous *circum/fessions.* Through his lyrics, Cohen makes a series of cuts that bind: cutting himself off from his father's Judaism, from his father's Zionism; and later, from his own mask of masculinity as a Jewish Don Juan. That mask of machismo is stretched even further with the onset of the Yom Kippur War, when in October 6, 1973, Leonard takes leave of his family (who at the time lived on Hydra) the next day, flying from Athens to Tel Aviv to enlist in the Israel Defense Forces. As will become evident further on in this book, Cohen responds to the call while rebelling against the expectation of his father, an ardent Zionist. At the same time, though, he yearns to move beyond the path of his father to discover his own meaningful encounter with a Zionism and a Judaism unafraid of the world. This struggle manifests itself in 1974 on Cohen's fourth album, called *New Skin for the Old Ceremony,*[4] where Cohen asks his father in heaven and on earth to change the key to his spiritual identity his name. In "Lover Lover Lover," Cohen sings:

> I asked my father, I said, "Father change my name." The one I'm using now it's covered up with fear and filth and cowardice and shame. . . . He said: "I locked you in this body, I meant it as a kind of trial. You can use it for a weapon, or to make some woman smile."

As a Jew, Cohen received his name on the eighth day of his life following the ritual cutting of his foreskin, or circumcision. Forty-some-odd years later, in search of a new name for his soul, Cohen writes one of his most moving books of prayerful poetry, *Book of Mercy,*[5] as he follows the call of the prophet Jeremiah, whom he relished reading with his grandfather, Rabbi Solomon Klonitzki-Kline, while living together for a short time in Montréal: "Circumcise yourselves to YHVH, and surrender the foreskins of your heart. . . ."[6]

Awaiting liberation is the name of the soul caged in the prison of the body. This classic gnostic motif, common in alchemy, also speaks in a deep and direct way as Cohen's prophetic self rallies against his priestly lineage to envision "a new Jerusalem glowing." This new name also prophesizes Cohen's move beyond the shackles of being a "lady's man" (using himself to "make a woman smile"), toward an equanimity between the masculine impulse and the feminine *eros.* Reflective of this tension is the cover art for *New Skin for the Old Ceremony,* featuring the union of male and female and the four elements, adapted from the alchemical text *Rosearium Philosophorum* made popular by Carl Jung in his attempt to rebalance the primacy of the psyche within psychology.[7] The soul, for Jung, is composed in its essence of the feminine *Anima* and the masculine *Animus.* This dichotomy represents the true self as opposed to the masks worn daily. Cohen follows Jung in the belief that the source of creativity remains lodged in the soul, awaiting liberation. The purpose of the *Rosearium Philosophorum*, then, is to enable:

> the task of alchemical transmutation to unite these facets in a new harmony, into a perfected state of being where Body, Soul and Spirit mutually interpenetrate and work together. Man's soul is thus the bridging element between the outer realm of the physical body and the spiritual world. This bridge must be built out of integrating the primal polarities of the soul, so that it becomes both a vehicle or vessel for the spirit and the master and moulder of the physical realm.[8]

The language of alchemy serves as Cohen's palate as he attempts to paint a bridge for integrating the primal polarities of his own soul. The shift from alchemy to Rinzai Buddhism is not as stark as it may first seem. For it is but three years later, in 1977, following his first encounter with

Roshi in Japan, that Cohen then returns to record *Death of a Lady's Man*.[9] At this moment within the arc of Cohen's songbook, we hear his longing to move beyond integration of the primal polarities of his own soul's masculine impulse that circumscribes the feminine, to die and be reborn in a more balanced way.

For Cohen, each album and newly recorded song marks a "day" in his spiritual development. With *New Skin for the Old Ceremony*, Cohen illustrates how each of these "days" become woven into a new garment to shroud his soul. As the Zohar, the preeminent Jewish mystical text, teaches, birth and death are marked by a visitation from the "days" of one's life. When one is born, all the "days" of one's life emerge and as each day unfolds, the celestial "day" descends, awakening the possibility of living that day to its fullest. When one is about to die (to enter and experience higher dimensions) the soul is enveloped in a radiant garment, such a garment is woven out of one's virtuous days.[10] Thus, the garment of one's soul is either fully woven of one's days lived virtuously or the garment is rent from one's days lived shamefully. It is no small coincidence that one traditionally begins study of the Kabbalah, the Jewish mystical tradition, at forty years old. At forty years old, there are 14,600 days that stand before Cohen. With *New Skin for the Old Ceremony*, Cohen seeks to accumulate the "days" lived with virtue. It is by virtue of any modicum of equanimity within *eros* that Cohen yearns to make his "days" count.[11]

If, as I argue above, Cohen's lyrics dance us along on our own steps to self-discovery, then how has his songbook revealed my own journey as a Jewish philosopher, rabbi, musician, and artist? Within weeks of my arrival in the "American Jerusalem" known as San Francisco, for my first experiment with spiritual community I invoked the tantalizing "secret chord" of a broken *Hallelujah* over the Jewish New Year of *Rosh HaShannah* 5775. Albeit somewhat unconventional if not completely unorthodox for a rabbi to sing Leonard Cohen on the High Holidays with his/her community, I sought, nonetheless, to touch on something that the remainder of the Hebrew, *piyyut*-laden service no longer manages to realize for most of those gathered—a direct heart-to-heart connection. No one in the standing-room-only, 700-plus seat synagogue of Congregation Beth Sholom could resist this *Hallelujah* moment. Everyone was present; no voice remained silent for the seductive chorus.

It is this question as to the possibility of prayer that Leonard Cohen's songbook is so adept at addressing in his testimony that: "There's a blaze of light/In every word/It doesn't matter which you heard/The holy or the broken *Hallelujah*."[12] It is only possible for the illumination to abide in "every word" if prayer itself becomes a *circum/fession* that the words of prayer themselves are the "holy or the broken." Prayer must begin from this place of brokenness, for as the bard sings: "There is a crack in everything/ That's how the light gets in." [13] Philosophers, like Jacques Derrida and Michal Govrin, argue further braking or interrupting the prayer is essential to opening space for conversation with the *Other* in that:

> . . . a prayer should be interrupted. There is a moment of preparation; we have to be ready for the prayer. But, on the other side, when we pray, the prayer should not come to an end, because if the prayer is complete it is not prayer. So, the address of the other must remain interrupted. The interruption is the mode of our relation to the other. The prayer should remain interrupted. Not simply because someone has interrupted the prayer but because the meaning of the prayer remains undecidable. Must remain suspended . . . because it depends on the other. On the response of the other.[14]

To gain more of an appreciation of why such interruption and brokenness is so heartfelt for my journey, I share a brief sketch of how my prayer itself has become a *circum/fession* by way of Leonard Cohen's songbook. In the midst of my first leave-taking from the world of arts school to the study of architecture, I befriended a devout Catholic student, Bernardo Campos Pereira, hailing from Portugal. While studying architecture together at the University of Waterloo, I found myself in constant dialogue with him over how our study of iconography was systematically effacing our devotional lives. The effect of this systematic de-programming of any remaining sense of religiosity was felt most strongly over the many all-nighters in studios when our survival through these long stretches was made possible with an elixir of music. There was no time to pray as we were so immersed in study; but study was not seen as a devotional mode of prayer—yet . . .

Bernardo and I inevitably found ourselves returning time and again near dawn to Leonard Cohen—usually, to those knowing incantations of: "Everybody knows that the naked man and woman/Are just a shining artifact of the past/Everybody knows the scene is dead/But there's gonna be a meter on your bed/That will disclose/What everybody knows."[15] Of course it helped that as we were coming to terms with the role of such artifacts in our present creations, we were also studying Dante's *La Divina Comedia*. Somehow, it was only in the company of this devout Catholic student that I was able to find my bearings, otherwise feeling completely adrift within the virulent secularization that was rampant in our studios at that time. So as it was through Cohen's lyrics that I was invited to confront the deeper reality that: "Everybody knows the scene is dead," which empowered me to eventually leave architecture behind and return to an archaeology of self. One of the first parts of this excavation in my archaeology of self would beckon me to confront my Canadian identity and begin studying French again.

Pursuing this "archaeology of self"[16] was a challenge, given that I had given up the mandatory study of French in tenth grade to complete all my requisites in math and science required for architecture. Yet, in the language of my lost Canadian self I found the time necessary to perform an archaeology of self. I eventually became capable of reading Arthur Rimbaud and Charles Baudelaire in their original tongue, while experimenting in film by joining the infamous Cinema Club at University of Toronto—the same club that boasted august members like David Cronenberg and Atom Egoyan. It was a reputable path to follow.

My first short film, *Lines of Oblivion* (1992),[17] was its own experimental *circum/fession* on the lines of the city and how these lines circumscribed one's self—all by way of the prayerful poetry of Leonard Cohen's "Who by Fire."[18] I knew intuitively that this song was meant to be the soundtrack to this archaeology of myself, but little did I realize how impactful this experimental *circum/fession* would be on the course of my life. *Lines of Oblivion* did its tour of duty, traveling from Grenoble to Montréal on the art house circuit. It led me to my next station in the archaeology of self, the next experimental *circum/fession,* another short film, somewhat longer, entitled, *Fire on the Water* (1994), a retelling of the biblical story of Abraham sacrificing Isaac.[19] This time around, while I thought I had left Leonard Cohen behind, it turned out I was channeling his prayerful poetry even deeper. In my collaboration with Phillip Hoffman's renowned director of photography, Garrick Filewod, I decided to let go of the lyrical and move to a more primal expression in music. This led me to an encounter with a remarkable jazz saxophonist and world music expert, Ernie Tollar. As I described the visual mood I was attempting to evoke with the steady-cam foray into the brush at the shore of the stream, Ernie decided to play reedless sax. This allowed him to evoke the broken, sacred, primal sounds of the *Shofar.*

Abraham's willingness to sacrifice stood clearly before me as I completed *Fire on the Water.* So I wondered about my sacrifice—should I enter into the world of commercial filmmaking or should I enter the rabbinate? Each path, from my perspective, offered me an opportunity to enter deeper into that archaeology of self. In the end (which was another beginning), I chose the rabbinate. In my *(dis)placement* from Toronto, especially from all those forays with fellow writer, Jon Papernick in to post-punk clubs that were constantly closing down, like Ildiko's and The Siboney, I entered the Jewish Theological Seminary of America in Manhattan. My entry into the ivory tower of Jewish scholarship at 3080 Broadway concatenated with Leonard Cohen's lyrics: "I'm the little Jew/who wrote the Bible."[20] And with my first autumnal communal celebration of the Feast of Booths in JTS's monstrous *sukkah*, one late night I encountered Leonard Cohen again. This time Leonard Cohen emerged as I joined the midnight stragglers in the *sukkah*, led by a handful of Canadian ex-pats, singing and playing "Suzanne" together. I continued to encounter those chosen few who sang such songs of the heart, whether at the conservatory across the street, the Manhattan School of Music, or various jazz clubs scattered along the Upper West Side to the Lower East Side. Those New York years were marked by a schizophrenic immersion in traditional Jewish texts as well as an exploration of John Zorn's emerging Radical Jewish culture, especially at his now defunct experimental clubs, like Tonic. My eventual departure from New York, after a brief return to Toronto, coincided with Zorn's final performance of *Electric Masada* before it was closing time for his Tonic.

Cohen's melodies and lyrics urge us to dance ourselves into partnership with the Divine presence that is present at any moment, the *Shekhinah*. A pillar of rabbinic Judaism and its discourses as recorded in the Talmud teaches:

> . . . the *Shekhinah* hovers over one neither through gloom, nor through sloth, nor through frivolity, nor through levity, nor through talk, nor through idle chatter, but only through a matter of joy in connection with a precept, as it is said: "But now bring me a minstrel. And it came to pass, when the minstrel played, that the hand of the Lord came upon him" (II Kings 3:15).[21]

Listen to Cohen's images, see his melodies, and you will notice two dancers hovering. They dance on their own—together, they sing together—alone. One is called the Shekhinah—she is a strange-looking being, as old as creation and as new as an exile yearning for homecoming. This being, the

Divine Presence, dances in secret from the edge of the stage. She is veiled in mystery. In her arms dances Leonard Cohen. They make an unlikely pair: they syncopate in strange—even uncanny—rhythm. Yet somehow Leonard Cohen and his partner connect. Through Cohen, the Montreal bard, the exile-itinerant Jew who practices Rinzai Buddhism, the Divine Mystery may unveil Herself of some of her secrets. Together, they offer us another path home…

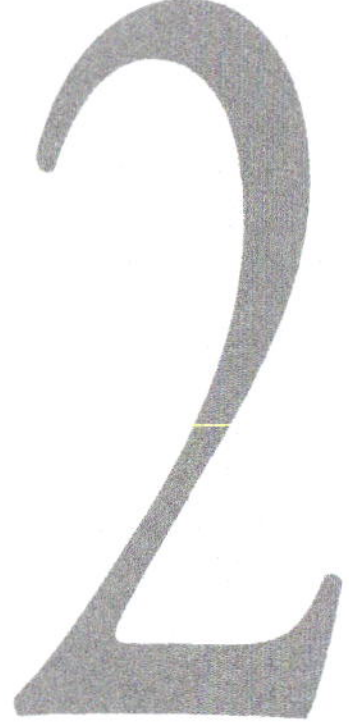

On Exile as Redemption in (Canadian) Jewish Mysticism

Exile as Redemption: (Canadian) Conundrum of a "Third Solitude"

Exile as redemption—despite its paradox—is a strange but true experience in the contemporary period, especially in Canada.[1] If indeed "home is a place where people practice identity and intimacy,"[2] then exilic living serves as a kind of homecoming. The question remains whether the vision of Montreal's prophetic poet, journalist, novelist, short story writer, and lawyer, Abraham Moses "A. M." Klein (1909–1972) continues defining Canadian Jewish identity as being "snatched from the center, we learned circumference"[3]—and whether such circumference enables a unique mystical experience. What is it about the Canadian psyche that uniquely positions its visionaries to write so that "in exile they write home"?[4] If indeed Canadian Jewish writers are "alternating between dystopia and utopia, [so that] the Diaspora's labyrinth frustrates Zion,"[5] can the claim be substantiated that alternations of Canadian Jewish mystics do more than frustrate but actually create an *imaginal* Zion—that space between imagination and reality— within the Diaspora? To address this particular question of mystical experience and the creation of an *imaginal* Zion from the perspective of two Montreal Jews' "third solitude,"[6] the larger debate surrounding homecoming from Diaspora to Zion in Israel first needs to be outlined.

On the one hand, a cluster of scholars suggest that in this post-modern, post-Zionist age, and given the evolution of the inherited model of homecoming that crosses "the borders between real and imagined spaces" with the founding of the State of Israel, there is an inherent danger "that comes from the fulfillment of desire, the actualization of imaginary worlds."[7] The dialectic between exile and redemption requires a much more nuanced set of grammars.[8] Not only are "the workings of the imagination" in Jewish diasporic life overflowing with its own cultural creativity, but these "new Jews" and their millennial Judaism are flourishing as alternative paradigms borne of *substitution*, no longer dependent upon Israel as its center for cultural renewal radiating outward to its perceived periphery of Diaspora.[9] No longer is exile in the periphery. Rather, the Boyarins go so far as to suggest that "Diaspora as a theoretical and historical model [should] *replace* national self-determination" to be celebrated not just for Jews but for all people.[10] Furthermore, Kol Dor, a recent international network of Jewish leaders from twelve countries including Israel, actually refuse to use any kind of "Israel-Diaspora" discourse and instead would speak in terms of "global Jewish discourse."[11]

On the other hand, some scholars are still holding fast to recover the Zionist project as retaining its central power for meaning-making that extends a determinative Jewish culture and identity to the periphery.[12] Somewhere in between—howling to crack Zionism's vault—the voices of lone pragmatists are attempting to weigh in over the struggle to recover a centrist space for the meaning-making potential of this rapidly fading dialectic.[13]

Amid this ongoing debate, I will argue for the abiding spiritual relevancy of the exile-redemption dialectic and how "the Jewish diaspora is the repeated experience of *rediasporization*"[14] leading to the transformation of exile as redemption through Canadian Jewish Mysticism. In the course of this comparative analysis, I will present and reflect on a working definition of contemporary mysticism, and then make the case for a Canadian Mysticism that should include its own subgenre of Jewish Mysticism. The majority of our present analysis will then engage in a comparison between two of the most diverse Canadian mystics from Montréal—a Hasidic rebbe, R. Meshulam Feish Segal-Loewy (1921-2015), and a Jewish monk, Leonard Cohen (1934-2016). Each Canadian mystical exemplar transmits, challenges, and transforms this dialectic of exile-redemption in remarkably innovative ways. These Canadian mystical exemplars problematize the dialectic of exile-redemption in ways that are both "classical/continuous" and "contemporary/discontinuous" with the flow and transmission of Jewish Mysticism known as Kabbalah.[15]

Canadian Jewish Mysticism: Toward the Definition of a Subgenre

To begin our investigation, a working definition of mysticism as "mystical experience" is in order. If indeed mysticism is to be considered an "interpretive category" that records, reflects, and transmits the unitive experience, then let us consider Robert Ellwood's definition as a possible framework:

> Mystical experience is experience in a religious context that is immediately or subsequently interpreted by the experiencer as a direct, unmediated encounter with the ultimate divine reality. This experience engenders a deep sense of unity and suggests the experiencer was living on a level of being other than ordinary.[16]

Ellwood necessarily admits in his definition of mysticism that this category of "religious context" needs to be nuanced, if not expanded, for it is "a matter of language in the broadest sense (perhaps symbolic expression would be a better term: while language is the fundamental model and vehicle for communicating what we think, nonverbal media—music, art, rites, styles of groups—are also such communication)."[17] In this sense, whether the mystical experiences under consideration as transmitted in the discourses of a Hasidic rebbe or the poems and lyrics of a Jewish monk are to be classified as "peak experiences" or "classical mystical experiences" is less the issue than the reality that both are "self-validating" and reflect the language of their particular host culture.[18] What then are the boundaries of such a working definition?

By deliberately choosing to compare exemplars of "discontinuous kabbalah" with "continuous kabbalah"[19] as embodied in two Montreal Jews, I am attempting to expand the usefulness of the working definition for the diversity of contemporary mystical experiences. The peculiar case of Leonard Cohen's contemporary mysticism, for example, especially evident in his musical lyrics and poetry, has been chosen for analysis to challenge the limits of duality in "peak theory" or "high experiences" by being both "joyous and fulfilling," as well as fulfilling the need to be "focused [on] moments of stunning ecstasy and clear realization."[20] This kind of categorical dualism will be further challenged by the classical Kabbalah embedded in the Hasidic teachings of the Tosher Rebbe as well as other dualities, such as: exile/redemption; profane/sacred; Babylon/Jerusalem.

Further, in comparing the mysticisms of a Jewish monk and a Hasidic rebbe from Montréal, the question must arise whether their unique experiences as and within Canada's "third solitude" have in any way affected their mystical visions and/or intensified their messianic fervor. On the one hand, Cohen ingeniously subverted the 1960s genteel, "hushed cosmopolitanism" of a predominantly Anglophone Protestant Westmount.[21] On the other hand, the Tosher Rebbe confronted the rising tides of nationalism of *La révolution tranquille,* reverberating and even revolting against these Quebécois Catholic cultural roots to create an insular community of Kiryas Tosh, set apart while nestled within the suburb of Boisbriand. Between such diverse Quebécois cultural mosaics, I am interested in the emergence of a unique texture of Canadian Jewish Mysticism. Are these mystical visionaries reacting to the "legacy of the Quiet Revolution, and the moral, spiritual vacuum that has followed the collapse of clerical power in Québec,"[22] or are these mystical visionaries *sui generis*? The oscillation of such textures within a diverse Quebécois cultural mosaic is what this investigation attempts to explore.

Building on this working definition of mysticism, let us consider the possibility of "Canadian Mysticism." Some of the major trends of mysticism within Canadian philosophical circles attempt to locate its unique core in dissecting mystical visioning and ethics.[23] On the surface, nothing seems to be terribly unique or striking in perusing the Canadian philosophical debates surrounding the nature of mystical experience, its perhaps endangered relationship to ethics, and how philosophy might move beyond the quagmire of categories and definitions that are ultimately limited by local religious culture or transcendental ineffabilities. The outlier in such a conversation about Canadian Mysticism, of course, is Richard Maurice Bucke (1837-1902) and his important contributions to the formulation of a new paradigm of modern mysticism, known as Cosmic Consciousness, revealed to him in London, Ontario in Canada.[24]

On the one hand, what is most intriguing about such an idiosyncratic category of Canadian Mysticism is the way it has been used to address *everything but* Jewish Mysticism. For example, Canadian Mysticism most often is addressed through the medium of painting in the renowned Group of Seven.[25] Each member of this painting fellowship—including original members from Toronto that extended to Winnipeg and Montréal in becoming a national school[26]—used "mystical form rather than aesthetically invented or initiated form, in their painting,"[27] transforming that form through their transcendentalist experiences in painting the mystical North into a kind of theosophical landscape.. Beyond what could be argued as an isolated case of Canadian Mysticism predominant within the art world, there are also trends of theosophy spreading rampantly throughout Canada in the early part of the twentieth century, with its ties to nationalism and mysticism. From the establishment of the first Canadian Lodge of the Theosophical Society in 1891, to eighteen more lodges sprouting up throughout Canada by 1920, there were nearly a thousand such adherents in Canada by 1922.[28] Coupled with the publication of its own journal, *The Canadian Theosophist*, in 1920, the mysticism of theosophy begins to embed itself in aspects of the Canadian psyche and becomes an early recurring motif in Canadian Mysticism, specifically in Montréal.[29] What remains absent in almost all of the current research on theosophy, however, are the Jewish mystical roots in this process of theosophical universalization.[30]

On the other hand, the renaissance of the particularistic manifestation of Jewish Mysticism in Canada, specifically in Montréal, deserves further reflection. In his insightful study of R. Yudel Rosenberg (1859-1935), Ira Robinson observes the cultural importance of this Montréal rabbi's translation of and commentary on the *locus classicus* of Jewish Mysticism, the Zohar.[31] Given its numerous reprints, Rosenberg's Zohar translation project into Hebrew remained, according to Robinson, as significant as Gershom Scholem's academic project of resuscitating the Jewish mystical tradition from Hebrew University in Jerusalem, making it accessible to a new generation of seekers.[32] The question arises whether R. Rosenberg's Zohar translation emerged from Montréal in response to the "third solitude" or if this work was *sui generis*.

In the "increasingly globalized mystical culture of the twentieth and early twenty-first centuries"[33] this question about the nature of mystical visionaries amid the "third solitude" of Montréal Jewry lingers. Given the "hybridity" of contemporary mystical visionaries and their yearning to "touch God,"[34] the question remains whether the mystical quests under investigation here are in any way anchored and influenced by this "third solitude" of Montréal Jewry, uniquely positioning them to be in the world of Canada, but not of it. Turning to our two mystical exemplars at hand, this tapestry of exile and redemption is masterfully woven from the prayerful poetry of Leonard Cohen to the Hasidism of R. Segal-Loewy (the Tosher Rebbe). Each one is a mystic in their own right, constantly engaged in the exilic search for the elusive site of redemption—the concealed Zion, their hidden Jerusalem. Seeking that space between imagination and the reality of Jerusalem—an *interworld* of the *imaginal*—forever seen through the reality of Babylon, remains the challenge. If indeed Canadian Jewish writers are writing home in exile,[35] then I would argue that Canadian Jewish mystics need to be read with a similar lens to really appreciate their nuanced take on exile as homecoming.

Exile is always just a step away from redemption—much of the spiritual life is a subtle dance in and out of redemption. But what happens when being in exile itself produces the possibility of its own redemption? Or what happens when the homeland of Jerusalem is to be found in the exilic state of Babylon? Such an oscillation from exile to redemption brings with it immense creativity and inspiration. Cultures both religious and secular have their narratives of exile and redemption. Some return home, but many remain and flourish as a result of being in exile. Such exilic consciousness is a quintessentially Jewish way of looking at the world. Such consciousness has implications for the creative spirit, especially for the mystics who envisioned God's exile as a necessary precursor to redemption. While the claim that "Everything is in Exile!" is affirmed by some Canadian Jewish thinkers, such as Emil Fackenheim[36]—never mind the Dalai Lama[37]—it serves as an important catalyst for creativity. The yearning to reunite with the extraordinary experience of unitive consciousness allows both mystic and poet to envision the redemption of *something beyond*, all the while grounded *in the exile of here and now.*

Relating to this subtle oscillation of exile and redemption is a question very rarely asked, namely—what is the nature of mystical inspiration within the Canadian mystical psyche? How is Zion mystically envisioned and lived in the exile of the Great White North's Diaspora? When considering the dichotomy of exile/redemption, there are a number of thematic models that have affected many artists and writers, including: (1) choosing exile from Canada to go and shape the culture of a new homeland;[38] (2) exile as refuge in Canada from persecution in adapting the present place as the new homeland;[39] (3) exile as refuge in Canada as a home base for further return traveling to other homelands. Or one can look at the Great White North's Diaspora from a synchronic perspective that ascends from: (1) pioneers; (2) modernists; (3) inheritors; to (4) poet-novelists and musicians.[40]

This brings us to the thrust of the argument, namely, that the mystic is one exceptionally equipped to transform exile into homecoming, all the while succumbing to the transformation of his/her soul within the host culture. The experience of homecoming in Babylon redeems its inner Zion so that through the process its very demarcations (*ziyyonim*) are transformed. If the role of the mystic is to interpret living in that extraordinary "deep sense of unity," then what exactly is the texture of light that radiates from such Canadian Jewish mystics? To sharpen the question: how is the texture of such mystical visions affected in Québec for those writing by a cultural preoccupation with "exile, dislocation and memories of an abandoned homeland"?[41] The variety of Judaism(s) that are in continuous formation and evolution exemplify the pluralism of the Canadian mystical psyche, which will now be explored in two Jewish mystics from Montréal.

Continuous Kabbalah of Komarno in the Tosher Rebbe

The mysticism of the Tosher Hasidic Dynasty is unique in that it remains inflected by the hybridity of the Komarno Hasidic tradition set apart within the local host culture of Boisbriand, Quebec. The hybrid approach of the continuous Kabbalah in the Komarno-Zidichov Hasidic lineage is renowned for its intensive correlations of Beshtian Hasidism with Lurianic Kabbalah.[42] These intensive correlations are revisionary in the sense of formulating a reconciliation between the two seemingly divergent mystical schools of Kabbalah and Hasidism. This is by no means incidental to the texture of mystical visions in this lineage, especially in the case of the current Tosher Rebbe, R. Segal-Loewy. The Komarno-Zidichov Hasidic lineage[43] retains its long-standing connection to the devotional aspects of Hasidism,[44] while transmitting its own form of hypernomianism to which we shall return shortly.[45] To what degree does this devotion to reconciling Beshtian Hasidism with continuous Lurianic Kabbalah inspire the Tosher Rebbe to envision exile as homecoming?

Nestled just outside of Montréal in a suburb known as Boisbriand is Kiryas Tosh, the home of this "third solitude" enclave, a community of Jews caught between the Anglo and Francophone worlds, neither of which fully accepted them for decades. Kiryas Tosh realizes the homecoming that resurrects the Hasidic dynasty originating in Nyirtass ("Tosh"), Hungary,[46] that all but perished in the *Shoah*. Tosh is considered to be one of the largest Hasidic groups in the world today, with its settlements and synagogues across New York in Borough Park, Williamsburg, Brooklyn, Kiryas Joel, New Jersey and Monsey, New York. This tremendous growth is in no small part due to the pioneering vision of the Tosher Rebbe, who emigrated to Montréal 1951 and by 1963 envisioned the creation of Kiryas Tosh. That vision of homecoming to Kiryas Tosh was a double exile—namely, after being exiled from Nyirtass, the Tosher Rebbe took on his own exile from Montréal to Boisbriand.[47]

A good part of the Tosher Rebbe's devotional talks or *sihot qodesh* have been transcribed and written down in Hebrew in a series of five books, entitled *Avodat Avodah: Dibrot Qodesh*, which will form the basis of the present analysis. This series of devotional discourses or *sihot* printed in Hebrew are organized around the weekly Torah portions and Jewish holidays with guidance for spiritual practice. The *Imrot Qodesh* in Yiddish parallel the aforementioned Hebrew version in scope and structure. It is in the Tosher Rebbe's *sihot qodesh* where the contours of a recurring dialectic of exile/redemption are encountered. The terms of this dialectic are salient if one is to appreciate what demarcates this continuous Kabbalah of Komarno-Zidichov within Tosher Hasidism as a unique expression of Canadian Mysticism. Is it possible that exile and redemption take on a new, more radicalized meaning once re-contextualized in the local Canadian culture of Boisbriand rather than say the American Borough Park?[48] Is the pronounced ambiguity toward Zionism—an a/Zionism bordering on an anti-Zionism—a reaction to the anti-Semitism "that lies just beneath the surface of [Québécois] society,"[49] or is it a veiled critique of the secular nationalism in the wake of *La révolution tranquille*? Or is such ambiguity about Zionism already present in the spiritualization of the Land of Israel in Komarno-Zidichov Hasidic lineage?

The source of all spiritual effulgence, for Komarno-Zidichov Hasidic lineage, flows directly from the Holy One through the Land of Israel,[50] so that language itself is even transformed by this flaw. Upon articulation, the revelatory capacity of language to disclose the otherwise concealed divine presence of the exilic *Shekhinah* is only possible in the Land of Israel.[51] Yet there remains a lingering ambiguity in the Komarno-Zidichov perspective—the true holiness of the Land of Israel can only be experienced once its current state of desolate land and ruined cities (i.e. secular State of Israel) is redeemed from such exile back to its pristine state of divine lands and cities (i.e. messianic sovereignty).[52] Paradoxically, many *rebbeim* within the Komarno-Zidichov lineage displayed an abiding love for Zion in their dress,[53] their yearning to emigrate to the Land of Israel,[54] and their realization that the most robust innovations in thinking through Torah happen in Israel.[55]

Given this fluid Komarno-Zidichov mystical perspective on the Land of Israel, let us now consider how this is absorbed and retransmitted by the Tosher Rebbe; namely, is his highly spiritualized stance toward the Land of Israel to be read as anti-Zionist, or a/Zionist, or some other hybrid? The contours of a recurring dialectic of exile-redemption will now be explored, first in terms of exile and then in terms of redemption and messianism, within the Tosher Rebbe's *sihot qodesh*. The degree to which this Hasidic dynasty has flourished and its mysticism blossomed on the margins of Montréal should come as little surprise. After all, the Tosher community has made valuable inroads with the Québécois political system.[56] What is remarkable, however, is the degree to which an otherwise particularistic community—one that prides itself on being set apart—fails to recognize the particularity of its host francophone culture. Otherwise, how is the Tosher Hasidim's nuanced diasporic existence in the charged political context of Québec glossed over with such general terms for exile, like "America" in North America? Notwithstanding the adept political maneuvering of the Tosher Hasidim, exile as homecoming takes on new meaning once recontextualized in Boisbriand. Should not the place of Boisbriand then translate into an equally nuanced discourse about its spiritual homecoming in the Diaspora of Kiryas Tosh?

The dialectic of exile-redemption takes on new meaning as recontextualized in Boisbriand by the Tosher Rebbe's *sihot qodesh*. The diaspora of Boisbriand, Québec is contrasted with the diaspora of bygone days of Nyirtass, Hungary. Amidst the rampant poverty of Nyirtass, the greatest trials over desires of this-worldly materialism there were all about necessities for survival, whereas the "American" cultural context is altogether different. "By habituating oneself to be satisfied with eating less [in Nyirtass], they would sanctify themselves even in the permissible desires, for that was the way they were raised and educated—namely, that this-worldly desires are engaged only by necessity."[57] The Boisbriand context is altogether different because of "the overwhelming negative energy of the American context to beautify and stimulate whatever one sees through [the lens of] the desires and delights of this world, deluding one to think that these delights are the ultimate bliss of this world."[58]

This body/soul dualism of "a desire for the spiritual life takes place amidst a highly materialistic culture to continually high levels of insatiable desire for more."[59]

Even more curious, notwithstanding this dire cultural context, the Tosher Rebbe suggests that personal redemption is possible—how? Every seeker has the potential to leave their personal exile in Egypt to be redeemed at any moment through one's personal conduct and deeds.[60] While remaining emphatic that this is possible—". . . by way of the power of Torah, every individual has the power to leave Egypt *even while in exile*"—[61] the path of love alone will not suffice. The perceived austerity of the Tosher Hasidic path may in part stem from this conviction that love alone will not suffice to melt through the power of negative energies that permeate the exile of Egypt *qua* Boisbriand. The personal potential for redemption is felt in this double exile of Egypt *qua* Boisbriand,[62] where the Tosher Hasidim are surrounded by more French than English, while unabashedly continuing to speak Yiddish and pray in Hebrew. Even though the Tosher Hasidim live in a place permeated by the negative energies of "American exile," their own self-perception of a double exile of knowledge and speech requires a balancing dose of reverence and wonder.[63]

The oppositional energy of the *qelipot* is manifest in many ways, but most striking is the acknowledgement of the overwhelming influence of the media and overeating, both of which seduce the mind, incessantly distracting it from the spiritual practice of prayer and study.[64] It is the latter manifestation of the oppositional energy of the *qelipot* through improper consumption that is a recurring challenge in the Tosher Rebbe's devotional life. When these oppositional forces of the *qelipot* are not properly dealt with, either by reducing food intake or abstaining completely, then such a person is actually delaying redemption, as the Tosher Rebbe teaches:

> In *Nissan* we were redeemed and in *Nissan* we shall again be redeemed, and so one needs to contemplate this deeply, how to redeem one's soul

> from the forbidden realm, lest one delay redemption through one's deeds.
>
> And one is never exempt from sitting and lamenting over the delaying of the advent of the messiah, from being perplexed why the Son of Jesse [i.e. Messiah] has still not come, and from wondering why exile has been so extended? For as soon as one does a spiritual stock-taking, one comes to see how much s/he is actually causing the delay of redemption. If one eats for the sake of libidinal impulse alone, consuming whatever sweet things that appeal, then such a person is causing his/her own interior divine portion to descend into the evil within the sparkles of the oppositional realm, causing the exile of the *Shekhinah*.[65]

Furthermore, amid the darkness of this present exile,[66] there is light, but the question remains: in what direction does it shine—inward or outward toward Zion? Just as the Redeemer salvages the first and the last, so too the final remnant in Boisbriand will be redeemed from their exile amidst that very exile in their last place on the map.[67] Zion has become utterly spiritualized as an ideal—a spiritual ideal no longer tied to the physical *topos* of the Land of Israel. Holiness through the space of Zion is superseded by the site of holiness in time of the Sabbath. The "Sabbath demarcated and celebrated in the exile [of Boisbriand] is holier than any Sabbath of Temple times."[68] Once again, Ezrahi's observations on the transvaluation of exile as sacred center are valuable here:

> In traditions culminating in the Kabbalah, time and space become conflated so that the sanctity of place is projected not only onto texts but also onto the rhythm of weekly ritual: the Sabbath becomes a sacred center, analogous to Jerusalem and the Garden of Eden, and the synagogue a miniature temple (*mikdash m'at*), allowing for a regular re-creation of cosmos out of chaos.[69]

On the hypernomianism of the Tosher Rebbe's devotional practice, some preliminary observations in the fieldwork by Lewis and Shaffir[70] are illuminating and suggestive. The Tosher Rebbe stresses the importance of prayer and its capacity to redeem one from exile if enacted with the "proper focus."[71] There is an operative distinction between the levels of prayer, both nomian and hypernomian. On the one hand, there is the nomian level, where prayer is a thrice-daily spiritual practice that follows the paradigm of patriarchal temporality (i.e. Abraham symbolizing dawn, Isaac symbolizing midday, and Jacob symbolizing night).[72] By all appearances in the Tosher Rebbe's discourses, it is assumed that "praying in a regular *quorum*, day after day, without any change whatsoever, as well as eating according to a regimen only what is absolutely necessary for health, is what strengthens one's powers for study and prayer"[73] means *just that.* Even if this is to be understood merely on the nomian or legal level, the linkage here between increased spiritual power through a decrease in consumption amid regular prayer beckons further questioning. This decrease in consumption leads "to an overall lack of desire to eat at all"[74] and "through afflictions at the moment of consumption, it is as if one has fasted the entire day."[75] The careful editing of these discourses, according to Lewis and Shaffir, reflects a more toned-down version of ascetic devotion, lest the contemporary Tosher Hasidim be intimidated by the rebbe's austerity.[76]

On the other hand, there is the hypernomian level, where prayer must include the spontaneous "openings of the heart like fire through the letters."[77] Prayer of the devoted one has the capacity to overturn divine decrees and change the nature of reality.[78] Building on this classic Hasidic trope regarding the *tzaddik's* prayer, it is known within his community that the Tosher Rebbe does not complete his prayers at the appointed times of morning, afternoon, and evening. Rather he engages in regular daylong fasts, culminating in being joined by a rotation of nine other Tosh *yeshiva* students, who are also instructed to fast for their rotation in order to participate in a private quorum to enable the rebbe's recitation of the entirety of the regimented daily prayers—all well beyond their due time.[79] In creating such a hypernomian devotional space of spiritual intimacy through constant rotation of his *yeshiva* students,[80] the Tosher Rebbe reveals his spiritual site of a concealed Zion to his community on a regular, rotating basis. The site of this Zion accomplished through hypernomian devotional space is only possible when one accepts that "every person should cultivate a miniature temple within one's own body, so as to be a vessel for the *Shekhinah*." [81] Not only is Sabbatical temporality infused with this redemptive capacity of Zion, but now exile is overcome in weekday prayer through the redemption of hypernomian devotionality surrounding the Tosher Rebbe in his din prayer.[82]

Kabbalah in Poetry & Lyric: Leonard Cohen's Redemption of Exile

If there is a pop-saint, poet laureate of Montréal, it would undoubtedly be Leonard Cohen.[83] The Montréal bard's journey through the recording of an 1840s patriotic folk song, "Un Canadien Errant," captures the deeply exilic landscape that typifies his paradoxical yearning for homecoming. New layers in the theme of exile are revealed in it: a lyric about a rebel from Québec, banished to America and longing for home, it then becomes a song sung by a Canadian Jew who had wandered away and lives in Los Angeles, accompanied by a Mexican Mariachi band.[84] At this very moment in his exilic wanderings, the nearest home Cohen had was in the presence of spiritual intimacy with his Rinzai Zen master, Joshu Sasaki Roshi.[85]

Over the course of his career, the Montréal bard has claimed that "he is tired of moving around" and he would like to "stay in one place for a while," yet "there always seemed good reasons to move."[86] Cohen's life as a poet has been a peripatetic one that has followed a course of continuous, self-imposed exile from his homeland in Montréal to sparse rooms in hotels from Manhattan and Mumbai, to a house on the Greek island of Hydra, and a monk's cottage at the Zen Monastery of Mount Baldy, just east of Los Angeles. The ascetic aesthetic of bare rooms has always attracted

Cohen and informs his lyric and poetic *imaginality* of Jerusalem and Babylon.[87] Through all of his decades of peripatetic wanderings, Cohen remains consistent in: "a longing beyond/flesh and loneliness."[88]

Montréal as homecoming for Cohen was always brimming with redemption, as he claims to have had "a very messianic childhood."[89] Growing up on Belmont Street in Westmount, a classmate recalls how much "Leonard was embedded in religion, deeply connected with the *shul* through his grandfather, who was president of the synagogue, and because of his respect for the elders; I remember how Leonard used to recount how his grandfather could put a pin through the Torah and be able to recite every word on each page it touched. . . ."[90] Throughout his spiritual journeys in meditation, it is inevitable that the image of his grandfather as sage and teacher would emerge:

> My grandfather appeared
> and demanded:
> "What have you
> done with my
> books? My
> 'Lexicon of Hebrew Homonyms,'
> my 'Thesaurus
> of Talmudic
> Interpretations,'
> my unfinished
> 'Dictionary'?"[91]

While the tradition and its loss weigh on Cohen as he takes leave of it, it is precisely within the stream of his ancestral tradition into which he steps, to confront that part of himself in the mirror. His unfinished "dictionary" of spiritual ascent and descent, of negation and affirmation, of *thanatos* and *eros*, and of exile and redemption—which is the key to Leonard Cohen's post-secular song book, at home, both in the street, and in the house of worship. In addition to a regular exposure to traditional synagogue life through his grandfather, Rabbi Klonitzki-Kline, Leonard expressed solidarity with his grandfather who was also a writer. The two of them would sit together many evenings "going through the Book of Isaiah, which the rabbi knew by heart which Leonard came to love for its poetry, imagery and prophecy."[92] Early on,—much like Dublin was to Joyce—Montréal came to serve and symbolize exile as homecoming for Cohen.[93]

During his wanderings to New York, London, and Greece, Cohen always viewed Montréal as a homecoming, albeit with the ambivalence of exile. For example, "in December 1963 at a symposium held in Montréal on the future of Judaism in Canada, Leonard's address, entitled 'Loneliness and History,' castigates the Montréal Jewish community for abandoning the spiritual for the material."[94] This recurrent material-spiritual dichotomy is echoed in its Babylon-Jerusalem counterpart. Early on in novels like *The Favorite Game*, Leonard turned the spotlight on those who succumbed to the material at the expense of the spiritual, "like his uncles, who occupied the front pews at the synagogue were pledged only to their businesses; religious observance was an empty masquerade. They did not believe their blood was consecrated. . . They did not seem to realize how fragile the ceremony was. They participated blindly, as if it would last forever. . . Their nobility was insecure because it rested on inheritance and not moment-to-moment creation in the face of annihilation."[95] This castigation of his hometown Jewish community made national headlines, ultimately reinforcing a sense of exile as homecoming. His attempt to bridge the irreconcilable gap between the material-spiritual dialectic, as an echo of Babylon-Jerusalem, leads Leonard into the mystical orchards.

Reading Leonard Cohen as a non-dual Jewish mystical poet and songwriter has already been astutely and comprehensively analyzed by Elliot R. Wolfson.[96] Wolfson characterizes the Montréal bard as a mystic attracted to "celibate piety," thus enabling Wolfson to masterfully display the poet's attunement to "the insight regarding the erotic nature of asceticism, which implies the ascetic nature of eroticism."[97] Cohen stands as a poet who, in Wolfson's reading, unabashedly utilizes Jewish mystical imagery (whether Zoharic, Lurianic, or Hasidic Kabbalah).[98] Consider the following prelude of Jewish mystical imagery to a song proffered by Cohen during his concert in Jerusalem at *Binyanei Ha'uma* in the early 1970s:

> "It says in the Kabbalah that if you can't get off the ground you should stay on the ground. It says in the Kabbalah that unless Adam and Eve face each other, God does not sit in his throne, and somehow the male and female part of me refuse to encounter one another tonight and God does not sit in his throne and this is a terrible thing to happen in Jerusalem. So listen, we're going to leave the stage now and try to profoundly meditate in the dressing room to try to get ourselves back into shape if we can manage," Leonard said, "we'll be back."[99]

It is this kind of mystical imagery that "both expands and constricts the boundaries of his Judaism *vis-à-vis* other traditions [especially Buddhism] in an effort to legitimate the validity of the *other* on the basis of affirming the distinctiveness of his own cultural formation."[100] Intimations of this approach are present also when he says that "we are creating a loose church where each man can have his own vision."[101] Such a vision oscillates between Jerusalem and Babylon, between Buddhism and Judaism. As a novelist, poet, and singer-songwriter, Cohen uses diverse media to expose the anarchic landscapes of life with a healthy dose of Canadian suspicion—believing in God without knowing what God purposes.[102] Decades dedicated to Zen practice by Cohen can be seen as a commitment to redeeming the frequently xenophobic, triumphalist strains within the Jewish tradition through the rigor of an atheistic, acosmic Buddhist lens. His master, Sasaki Roshi had instructed Cohen that there is ultimately no contradiction between the prayerful worship of Judaism and a/theistic practice of Zen. This unquenchable desire to explore wider horizons of spiritual experience caused a questioning of the boundaries in tradition, as evidenced in an early morning *koan* recorded by Cohen: "Secure in a tradition—possible?"[103]

The self-interrogation is open: can one remain truly secure in the sense of really *knowing* the universal truth while embedded in one's own particularistic tradition? What are the limits of knowing one's true self within such a tradition? Is that boundary violated when, as a Jew, one takes part in Rinzai Buddhist practices such as *sanzen, koan*, or *zazen*? Notwithstanding his deep involvement with Buddhism, Leonard continues to insist to anyone who asks that he remains a Jew, more than satisfied in having a perfectly good religion, as he writes in his poem:

> Anyone who says/I'm not a Jew/is not a Jew/I'm very sorry/but this decision/is final.[104]

Cohen also pointed out that Sasaki Roshi never made any attempt to give this Jewish monk a new religion.[105] Rather this exiled monk and teacher, Sasaki Roshi, became an anchor amidst the tumult of Cohen's wanderings, helping him become centered and feel at home, to the point where this Zen master becomes interwoven in the lyric of "Bird on the Wire"—from "a worm on the hook" to "a monk bending over a book."[106]

Being anchored by his Zen master, the exilic Leonard finds his Zion on every road he travels. This is all the more remarkable given Cohen's suspicion of holy men and his first criticism of Sasaki Roshi as a kind of false messiah like Sabbetai Tzvi.[107] Furthermore, the complementarity of Zen practice within a Jewish mystical path traversed by Cohen, as Wolfson's study shows, is what allows for the Montréal bard to manifest his deepest appetites concerning the absolute. Then the nameless unity and the nothingness of being coincide "with the monotheistic idea of one God as the ontic source of all reality."[108] The rigor of *zazen* practice enabled Cohen to grow spiritually in a way that seemed unavailable in the rabbinic Judaism he inherited growing up in Westmount, Montréal. To traverse these American Rinzai pathmarks [*ziyyonim*] would mean following Sasaki Roshi along any part of his extensive "winter and summer retreats and training periods at Mount Baldy Zen Center as well as extensive training at Jemez Springs in the fall and spring. As well as *Dai-sesshins* at Rinzai-ji, Los Angeles, and on the road, Vienna, Princeton, Ithaca, . . . and still there is *sanzen* four times a day and daily *teisho*. And still there is the constant nurturing of those who come to have their true situation clarified, their minds put at ease."[109]

The American Rinzai pathmarks [*ziyyonim*] shared by Leonard and Sasaki Roshi also led the faithful disciple to dedicate resources early on to the dissemination of Sasaki Roshi's teachings in English. Following his voyage to Japan in 1976, by mid-July 1978 Cohen had been supporting an incumbent scholar, Neal Donner, to work on the dissemination of Sasaki Roshi's teachings for an American audience. In that short period as Cimarron scholar-in-residence in Colorado Springs, Donner attested to his good relations with Sasaki Roshi and the students. He also records having "begun a number of important projects (the Bassui translation; the gathering together of *teisho* transcripts and publications of Roshi's talks; the class on Chinese Buddhism, which has so far met twice and been quite well received, with about a dozen students each time, including some from the outside, i.e. non-residents; oral translation of Roshi's *teisho* here at Cimmaron and at Jemez Springs and Colorado) and generally [*having*] given everyone a good chance to see what sort of a person and scholar I am. . . ."[110] Having established "a personal relationship with Roshi," in his capacity as Cimarron scholar-in-residence, Donner said that he "would be pleased to keep working on his material (aiming towards publishing books containing his thought) at other places besides Cimmaron, or let us say on a part-time basis."[111]

Another window into the spiritual intimacy shared between Leonard and Sasaki Roshi—amidst the rigor of the master-disciple American Rinzai "pathmarks" [*ziyyonim*]—appeared when Sasaki Roshi entered the hospital for laparoscopic surgery for large gall bladders on June 30, 1992, an event that created much trauma for disciples like Cohen. "When Roshi first came to after his surgery, he looked at me sitting beside him and said, 'Leonard, you don't look well—a little blue. Roshi worried about you, maybe you fall down?' Roshi was lying in bed with oxygen tubes in his nose, draining tubes in his throat, draining tubes in his incision, intravenous needles in his arms, monitors attached to his body. . . After a while Roshi said, 'Sickness very interesting, life much suffering.' I asked him, 'Is it worth it, Roshi?' Roshi replied, 'Value just human imagination.' That's when I knew the old man was back. Eight days later, Roshi gave sanzen at Mount Baldy."[112]

As a Jew brought up in a monotheistic environment, naturally questions would emerge about how to reconcile these roots with Rinzai Buddhism. The self must be purged and polished, in part through practice of *zazen*, including meditative recitation of the *Heart* and *Lotus Sutras*.[113] Sasaki Roshi articulated a kind of openness to evolving with his students, reflecting their challenges like a finely polished mirror:

> *Int*-How does a God-affirming type differ in the way he comes to Zen from a God-negating type in depth of interest or in way of practice?
>
> *Roshi*-Well, the people that affirm God manifest in a self-affirming way, and people who negate God manifest in a self-negating way. The people that affirm God feel that God affirms them. That's why those kinds of people appear more in times of peace. And the God-negating people are the ones who suffer or fear wars. In other words when people get unhappy, they negate God. For the people that negate God you have to give the practice that asks, "Where are you when God negates you? Where does the self go when it is negated by God?" Things like that make practice interesting. And when you are affirmed by God, what kind of affirmed self manifests? According to Zen we don't negate either of those perspectives.[114]

This tension along the spiritual journey between affirmation and negation, of self and of God, between *kataphasis* and *apophasis,* clearly struck a chord with Cohen. From that first step along the Rinzai path to Japan, encountering Sasaki Roshi in 1977, as well as on subsequent journeys back as late as 1996, Cohen's ability to straddle both affirmation and negation is the very exile that brings glimmers of redemption:

My sun sweet
dark religion
of drunk religion
all for the sake
of poetry
My whole life
burning on the
altar of poetry
my robes
my sandals
my circumcision
my shameful prayer
and Mexican candles
all for the sake
of this moment
at the bar of
the Takanawa Prince Hotel
the opening of poetry
slipping down
into the pure land
of God
into the earlobes
of Buddha
and the blue tiles
of the one Allah
into the
twenty seven hells
of my own religion.[115]

Cohen's sincere stripping away of self could not be more heartfelt and any less heart-wrenching. In one of his daily Zen practices of contemplating his true self by looking at the mirror and emerging with a singular etching and *koan*, over the course of an entire year, Cohen writes:

> לאל ברוך נעימות יתינו
> just to have been one of them/even on the lowest rung[116]

The journey through each and every "pathmark" [*ziyyon*] of self requires a willingness to confront that image in the mirror, straddling at once affirmation and negation. The fusion of this *koan* with an excerpt of traditional Jewish liturgy that demarcates the turn to unified consciousness in love that prefaces with the *Shema* is noteworthy.

Even the Montréal bard was strongly influenced by the turning point of North American Jewry's renewed sense of ethnic pride, in 1967 the six day war emboldened through a strident Zionist response and awakening. As one first encounters Leonard Cohen's poetry and songwriting on Jerusalem, especially in the 1970s, the imagery appears idyllic, if not intoxicated by a naïve romanticism of a genteel nationalism. Jerusalem comes to the forefront of Cohen's own self-interrogation:

> Between the mountains of spices/the cities thrust up pearl domes and filigree spires./Never before was Jerusalem so beautiful./In the sculptured temple how many pilgrims, lost in the measures of tambourine and lyre,/ kneeled before the glory of the ritual?/Trained in grace the daughters of Zion moved,/not less splendid than the golden statuary,/the bravery of ornaments about their scented feet.[117]

With the onset of the Yom Kippur War on October 6, 1973, Leonard takes leave of his family (who at the time lived on Hydra) the next day, flying from Athens to Tel Aviv to enlist in the Israel Defense Forces. In 1974, Cohen described his motives for the sudden leave-taking from Hydra to what he called his "myth-home" as a complex commitment: "I've never disguised the fact that I'm Jewish and in any crisis in Israel I would be there . . . I am committed to the survival of the Jewish people."[118] For the next few weeks, Leonard joined up with Israeli musicians Oshik Levi, Matti Caspi, Mordechai "Pupik" Arnon, and Ilana Rovina to sing for the IDF soldiers in "outposts, encampments, aircraft hangars, field hospitals, anywhere they saw soldiers, and performed for them up to eight times a day."[119] While Cohen appears to be a prolific songwriter, he generally goes through grueling stretches of agonizing rewrites until the song emerges complete. By contrast, this early trip to Israel stands out as one of the few times where Cohen was miraculously able to write a song so quickly. Leonard improvised the song "Lover Lover Lover" in front of the soldiers during his second performance with the band of Israeli musicians and the lyrics revealed to him the effects of war in Zion:

> May the spirit of this song/May it rise up pure and free/May it be a shield for you/A shield against the enemy.[120]

What is remarkable about Cohen's ongoing struggle with the dialectic of exile-redemption is that by his 1974 tour, the Montréal bard would introduce "Lover Lover Lover" as a song "written in the Sinai desert for soldiers of both sides."[121] Just as the dialectic of exile-redemption merges into exile-as-redemption, Israel and her Arab neighbors merge into one family of people.

After Israel, Cohen kept journeying onwards, delving even deeper into the war-torn zone of Ethiopia. The self-imposed exile from his self-proclaimed "myth-home" of Israel into Ethiopia raises the question of why Cohen needed to continue journeying if, like all Jews, he was supposed to finally be at home in Israel. This journeying for Cohen in search of his "myth home" was more than merely avoiding marital battles at home,[122] but an attempt to exhaust the narratives of nationalism swirling around him in the Zionist circles of Montréal. By 1975, within this triadic cultural context of Montréal-Jerusalem-Asmara, there is an evolving nuance of negation. It is most prevalent in the way Cohen addressed the dialectic of exile-redemption through the symbol of Zion in Jerusalem.

Cohen's language seems to almost interrupt its own thought pattern midflight:

> I won't be sitting here long. I'm in a terrible hurry. I'm going to Jerusalem. I'm going with the happy Israeli soldiers and I'm going with the King of Saudi Arabia to kneel down in the place that we were promised. . . *I won't be going to Jerusalem after all.* You will have to go to Jerusalem alone. It is yours. It was *given to you by the angels of culture and time.* But I can't go.[123]

Early on, the poet marked an ironic contrast between the physicality of Jerusalem "with the happy Israeli soldiers" and an inaccessible supernal and eternal Jerusalem. Throughout his oeuvre, whether in prose, poetry, or lyrics, Cohen is constantly searching in exile for the elusive site of redemption—the hidden Jerusalem. What keeps this Montreal mystic from disclosing this redemptive site is the prevalence of Babylon or the pervasive exilic experience, which he names anew—not as Rue St-Denis, or St-Catherine of Montréal—but as "Boogie Street." As the Montréal bard reflects, Boogie Street is the mundane routine of life, and we believe that we leave it from time to time. "We go up a mountain or into a hole, but most of the time we're hustling on Boogie Street one way or another."[124] Cohen observed a double exile at play, in that even a monastery is also part of Boogie Street. Closing one's door at home allows for an elimination of the world, whereas "a monastery is designed to eliminate private space," leading the bard to ruminate paradoxically that ". . . there's really *more respite from Boogie Street on Boogie Street* than there is in a monastery."[125]

Unsurprising then that the myth of homecoming for a mystical recluse in a retreat center like Mount Baldy—far away from Montréal—was shattered. The "three solitudes" that informed Cohen's Canadian Jewish upbringing are extended—beyond the Anglo-Protestant and Catholic-Francophone sphere for the Montréal Jew—now through the fourth solitude of Zen Buddhism. Retaining a disarming sense of irony when discussing his foray into Zen Buddhism, Cohen is consistent in his continuing loyalty to the Montréal Judaism of his upbringing, even when it is in need of a real spiritual reboot.[126] Such a re-orientation for Cohen was realized most efficiently through the spiritual technologies of fasting shared by Judaism and Zen Buddhism. Early on in his wanderings as a peripatetic poet, Cohen becomes aware of the pull that the ascetic life has upon his soul. In his 1961 poetry collection, *Spice Box of the Earth*, Cohen claims:

> I have not lingered in European monasteries/and discovered among the tall grasses tombs of knights/who fell as beautifully as their ballads tell . . . I have not held my breath/so that I might hear the breathing of G-d,/or tamed my heartbeat with an exercise,/or starved for visions.[127]

This "celibate piety"[128] that Cohen both craves and flees from is most cogently expressed through his exilic wanderings as a homecoming. The devotional posture of fasting as already seen with the Tosher Rebbe is what also brings Cohen most directly into alignment with exile as homecoming. Before entering into retreat at the monastery on Mount Baldy, even on the island of Hydra, Cohen was already "a monk with benefits"[129] who observed the Sabbath. Cohen's lifelong observance of the Sabbath, one of an erotic asceticism amid his self-imposed exiles, brought him great meaning. This recurring image of the Jewish monk evokes Cohen's favorite book of biblical prophecy, Isaiah, who envisions such celibate piety through the symbol of those "Eunuchs who observe the Sabbath."[130] While never marrying Suzanne Elrod, the material-spiritual dialectic deepened, forcing Leonard into deeper yearning for exile—continually hungry for emptying power of hunger.[131] Fasting continued to hold sway over Leonard as a spiritual discipline that complemented his self-imposed exilic wanderings.[132]

This process of celibate piety reached ecstatic heights early on in Cohen's writing of his most provocative novel in 1966, *Beautiful Losers.*[133] This novel of Canadian Jewish mysticism, *par excellence*, envisions a "postmodernism grounded in Canadian history, Indian myth, and Cabbalistic [*sic*] games,"[134] expanding its mysticism into new horizons of the Canadian *imaginality*. This recasting of the third solitude now invokes the triad of Jews, Catholics, and aboriginals by masterfully repainting the opening portrait of Catherine Tekakwitha (1656-1680), Iroquois Virgin or Lily of the Shores of Mohawk River.[135] It is Cohen's mystical vision in this novel that allows for the "postcolonial recuperation of seventeenth-century native Canada, complicated by and aligned with a 'post-diasporic' Jewish sensibility" whereby "Jewish tribes lie behind Indian tribes."[136] Notice how the third solitude of Montréal Jews, between British and French colonial legacies, is extended and challenged now by the Jew's separation from the aboriginal Canadian. This daring excavation of one dyad within the third solitude triad opens an *imaginal* stream—between the St. Lawrence and Sambatyon Rivers, between aboriginal and Jew—that positions Cohen on a uniquely Canadian mystical journey to expand Zion.

The mystical process of writing *Beautiful Losers* also expands the spiritual landscape of Cohen's exile as homecoming through Zion. If indeed Cohen considered *Beautiful Losers* a prayer, one immediately senses the intimate linkage to the process of a saintly, erotic asceticism of fasting in exile:

> *Beautiful Losers* is a prayer—at times a hysterically funny, filthy prayer—for the unity of the self, and a hymn to the loss of self through sainthood and transfiguration. . . . It was "written in blood," said Leonard. He was writing, at various points, ten, fifteen, twenty hours a day. . . . When he finished typing the seven last words—"forever in your trip to the end"—Leonard went on a ten-day fast. He says, "I flipped out completely. It was my wildest trip. I hallucinated for a week. They took me to the hospital in Hydra." He was put on a protein drip. After they sent him home, he spent three weeks in bed, hallucinating, he said, while Marianne took care of him. "I would like to say that it made me saintly," he said.[137]

To become the saint of celibate piety, Cohen must dare to excavate his own *imaginal* experience of the aboriginal Canadian from the dyad of his Jewish tribal roots within the third solitude triad. This process of excavating his own Jewish tribalism leads to the lost root of his Canadian aboriginal tribalism. In this early, almost prophetic gesture in his novel, Cohen affirms lyrically later on that "coming up against someone else all the time is *Boogie Street*."[138] It is through his encounter with the *other*—in the figure of Catherine Tekakwitha—that enables Cohen to break down the dualism of Babylon-Jerusalem and complicate his third solitude as a Montréal Jew in order to break through to his truer spiritual self by recovering the aboriginal impulse his ancestors settled.

The more distance Cohen traverses in escaping his Montréal Jewish home, the more he is drawn back into that exilic place of *no-place*. Cohen captures this exilic sense of place that is no-place in another recent refrain:

> So let's drink to when it's over/and let's drink to when we meet/I'll be waiting on this corner/ where there used to be a street.[139]

Standing in the place of no-place, evokes a sense of *(dis)placement* coupled with an impossible yearning to return to place:

> I believe you are standing in the place where I am supposed to be standing.[140]

The street, then, is not simply physical topography, but part of the mapping of the greater Self along the path of negation and affirmation, that exilic journeying in search of the beloved, across time and space, evinced in this *koan*:

> I spoke to/you/yesterday/on my/long/walk/I spoke/to you,/beloved.[141]

Forever the peripatetic poet, Cohen's exilic journeying in search of the beloved—much like early Hasidic itinerants and their exilic wanderings through Eastern Europe[142]—is a search for Zion found in exile. Through his wanderings to London and New York, Cohen came to a remarkable realization—that the self-discovery of his personal Zion was linked to disclosure of his own self before the *other.* Moreover, this self-discovery takes place amidst moments of deep rupture. This is captured in his famous song, "Famous Blue Raincoat," which for Cohen came to symbolize "that unassailable romantic life, the opposite of a cloak of invisibility, the garment that would lead you into marvelous erotic and intellectual adventures."[143] In confronting the double disclosure of this revealed raincoat of visibility, Cohen comes to terms with the exilic nature of his spiritual quest for Zion. Namely, that exile is a necessary part of the return to true self as, "homecoming." The poet was almost eighty years old, yet this exilic experience of *self* continued to drive and inspire him on his journey.

The exilic reality of Babylon colored and confounded the poet's seeking of the *imaginality* of Jerusalem—the netherworld between imagination and reality. In that place of no-place, the poet yearned to reveal what is concealed, "a secret meeting, a warning, a Jerusalem hidden in Jerusalem."[144] While the poet had never sought the topography of Jerusalem *per se,* for him symbolic Jerusalem hides within it another secret symbol. The *imaginal* experience of "a Jerusalem hidden in Jerusalem" is doubly concealed from most seekers, leading to delusions of grandeur. If strains of the Jewish religion are concerned solely with the physical topography of Jerusalem, then the deeper spiritual "Jerusalem hidden in Jerusalem" will remain in exile. This kind of nationalistic, exoteric reductivism that often passes for religion— and Cohen is unabashed about seeing Judaism as one prime exemplar—cannot reconcile itself with the spiritual longing of the doubly concealed Jerusalem.

From the revelation that is doubly concealed, there also is the real desire for a double revelation of a redemption. It is that redemption that then brings its own concealment of exile in the *imaginal* symbol of Babylon. This symbol of Babylon recurs from his earlier musings and is refined, especially in Cohen's latest songwriting. At an earlier phase, the poet succumbs to the intoxication of exile, forgoing any redemption beyond the time-space of his present experience, as he writes: "I really hope you stumble on/The Great Red Whore of Babylon/Forget the Grace/Enjoy the Lace. . . ."[145] This same sense of abandonment is evident in his more famous song, "Chelsea Hotel," in which New York serves as a contemporary Babylon:

> I remember you well in the Chelsea Hotel,
> you were talking so brave and so sweet;
> giving me head on the unmade bed,
> while the limousines wait in the street.
> And those were the reasons, and that was New York,
> we were running for the money and the flesh;
> and that was called love for the workers in song,
> probably still is for those of them left.[146]

New York symbolizes yet another recurring exilic experience along the path of this peripatetic poet. Notice how rarely Cohen pines for the Montréal of his childhood; rather, Babylon has many more stations along the journey of meaning-making. What matters is the underlying desire, the insatiable yearning that is Jerusalem despite being stranded for the moment at the bohemian refuge of Babylon, symbolized in the form of New York's Chelsea Hotel.

The evocation of the exilic *imaginality* of Babylon continues to grow more intense in Cohen's lyrics; the more insatiable the yearning for Jerusalem, the more Babylon is evoked, as in another renowned song, "Dance Me to the End of Love":

> Let me see your beauty
> when the witnesses are gone
> Let me feel you moving
> like they do in Babylon

Show me slowly what I only
know the limits of
Dance me to the end of love.[147]

Babylon is troped here as the site of a deeply dynamic desire, even while the poet desires so much more. The yearning displayed here is to be shown beyond what he "only knows the limits of" and to take that dance "to the end of Love," ultimately reuniting with the *unsaid* Jerusalem. As he wrote early on in Hydra: "we need eman-/cipation from/desire & no-desire."[148]

This journey to the end of desire and immersion into the deeper love of Jerusalem is evident in the poet's more recent lyrics. These words are marked by a deepening spiritual journey of retreat and return. The retreat and return to Babylon is noted in the lyrics of his recent song, "By the Rivers Dark":

Though I take my song
From a withered limb,
Both song and tree,
They sing for him.

Be the truth unsaid
And the blessing gone,
If I forget
My Babylon.[149]

Through this song, Cohen is inverting the *imaginality* of desire that links exile and redemption within its dialectical dance that begins in the exilic psalms of the bible.[150] Cohen early on identifies deeply with the Davidic Psalmist:

> Like the Psalmist/I know nothing/but to turn aside/and mark the longing down/and by this I say nothing. . . I turn away/and hear the music in your mouth.[151]

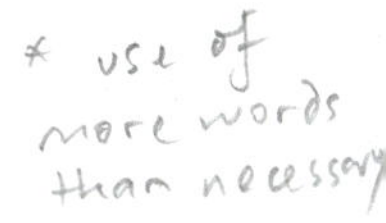

Whereas the Psalmist yearns for Jerusalem in exile "by the rivers of Babylon *there we* sat down and cried"—the pleonastic "there" defines exile as the place that is always *elsewhere*, far away from Zion, and as Ezrahi suggests, this becomes "the pre-text for poetry."[152] Cohen seeks to discover the *imaginal* crown of Jerusalem "by the rivers dark" in Babylon—that is, in exile as homecoming. Precisely in that dialectic lies the key to redemption. Namely, the Babylon of exile becomes the exilic site of redemption—Zion. No longer is Babylon the place from which one yearns for Zion as in Psalm 137:1. Instead, this exilic existence evolves from having lived there *to belong there at last,* as the song itself suggests: "I lived my life/in Babylon. . . ./And I had no strength/In Babylon. . . ./I belonged at last/ to Babylon." Once that sense of succumbing to exile has overtaken the poet, and his heart is broken open does he truly come to understand the necessity of exile in realizing redemption: "Be the truth unsaid/And the blessing gone,/If I forget/My Babylon." While exile can lull any seeker into a deep state of spiritual coma, the poet is awakened by his encounter with the darkness of Babylon. In that process of encountering the shadow side of desire, the poet opens and realizes the underlying unity within the dichotomies to which he was once enslaved: "Then he struck my heart/ With a deadly force,/And he said, 'This heart:/It is not yours.'" The key to the redemption that Cohen seeks is a classic mystical paradox—the redemption of Jerusalem is found in the exile of Babylon—where "singing becomes mnemonic compensation for absence"[153] so that exile becomes homecoming.

But this spiritual quest that began in Montréal and has taken Cohen the world over and back again is much more complicated than any simple dualism of Babylon-Jerusalem and exile-redemption. This is most evident once the Montréal bard actually returns again to Zion despite his earlier, post-Yom Kippur War poetic reflections on the impossibility of reaching Jerusalem: "I won't be going to Jerusalem after all. You will have to go to Jerusalem alone. It is yours. It was given to you by the angels of culture and time. But I can't go."[154] This early realization of the impossibility of reaching the "real" Zion in traveling to Israel recurs three decades later when Cohen reached Israel at the end of his European Tour in 2009.

This return to Zion, with its invocation of the Priestly Blessing in Tel Aviv rather than at the Western Wall in Jerusalem, is telling of Cohen's own exilic journey to redemption. The universalist tone of his poetics, incubated in the early 1960s in Montréal, resounds decades later while remaining embedded in his particular religious path. After the finale to end all finales—with the High Priest invoking his Priestly Blessing in Tel Aviv—the particular has become universalized with "*Leonard Cohens* everywhere."[155]

Ultimately here one encounters the divergence between the two Canadian mystics we have been exploring thus far. Leonard Cohen crosses cultural boundaries from the hushed Westmount cosmopolitanism and privileged status of his Jewish upbringing blossoming into a bohemian bard-*kohen* and returning as a contemplative mystical Jew to Israel via Tel Aviv. By contrast, the Tosher Rebbe, R. Segal-Loewy, deepens the dualism that began in Nyirtass, Hungary as it is transplanted into the *"accommodement raisonable"* of Boisbriand. Cohen traverses his Judaism as a mystic who surpasses his precursor poets like A. M. Klein and Irving Layton along the path toward a non-dual mystical apperception. By contrast, the Tosher Rebbe was in the midst of developing a deeply devotional mystical dualism that cannot fully reconcile itself with the boundary-crossing visions of his master, R. Yitzhak Ayzik Yehudah Yehiel of Komarno, amidst the insular, self-imposed exile of Kiryas Tosh in Boisbriand. Regarding this heightening of dualism in the Tosher Rebbe, I have been arguing that such mysticism oscillates into a hypernomian radicalization of the holy/profane dichotomy, perhaps in part given its insular exile from surrounding local Québécois culture.[156] By comparison, Cohen revolts against the assimilation and apathy rampant amidst the Montréal Jewish elite of his upbringing. Without such a spiritual revolution, Cohen would have forfeited performing in Tel Aviv, given the irreconcilable dualism between Israeli and Palestinian members of the *Bereaved Parents For Peace*. Rather, what emerges for this Montréal bard is a dissolution of any illusions of dualism into a unified vision to heal the broken heart through an expanded Zion in exile.

Conclusion: Canadian Mysticism's Redemption in Exile

The dialectical *to and fro* between Babylon and Jerusalem, between living in and yearning for Zion, causes creative tension for the two Jewish mystics from Montréal—the Hasidic rebbe and the Jewish monk. Zion is transformed through each of their unique *ziyonim* of the exilic Babylon within Québécois culture. Whether in the form of prayerful poetry, song, or even Hasidic discourse, the Jewish mystic ensconced in the Montréal landscape is influenced by Canada and Québec's complicated politics of homeland and identity.[157] I have shown that there is a unique texture to the universal and particular lights that radiate from these two Jewish mystics who remain connected to their exile as homecoming in Montréal. Within the hypernomianism of each of these mystics, both curiously turn to fasting to construct and envision their devotional experiences of homecoming to Zion. The mystical variety of these diverse Judaism(s) are in continuous formation and evolution, exemplifying a pluralism of the Canadian psyche that extends beyond state-based multiculturalism.[158]

The dialectical tension that inspires Leonard Cohen to deepen his mystical apperception of the Zion concealed in Babylon, as I have been arguing, is that same creative tension in the Tosher Rebbe's vision of the final remnant of Hasidim in Boisbriand awaiting to be redeemed from their exile amidst that very exile. What is remarkable here is how each of these unique encounters with the spirit in exile retains a distinctly local cultural process for redemption of Zion within the third solitude of

Montréal Jewish culture. In each case, some part of that yearning for the redemption of Zion has become spiritualized as Zion in exile rather than embodied in the physical Land of Israel. I have argued that both mystic and poet find their possible pathways of redemption as a spiritualized Zion within an exilic Babylon. It is within this reconfigured third solitude that the unique mystical experiences and records of a Hasidic rebbe and a Jewish monk are expanding the path marks [*ziyyonim*] (Canadian) Jewish mysticism.

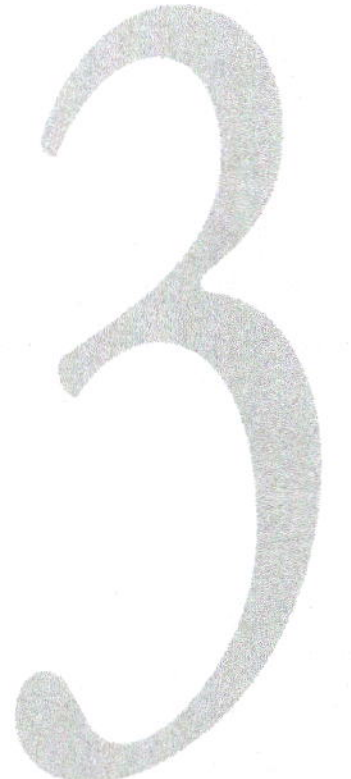

From Darkness, a Love of All This
Seeking the Sacred in Post-Secular Song

What is the nature of enlightenment and what is its purpose if, and when, it is achieved? Lao Tzu once sat under a tree, frustrated. He was frustrated for the fact that he had tried all that he could but still not attained the whole. He had attained a lot, yet there was a lack. He could not figure out what was missing. It was autumn, and as he sat frustrated under a tree, he saw a dry leaf fall slowly. The leaf was swayed by the wind. The leaf went along with wind in whatever direction it blew without the least struggle. Then when the wind stopped, the leaf slowly settled down on the earth peacefully. At that moment, something settled within Lao Tzu.Effort is required to become effortless; so effortlessness settled in Lao Tzu.[1]

This is pure *Wu Wei*—acting without acting, that is to "act naturally," "effortless action," or "non-willful action", so that there is no need for human tampering with the flow of reality—for the Taoist, this is a key to enlightenment. And yet, nothing could be more antithetical to the Jewish notion of *Ratzon* or "will," as my teacher of Taoism once remarked to me.[2]

If one looks through the Hebrew Bible for records of enlightenment, most often one will search in vain. Enlightenment is not a key concern there in its own time, but circumstances change and through the ages that concern comes to the fore in the way that Scripture is marshaled to give voice to the quest for enlightenment along the mystical path.

Its roots, however, are embedded in the Bible's appreciation for the power of music, its relation to the prophetic impulse and revelation. Revelation is a process of uncovering the ear (Ruth 4:4; Job 33:16; Job 36:10); uncovering the eyes (Numbers 24: 4, 6); and sharing a secret (Proverbs 20:19; Amos 3:7). To be revealed is the opening of what is sealed (Jeremiah 32:11), more than a secret being disclosed, the truth is disseminated and publicized (Esther 3:14, 8:13). While prophets like Ezekiel focus on the revelation of the divine body, much of what the pilgrim seeks through the psalms is to behold the light of the divine face (Psalm 27, etc.). Seeing the light of the face of the other is a process of *en-lightenment.* So if we reconsider this question from the perspective of music, something else emerges and remains embedded early on in the spiritual history of Judaism.

Fast forward to the twenty first century, *lo and behold,* those fleeting moments of singers and musicians seeking enlightenment has taken place, to a great degree, in America. This quest for enlightenment and illumination in jazz might include musicians like: Pharaoh Saunders; Miles Davis; Wayne Shorter; John Coltrane; George Russell; the fusion of jazz with *klezmer* by Andy Statman and Walter Zev Feldman; and Radical Jewish culture musicians like John Zorn, Ben Goldberg, and David Krakauer.[3] This same quest for enlightenment and illumination in rock music might include: the Beach Boys and the Beatles in their relationship with Transcendental Meditation through the Maharishi Mahesh Yogi starting in 1967;[4] Bob Dylan's conversion from Judaism to Christianity in joining the Vineyard Fellowship, along with band members Steven Soles, David Mansfield, T-Bone Burnett, and Mary Alice Artes, starting in 1978;[5] Dylan's return to Judaism through appearances on *Chabad* telethons; Matisyahu's re-orientation from his origins as Matthew Miller in Reconstructionist Judaism to a temporary return as *ba'al teshuvah* to and through *Chabad,* then *Karliner* and *Bratzlaver* Hasidism(s);[6] or the recent spate of American pop singers lining up at the Kabbalah Center.[7]

Regardless of how one draws up the list of musicians seeking enlightenment, there is something unique about the late capitalist American flavor of what Turkish Sufi poet Jelaludin Rumi once intuitively labeled, "spiritual window shoppers."[8] At its most extreme, the religion of America is no religion[9]—yet it still has a price tag! Somehow this search for the sacred post-Age of Aquarius has remained an abiding concern for Montréal bard and singer-songwriter, Leonard Cohen. In this post-secular culture he traverses, even record executives who sign and support his songwriting remain baffled, admitting to the Montréal bard: "We know you are great, Leonard, but are you any good?"[10] So the perennial response for decades now by the Montréal bard, as recorded most succinctly in the prolific oeuvre of song, remains the signposts that demarcate the road along this search for the sacred in a post-secular age. A deeper appreciation of what is meant by a post-secular age is necessary to address the opening question about the textures of enlightenment. But skepticism abounds when it comes to analyzing the emergence of contemporary spirituality, especially from the heart of disenchantment to re-enchantment on the West Coast, as Jürgen Habermas wryly remarks:

> The Californian syncretism of pseudo-scientific and esoteric doctrines and religious fundamentalism are thoroughly modern phenomena which may even express social pathologies of modernity, but which certainly do not offer any resistance to them. The missionary successes of a literal, but liturgically extravagant spiritualism are certainly also interesting from the sociological points of view. However, I cannot see what importance religious movements, which cut themselves off from the cognitive achievements of modernity could have for the secular self-understanding of modernity.[11]

While I argue that the songs of Leonard Cohen sit squarely outside the "literal, but liturgically extravagant spiritualism" Habermas is pointing to, there is a larger context of post-secular critique emerging amidst these seemingly dismissive remarks. Like Habermas, Slavoj Žižek is also disturbed, namely, by the withdrawal of the cognitive in favor of the emotional (read *spiritual*). Before arriving at the rupture of Žižek, it is necessary to define enlightenment as well as map out the contours of negative dialectics.

Now imagine you were visiting North America from another planet; how would you figure out what everyone around you means by "enlightenment"?

If you traveled to *Esalen* in Big Sur, you might hear one version; if you traveled to *Spirit Rock* nestled in Marin, you might hear another; and if you make your way to Death Valley for *Burning Man* or to Berkeley for *Urban Adamah*, yet another and another. . . . How can there be so many variations on what seems to be such a simple word—enlightenment?

Lest you become as frustrated as Lao Tzu, you might simply avail yourself of a dictionary to figure out exactly what anglophones really mean by "enlightenment." Since 1891 the definition in the Oxford English Dictionary had read as follows:

> 1. The action of enlightening; the state of being enlightened. . . . [I]mparting or receiving mental or spiritual light.
> 2. Sometimes used [after Ger. *Aufklärung, Aufklärerei*] to designate the spirit and aims of the French philosophers of the 18th c., or of others whom it is intended to associate with them in the implied charge of shallow and pretentious intellectualism, unreasonable contempt for tradition and authority, etc.[12]

How then did this word make the leap from German into English?

Moses Mendelssohn asked this question early on, and James Schmidt has recently noticed that Friedrich Hegel was quite interested in these discussions, so much so that "he'd copied Moses Mendelssohn's answer to the question into a notebook he kept while in high school and he carried this notebook with him throughout his life."[13]

When Schmidt decided to challenge the OED, he already had a growing suspicion that the preferred translation for *Aufklärung* appeared to be "mental illumination." Schmidt's archeology into the history of the word Enlightment takes us back to Paul Leopold Haffner, who would go on to become Archbishop of Mainz. And remarkably, it is the Archbishop of Mainz who began his account of the word by feigning some confusion as to what it meant to even attempt to write a history of "enlightenment":

> Enlightenment is a sublime word, if one goes back to its meaning; it means illumination of the spirit through truth, liberation from the shadows of error, or uncertainty, of doubt. Enlightenment is, in its deepest meaning, the transfiguration [*Verklärung*] of reason.[14]

And yet, as a thirty-five year old Catholic priest who studied at Tübingen and taught philosophy briefly, Paul Leopold Haffner became bishop of Mainz in 1886 and held the post until his death in 1899.[15]

In order to be counted among the truly enlightened, one must "know nothing," echoing the earlier teaching of the Ba'al Shem Tov from the mid-1700s:

> For the ultimate "purpose of knowing is *un*knowing."[16]

This is what is meant by *'emunah*, namely, that which is not cognitive and thus not conceptual and cannot be processed cognitively by the intellect; rather *'emunah* exceeds cognitive capacities and knowledge, which is why the "purpose of knowing through Torah is unknowing" is beyond the limitations of cognition.

Torah, in the deepest sense, refers to the primordial, gnostic wisdom of the most Ancient One. The Wisdom that undergirds such a primordial Torah thus emerges from this foundation of *'emunah*. Namely, the higher level of *'emunah* cannot be perceived cognitively, and thus requires a turning of the mind towards a nullification of the ego in contemplating No-Thing. This is not non-existence or nihilism, for the mind recognizes that there remains hope.

The miracle here is the possibility of *gnosis.* This is the circumstance whereby the mind can be healed and transformed from tainted existence and false belief. The self has to reformat its recognition of what was already hidden in plain sight. The mind is not the absolute arbiter of the spiritual relationship, for the purpose of *knowing is unknowing.*

To write a history of enlightenment, after the BeSH"T and Bishop Haffner of Mainz, one would have to "begin with God and end with God." As an interdisciplinary thinker, hernemeute, and ritual artist committed to a Jewish philosophic path, I have long been perturbed by Theodor Adorno's pronouncement that "to write a poem after Auschwitz is barbaric." By interrogating this philosophical maxim, I began discovering that it betrayed a history of misreading. Adorno returned to this aforementioned maxim at least four times over the course of his life, each time, interrogating his own thinking, applying his own method of negative dialectics. This moment in Adorno's thinking itself has been torn out of its original context where he once wrote:

> The critique of culture is confronted with the last stage in the dialectic of culture and barbarism: *to write a poem after Auschwitz is barbaric*, and that corrodes also the knowledge which expresses why it has become *impossible to write poetry today.*[17]

Through the dialectic of Jewish poetry and philosophy after such a critique, which remains? An epiphany took place for me in the process of thinking, writing, and translating into Hebrew my full length study in Jewish philosophy, called *A New Physiognomy of Jewish Thinking: Critical Theory after Adorno as Applied to Jewish Thought.*[18] This present study is intimately intertwined with *A New Physiognomy of Jewish Thinking*, which itself incubated over the course of a decade. What links both of these journeys together in thinking is their convergence through *(dis)placement.* Encountering this deep sense of *(dis)placement,* as Wolfson and Hughes have already astutely noted, is to "defang" the intellectual rigor of a living Jewish philosophy.[19] The unwillingness and inability of most current approaches to Jewish philosophy to engage in it as a "way of life," or see it as a "living and engaged practice,"[20] is precisely the malaise in most thinking today, causing a deep sense of *(dis)placement.* Part of the albatross that Jewish philosophy continues to carry forward is an outdated methodology that predates the ashes of Auschwitz. The continual resistance of Jewish philosophy to confront the need for "moving beyond the traditional *Wissenschaft* model"[21] needs to be redressed.

However, a concatenation of other sounds in musical thinking is emerging, its traces already found in a cluster of thinkers willing to engage in Jewish philosophy, and willing to relinquish obsessions about reading the past on its own terms. These thinkers are willing to move to "expand the contours of Jewish philosophy—redefining its canon, articulating a new set of questions, showing its counterpoints with other disciplines—as a way to demonstrate the vitality and originality of the topic."[22] There is a yearning to establish "new conceptual models, modes of analysis, and theoretical paradigms to apply to the study of Jewish philosophy . . . seek[ing] new and dynamic ways to engage the material both to specialists in the field and to those in cognate disciplines with an interest in Jewish philosophy and critical theory."[23] Thinkers like Elliot Wolfson[24] invite Jewish Thinking to continue traversing the by-path forged by German Jewish thinker, Franz Rosenzweig (1886–1929), directing our thinking especially to the "apophatic turn [that] challenges the theistic faith," whereby "[w]hat is lost is the personal God of the Jewish tradition."[25] That revelation becomes the "unfathomable ground where mysticism and atheism insidiously shake hands,"[26] which necessitates a complete re-orientation to the nature of Jewish Thinking. Not only must the God concept be rethought, but so too the nature of Torah,[27] as well as boundaries of alterity to be traversed in *Israel* if thinking continues to be negotiated from the standpoint of preserving the identity of difference in the difference of identity.[28]

My present argument is to consider how other methodologies—like Theodor Adorno's *Negative Dialectics*—might contribute to opening the horizons of future Jewish Thinking in the post-secular mystical songbook of Leonard Cohen. Within the complex constellation of Adorno's thinking, I will focus on the inner musical tension that he seeks to restore the dialectical turn within thinking, and consider how new directions in Jewish Thinking can evolve through this dialectic in a nuanced way. What follows is a sketch of the contours of the methodology of *Negative Dialectics,* that can be usefully applied to Leonard Cohen's post-secular mystical songbook, in three discernable theses:[29] (1) there is the move from positive to negative dialectics, a bold step mapping out the territory that distinguishes the Frankfurt School from Hegelianism at large; (2) this necessary form of negative dialectics seeks to rebalance the correlation and do justice to both the "object" as well as the "subject of knowledge"; (3) the method of contemporary philosophical thinking can only serve in the capacity of self-critique.[30]

Alas, it is the larger failure of philosophy itself after Auschwitz that Jewish philosophy must still come to terms with. That is, in light of philosophy's failure to provide illumination on both the practical and theoretical levels within and beyond the ashes of Auschwitz, its project must be restricted to self-criticism—for how else could philosophy remain relevant to its own concept?[31] The purpose of philosophy for Adorno, in general, and I would suggest for Jewish philosophy, in particular, is to align concept and actuality, spirit, and reality.[32] Adorno holds out that any hope of revolution needs to be mitigated into more gradual transformation arising through the path of thinking. Applying this insight to Jewish philosophy means that it is more of an evolution in thinking, which necessitates self-criticism, something Cohen has no shortage of in his songbook!. This is the hopeless hopefulness for redemption, "the prism in which its color is caught,"[33] that still hovers in the offing for critical post-secular Jewish mystics like Cohen. From within musical thinking, the Jewish philosopher and theologian must also appreciate the role of aestheticsand and this is precisely why the post-secular songbook of Leonard Cohen still continues to matter.

And so from these contours of negative dialectics, I turn momentarily to critic Slavo Žižek, who is then able to drill down even deeper to the heart of this upset by naming it as a divine recoil taking place in Judeo-Christianity. Whereas Habermas is reticent to see the importance of religious movements that are intentionally swerving away from the head-centered, cognitive approach to religion and are choosing to hover in a more heart-centered, emotional realm of the spirit that typifies the religion of no-religion that is America, Žižek is willing to peer into the abyss , albeit from a European context.

Notwithstanding the divide between the American and European cultural contexts, Žižek's reflections on the "divine recoil" taking place in Judeo-Christianity resonates in the former context as much as in the latter. While as a post-modernist, Žižek weaves his analysis from a stunning array of thinkers, his most recent analysis of dialectical materialism belies his grounding in Marxism fused with Lacanian psychoanalysis. It is precisely at the heart of the project of modernity that Žižek's critical thinking necessarily turns to the divine within an unabashedly post-secular context. Such a context is forever in the shadow of the project of Enlightenment, which for Žižek, is most lucidly indebted to Hegelian philosophy. In appropriating Hegel's term of "absolute recoil" to entitle his current investigation, Žižek draws our attention to the ways that the "ground/reason" [*Grund*] interconnects reason to the very dismantling of its own ground [*zu Grunde gehen*] as a "recoil, counter-thrust" [*absoluter Gegenstoss*]. What interests Žižek here is how and when the process of "positedness," the "here it is" of existence, "is self-sublated, an essence is no longer directly determined by

an external Other, by its complex set of relations to otherness, to the environment into which it emerged. Rather, it determines itself, it is 'within itself the absolute recoil upon itself'—the gap, or discord, that introduces dynamism into it is absolutely immanent."[34] From this process, Žižek seeks to "elevate the speculative notion of absolute recoil into a universal ontological principle."[35] It is through this interconnecting reason to the very dismantling of its own ground that Žižek seeks recoil as a path to unveiling the nature of being and existence.

Why is this recoil, this "absolute counter-thrust" [*absoluter Gegenstoss*], this negation of negation, necessary now in a post-secular context? Why is this "passage to the crucial dialectical reversal of 'there is no relationship' into 'there is a non-relationship'" so relevant to the emerging discourse of post-secularism? Žižek is carrying forward his innovative reading of a "true materialism [which] is a 'materialism without materialism' in which substantial 'matter' disappears in a network of purely formal/ideal relations. This paradox is grounded in the fact that, today, it is idealism which emphasizes our bodily finitude and endeavors to demonstrate how this very finitude opens up the abyss of a transcendent divine Otherness beyond our reach. . . ."[36] Reason, the project of modernity leading to secularization, has implanted within its self-reflective process the seeds of its own dismantling—opening space amidst the ashes for a new relationship to the divine.

Just as critic Harold Bloom was in search of a mythic guise for his literary theory,[37] here Žižek is also in search of a mythic guise for a new dialectical materialism—and curiously enough both choose to return to the pre-modern myth in Lurianic Kabbalah known as "the shattering of the vessels" [*shevirat hakeilim*].[38] Žižek sees in this cosmogonic myth what he calls the "primordial wound," a possibility for articulating how "the breaking of the vessel is the opening to its restoration."[39] The mystical myth Žižek seeks is precisely what allows him to enshroud this Hegelian *absoluter Gegenstoss* as a process which "stands for the radical coincidence of opposites in which the action appears as its own counter-action, or, more precisely, in which the negative move (loss, withdrawal) itself generates what it 'negates,'" which again draws (un)knowingly on medieval Kabbalistic language.[40] Notwithstanding his atemporal recovery of sources to inform a new dialectical materialism, Žižek exemplifies the recoil of the contemporary thinker's distance from traditional sources that allows for a different reading upon return. It is this outside/inside perspective that then allows Žižek to ask:

> Where do we find these living gods? In the pagan Thing: God dies in himself in Judaism and for himself in Christianity. The destructive aspect of the divine that marks a living god—the brutal expression of rage mixed with ecstatic bliss—is what Lacan is aiming at with his statement that the gods belong to the Real.[41]

The contours of the Real, which embody "the brutal expression of rage mixed with ecstatic bliss," indicate an imminent accessibility to the abode of the divine through an emotional rather than cognitive register. Precisely the shift that disturbed Habermas is what Žižek sees as the turn to the Real in a post-secular context. Through the "primordial wound," Žižek is willing to stake out a return to the divine recoil. But Žižek does not invoke or attempt to reconcile the Nietzschean dualism of the logical order and stiff sobriety of the *Apollonian* impulse nor the instinctual and amoral *Dionysian* impulse.[42] Instead, Žižek seeks a fused, albeit primordially wounded, divinity that embodies, at once, the brutality of rage and the ecstasy of bliss. Once this move is made, Žižek continues the interrogation by asking: "So what happens when these living gods withdraw, when they no longer operate in a collective libidinal economy?"[43] What emerges here for Žižek then is the insight that "our only access to universality is through the gaps and inconsistencies of a particular life form . . ."[44] Žižek is careful to avoid "the rise of a more authentic Sacred prior even to God, not yet 'reified' in a God."[45] Following this path of dialectical reversal, Žižek concludes that "[t]he final revelation is thus that God Himself suffers even more than us mortals: our struggles against our enemies are tearing apart God Himself, they are struggles fighting within Himself. However, this is not to be conceived as the struggle of an entity divided into multiple Selves . . . there is substantially only one God, the two-ness is that of the Hegelian 'coincidence of opposites' which has nothing to do with the 'eternal harmony' of opposed forces characteristics of pagan cosmology."[46] Žižek's critical radar allow him to avoid the pitfalls of paganism that, when taken to its extreme of earth worship, can lead to a fascist obsession with any homeland, to conclude that: "It is this reflexive reversal from the object hidden in the subject to the subject itself which defines love, the move from blind fascination to love."[47]

This necessary digression into absolute recoil of the divine according to Žižek evinces an abiding appetite for enlightenment as he deftly sifts through remnants of the sacred after "the cognitive achievements of modernity." This is both a response and an effort to build upon "the secular self-understanding of modernity" as a bridge toward the sacred remnant still glowing in the ashes of modernity. It seems that Žižek's absolute recoil of the divine is very much relevant to analyzing this quest in the North American cultural context. Furthermore, it is Leonard Cohen, as a respected musical artist who is uniquely poised—with both his Zen training and Jewish mystical intuitions—to compose the post-secular soundtrack that engages such "absolute recoil" in this religion of no-religion in America.

We return to our opening question inquiring into the nature of enlightenment in a mystical context. Enlightenment generally should be seen as the result of a process of perfection of personhood and soul in relation to a greater source. That source may be Higher Self or God. In either case, the thread that binds the fabric of the search is the travail itself. Precisely the very "social pathologies of modernity" emerge in enlightened leaders. Nevertheless, Jewish mysticism envisions a perfection of personhood that leads to a transformation of the soul into a *tzaddik*'s soul—one who brings to one's self, one's community, and to all people, the world, and to the divine.[48] Likewise, Japanese Zen Buddhism envisions a perfection of personhood that leads to a transformation of the soul into one that brings light (just as does the *tzaddik*'s), to one's self, all people, and the world. Enlightenment for the *tzaddik* is tasted in ascending to the *time-that-is-coming* or *'olam ha-ba* through a state of cleaving to divine consciousness known as *devekut.* Enlightenment for the Zen practitioner is achieved through the practice of sitting meditation (*zazen*), which provides a path to wisdom through a state of *satori.* The main path of cultivating such wisdom is one of compassion expressed in the mundane "life-world" so full of anxiety and suffering.[49] What I argue here is that Cohen's post-secular songs exhibit a unique interweaving of Jewish Mysticism and Japanese Zen Buddhism. The Rinzai methods of *koan* practice and extended sitting serve as a kind of anti-philosophy that aims at overcoming dualism, but it is in the returning to the mundane "life-world" following *satori* that the work of enlightenment can be said truly to begin. The Jewish mystical methods of practicing Sabbath as a foretaste of the *time-that-is-coming* [*ta'am m'ein olam ha'ba*]; repairing the world [*tikkun olam*]; and merging [*devekut*] with the divine, all enable the mystic to be transformed into *tzaddik*-consciousness. When this state is achieved, the *tzaddik* is then responsible for leading, caring for, and awakening others. The trace of such light from this process of creative shattering is known in Lurianic Kabbalah as *reshimu. Reshimu* emerges in the shards of another Cohen-*koan*, with *Chanukah*, the Festival of Lights:

> and yet there was/a certain/light/a radiance/as if there still/remained/ behind—Oh I don't know—/as if he/were still/alive.[50]

Once the seeker reaches that illumination point which causes a transformation of self into *tzaddik* or *bodhisattva*,[51] the paths share remarkably parallels—insofar as one comes down the mountain of enlightenment and awakens others. In coming down the mountain of enlightenment, how would you react in discovering that your entire life savings had been embezzled by someone you once loved? How did decades of practice under the supervision of Rinzai Zen Master, Joshu Sasaki Roshi, allow Leonard Cohen to come down from Mount Baldy retreat center in the 1990s into the catastrophe awaiting him on his Boogie Street in West Los Angeles? And what of Cohen's Rinzai Zen Master, Sasaki Roshi, and his alleged indiscretions in the midst of Zen instruction with female students? Was Cohen's passing reference to it merely the dark side of the sexual revolution that marked much of the Age of Aquarius? After all, during the 1960s, of the four major Zen teachers who came to the United States from Japan—Shunryu Suzuki,[52] Eido Shimano,[53] Taizan Maezumi,[54] and Joshu Sasaki Roshi[55]—at least three were involved in alleged sex scandals.[56] Cohen's response to Sasaki's alleged indiscretions with students raises questions about the "willful non-action" of *Wu Wei*:

> He is just what he is. And of course he's going to be an enemy to your self-indulgence, an enemy to your laziness, he's going to be a friend to your effort. . . . He's going to be all things that he has to be to turn you away from depending on him. And finally you just say: This guy is absolutely true. He really loves me so much that I don't need to depend on him.[57]

In a Jewish-Buddhist context, these scandals signal more than simply another case of BGS or "Bad Guru Syndrome." A question arises: does this kind of master-disciple dysfunction, leading to downfall, point to the fissure between Jewish and Buddhist mysticism? Is there something intrinsic to the cultivation of non-dual consciousness that leads to the erasure of ethics once enlightenment is realized? As Cohen was initiated on the Rinzai path, becoming ordained as *Jikan* ("Silent One"),[58] his spiritual world-view becomes more expansive, allowing him to see his master teacher as "just what he is." This view reflects the Zen attitude that "any stance that is fixed is one-sided and partial," which will "deprive Zen, for example, of an opportunity to utilize Zen-seeing in the actions of everyday life." In returning to the mundane "life world," the gap separating *satori* from the everyday becomes readily apparent, so the Zen practitioner learns to see how to navigate this gap—how? In the move from having transcended the ego as "trans-individual" to the form of an "individual" with dualistic desires of the mundane world.[59] The freedom that comes with enlightenment allows a sense of spontaneity, where an action may now arise out of self on its own from nothing, suggesting a groundless ground that is nothing.[60] Desires are to then be transformed from defilements to non-defilements of higher spiritual energy.

Defiling desires symbolized as the mystical experience of luminal darkness—themes common to Kabbalah—are also a recurring motif in Cohen's songs. The Jewish mystic occupies a kind of non-dual reality of a hypernomian transmorality. What I am suggesting here is that Cohen embodies such a figure clothed in the sacred garb of the profane. Likewise, Cohen's post-secular songs do not ultimately succumb to a false messianic mission, but instead give voice to the defiled inherent within the pure.[61] It is the paradoxically experience of darkness that can hold so many facets at once. As evinced in the following lyrics, darkness is never far from light and love. In "Love Calls You by Your Name"[62] there is that space "between the darkness and the stage,/between the hour and the age," where "love calls you by your name." That liminal space appears again in "Ballad of the Absent Mare,"[63] embodying that desire in the common mystical symbol of the feminine horse, "and she's there where the light and the darkness divide." What makes Cohen's confrontation with what would otherwise be a depressing and deathly abode so striking is how the singer is attuned to its unique music, so in "That Don't Make It Junk"[64] he can sing: "I'll listen to the darkness sing-/I know what that's about./I tried to love you my way,/ But I couldn't make it hold./So I closed the Book of Longing/And I do what I am told." Darkness as the Other Side of light evokes a maiden, like the *Shekhinah*, who is exiled to those hours when the sun has already set.[65] Cohen rends the veils round this darkness in "Lady Midnight"[66] where he realizes that "it is this that the darkness is for!/I cried, O Lady Midnight, I fear that you grow old,/the stars eat your body and the wind makes you cold./If we cry now, she said, it will only be ignored." The feminization of the darkness recurs again in "The Gypsy Wife,"[67] where the wandering woman is at home beyond the light: "Whose darkness deepens in her arms/a little more?/And where is my gypsy wife tonight?" The depths of those darkened desires, consistently emerging within Cohen's songs, leads him to then dedicate and entitle an entire song to it as, "Darkness":

> I caught the darkness/It was drinking from your cup/I caught the darkness/Drinking from your cup/I said: Is this contagious?/You said: Just drink it up.[68]

Immediately the lyric draws us in to wonder who offered the singer this cup of darkness—a lover? A teacher? Or is this a case of not-two, namely, the offer originates from a state of non-dual consciousness that is beyond such distinctions? Regardless of what image emerges in this stanza, it plunges the seeker who sips from this cup into a darkening night of the soul. Entering into this state of consciousness alters the seeker's perception of time:

> I got no future/I know my days are few/The present's not that pleasant/Just a lot of things to do/I thought the past would last me/But the darkness got that too.[69]

The further the seeker enters into this altered state of consciousness, the more unclear this darkness. Is this a darkness that obliterates light or clarifies where the light cannot reach? What is emerging here is the sense that this is a luminal darkness that envelops both past and future, thus creating a loss of pleasure, if not outright suffering in the present.

> I should have seen it coming/It was right behind your eyes/You were young and it was summer/I just had to take a dive/Winning you was easy/But darkness was the prize.[70]

The emotions in this stanza point to betrayal that emerges from the vulnerability the opens in a loving relationship. While there is a recurring battle between *eros* and *thanatos*, between love and death, throughout Cohen's oeuvre, something has changed. The death of self that leads to a witnessing from afar breeds self-awareness:

> I used to love the rainbow/I used to love the view/I loved the early morning/I'd pretend that it was new/But I caught the darkness baby/ And it got worse than you/I caught the darkness . . .[71]

While the seeker could once dwell in the wondrous, erotic luminosity of the multi-colored rainbow and bask in the light of dawn as a renewal of creation, everything changes once the darkness set in. What begins as a dark night of the soul catalyzed by the erotic encounter, soon consumes the entire self so that darkness becomes a contagion. Echoes of the prophetic poetry of Isaiah, which Cohen's grandfather, Rabbi Solomon Klonitzki-Kline, used to read to him when they lived together in Montréal, concatenate here, especially the Prophet's verse about darkness:

> I form light and create darkness; I make peace and create evil; I am YHVH.[72]

Just as the liturgist of the *Ma'ariv* evening prayer substitutes the word "everything" for "evil," given a supreme discomfort with a divine author creating evil in tandem with darkness, so too, Cohen envisions darkness as enveloping everything and emerging from everything, from the All. Along the journey into the dark night of the soul, the hope of the evening prayer is that light will emerge from darkness and prevail. If there is no separate existence of darkness from light, then there is the distinct possibility that sometimes this mixture can turn from illumination through the light to a luminal darkness. Where then could any song emerge in such a darkening night of the soul?

The Jewish mystical path of *tikkun olam* converges with Zen-seeing the actions of everyday life in this very process of transforming defilements and elevating them into higher spiritual energy. Jewish-seeing positions the *tzaddik* with the capacity to use the system of sacral deeds known as *mitzvoth* as vehicles for this transformation process that not only elevates individual spiritual energy, but also affects and adorns the divine. That is the dual nature of *tikkun olam* at play here, at once repairing and adorning the godhead that affects these multiverses of consciousness. This textured way of seeing as an opportunity for transforming defilements to higher spiritual energy is at play in Leonard Cohen's song, "Here It Is":

> Here is your crown/And your seal and rings;/And here is your love/For all things./Here is your cart,/And your cardboard and piss;/And here is your love/For all of this.[73]

In juxtaposing "your crown" and "your cart" in these opening stanzas, Cohen presents a mundane "life-world" that is dualistic to the core, but with a twist. The twist is that while "your cardboard and piss" are the lot of the homeless one experiences daily in transversing Boogie Streets, it is unclear where "your seal and rings" come from and whether they are still worn. Are these remnants of jewelry that descend from the heights of marriage into the workaday week of the mundane "life world," or are they indications of royal origins of the human soul that have been cast off neglected, or forgotten? Or is the master-disciple dynamic of cultivating prophecy, once marked by "your seal and rings" as with Elisha and Elijah, now transformed into "your cardboard and piss"—images that accompany the iconic ranting homeless person on Boogie street? The common perception of the ego mind-stream is to see spiritual and mundane existence as a dualistic reality—one separat from the other. The lyrics of each stanza challenge this tendency to separate experiences for the sake of convenience, comfort, and ease of navigating an otherwise messy "life-world." It is precisely in this messiness of "not two" that an enlightened world view of "And here is your love/For all of this" can emerge. The challenge that life presents is how to transform its messiness, especially in the transition from life to death, into that state of "not-two" abiding as a blessing:

> May everyone live,/And may everyone die./Hello, my love,/And my love, Good bye.[74]

The flow of this blessing is now only expanded by further interspersing moments of celebration with moments of sickness—another manifestation of embracing everything, namely, the all of non-dual consciousness, without judgment and without will. Celebration marking sacred time is tasted through elevating wine. But during the ascent this wider perspective already also sees and embraces the drunken descent:

> Here is your wine,/And your drunken fall,/And here is your love./Your love for it all./Here is your sickness./Your bed and your pan;/And here is your love/For the woman, the man.[75]

The sickness, which begins by afflicting the individual physiologically in "your bed and your pan" is juxtaposed with the non-dual love for "for the woman, the man." Sickness parallels love and the question emerges; is the seeker lovesick or suffering from a love that is sick?

> And here is the night,/The night has begun;/And here is your death/In the heart of your son.[76]

Death of the self begins with the onset of the night, known as the "dark night of the soul." But this death appears to be most devastating and liberating when the image of the father dies "in the heart of your son." While part of this absolute recoil of the divine may emerge from the particularity of Cohen's fractured family life, it is nonetheless curious then that the final stanza invokes the son about to be crucified before the father:

> Here is your cross,/Your nails and your hill;/And here is your love,/That lists where it will.[77]

Rebirth of the trans-individual identity is possible in the sacred union of masculine and feminine. From the dark night of the soul, in which the self dies and is reborn, there then emerges the possibility of further differentiating by the birth of the third, in this case, the daughter. Her birth as third evokes the feminine indwelling presence, already referred to as the *Shekhinah*. Whereas the father surrenders his son for crucifixion, the fate of his daughter is different. It is in her heart where death occurs, rather than originating in her father's heart:

> And here is the dawn,/(until death do us part);/And here is your death,/ In your daughter's heart.[78]

The transience of life through which everyone is rushing is really a veil covering the reality of the No-thing to which all sentient beings return. The foundation of existence stands as the love which has been coursing through all the ascents and descents of the song to this point:

> And here you are hurried,/And here you are gone;/And here is the love,/ That it's all built upon.[79]

Swimming on the sea of darkness is modeled as a way of navigating "the crown" and "the cart" of life. What Cohen is sketching out is a way of seeing the infinite within the finite, the non-dual within the "life world" of dualism. This is eloquently encapsulated in the following poem by long-time University of New Hampshire philosophy professor, Donald C. Babcock (1889-1986), called "Little Duck":

> Now we are ready to look at something pretty special.
> It is a duck riding the ocean a hundred feet beyond the surf.

> . . . And what does he do, I ask you. He sits down in it.
> He reposes in the immediate as if it were infinity—which it is.
> That is religion, and the duck has it.
> He has made himself part of the boundless, by easing himself into it just where it touches him. I like the little duck. He doesn't know much.
> But he has religion.[80]

The duck floating in the swells brings back into focus albeit ironically the possibility of religion in a post-secular age. The sought out gesture is about learning to repose in the "immediate as if it were infinity." Navigating existence by knowing that amid the "great heaving" in the world one is inextricably "a part of it" captures Cohen's gift as a songwriter. Cohen is always "easing himself into it just where it touches him"—this vulnerability is what draws in so many to hear the Montréal bard's post-secular songbook. Cohen evokes this masterful navigation through the next *topos* of luminal darkness in the sea through his song, "Banjo":

> There's something that I'm watching/Means a lot to me/It's a broken banjo bobbing/On the dark infested sea.
> Don't know how it got there/Maybe taken by the wave/Off of someone's shoulder/Our out of someone's grave.
> It's coming for me darling/No matter where I go/Its duty is to harm/My duty is to know . . .[81]

Unique to his songwriting style, Cohen captures something of Babcock's duck riding the swells by substituting it with something even more surreal—a banjo. While the banjo is not an instrument favored by any of Cohen's current minstrels—neither Javier Mas on twelve string *bandurria*, nor Alexandru Bublitchi on violin—still its symbolism resonates. The music Cohen wants to provide for navigating the storms of life as a journeying through the sea are found in the resonant sounds of that simple, accessible instrument of folk music—the banjo. Perhaps the symbolism harkens back to Cohen's first forays into music with the country troubadours, the Buckskin Boys, during his youth. Well into the winter season of his life, Cohen has surpassed individuation and may just be journeying back to origins. But this is not as simple as it appears, for this banjo is broken and bobbing, at once wounded, alive and dead. It is the music sympathetically resonating from this dualistic state of broken bobbing that returns to the non-dual sound enveloping the universe.

The remarkable courage of Cohen's lyrical embrace of the All, the *everything* of non-dual consciousness, enables him to discover sacred song amidst the dualism of the mundane life world. The dark night of the soul through which the broken soul is bobbing will emerge more clarified, more expansive in ascending from this descent. From darkness emerges light, from hopelessness emerges hope, and so for Cohen, this darkness is luminal, glowing with the capacity for redemption. It takes a master journeyman to navigate the waves of divine recoil in song. Only the Montréal bard could sing about it as deftly as he does that: "There is a crack, a crack in everything, that's how the light gets in."[82] Cohen's lyrics serve as what Žižek sees as the "passage to non-relationship," adding robust contours to the emerging discourse of post-secularism throughout his songbook. Only when the ensuing darkness of withdrawal from the cognitive within modernity is broken through, even by a crack of light, does a song of non-relationship re-emerge as truly sacred within this post-secular cultural context. And so in re-emerging, the sacred song being sung in a post-secular age will begin to *sing itself.*[83]

4

Tangle of Matter & Ghost

Objective Spirit & Non-Dual Reality in Prayerful Poetry

Oh chosen love, Oh frozen love
Oh tangle of matter and ghost
Oh darling of angels, demons and saints
And the whole broken-hearted host
Gentle this soul.

—Leonard Cohen[1]

Without music, life would be an error.

—Nietzsche[2]

Through the ages, mystics and philosophers, poets and singers, each in their own way, have marveled at the inexplicable entanglement of mind and spirit that somehow remains embodied as a singular human being. The path to truth is a creative quest, so much so that for a philosopher and musician, like Friedrich Nietzsche (1844-1900), it must be indelibly marked by a post-Romantic view that all creativity, and reality itself, is most vibrant when its instinctual, wild *Dionysian* energy is in force. Such a quest, for Nietzsche, is an entanglement of the *Dionysian* and the *Apollonian* energies, which are constantly pushing and pulling at the modern subject. What scars the modern subject is a Nietzschean lament over how the necessary *Dionysian* creative energy is all but eclipsed by the sobriety of the *Apollonian*. The basis of the malaise that plagues the disengaged modern subject, for Nietzsche, lies in this loss of the necessary *Dionysian* creative energy that so audaciously affirms the search for "the mysterious primordial unity" despite "the shattering of the individual and his fusion with primal being."[3] What Nietzsche dares us to rediscover is just how much the *Dionysian* creative spirit is never satiated by mere *Apollonian* pleasures with surface beauty; rather the *Dionysian* needs to feel the "pain and contradiction" of a more "blissful ecstasy."[4]

At the precipice of the ensuing analysis of the prayerful poetry of Leonard Cohen, some consideration should be given as to whether this singer-songwriter is more of an *Apollonian* artist, as a hero, or more of a *Dionysian* artist, one whose dissolution into nature transforms him into a "primordial artist of the world."[5] Whichever creative energy this Montréal bard embodies, to be impactful his lyrical art must realize that when this music is repressed, or removed, as the opening epithet suggests, then life itself is misaligned and errant. It is up to the subject, who, for Nietzsche, is "over-human" (*übermenschlich*), to harness the music of life. This opens a wider horizon of being that is a more viable, ambiguous, and thus beautiful world-interpretation.[6] We shall see shortly why Leonard Cohen's songbook fulfills that need in a post-secular world so bereft of the spirit.

For modern philosophers, expressions like *ésprit* and *Geist* portray the fluid nature of subjectivity—a zone where an embodied spirit hovers in a most mysterious manner, despite all attempts to lock it down by any rational means of thinking. To then to be so audacious as to even infer, never mind to talk about, an "objective spirit" is clearly a product of Enlightenment thinking, in general, and G. W. F. Hegel (1770-1831), in particular. Such audacity still draws the attention of contemporary philosophers, like Charles Taylor (b. 1931), as he continues to dedicate enormous energy to thinking through the possibility of an "objective spirit."[7] As Taylor is careful to note, the very spirit emerging in the modern period—whether within or beyond our awareness—follows a pattern and structure. To navigate modernity for Taylor is to be aware of a mapping that constitutes the self by defining "what it is to be a human agent: the sense of *inwardness, freedom, individuality*, and being embedded in *nature*."[8] This very same dissatisfaction Taylor experiences in his fourfold mapping out the contours of self through modern philosophy, I would argue, also fuels the prolific *oeuvre* of lyrics by fellow Montréaler, Leonard Cohen (b. 1934). As a respected musical artist— coupled with both his Zen training and Jewish mystical intuitions—it is Leonard Cohen who continues to compose the post-secular soundtrack of the search for spirit in America. Whether a shared "third solitude" inspires the work of both philosopher and bard from Montréal is beyond the scope of the present investigation.[9] Our focus will remain on the following question: why does a philosopher like Charles Taylor continued to dedicate significant thinking to the archaeology and constitution of an "objective spirit," just as a songwriter like Leonard Cohen continues to produce lyrical reflections on the "tangle of matter and ghost"? To better understand the disengaged subject of modernity, I argue that both philosopher and singer-songwriter from Montréal provide unique lenses through which to think, contemplate, and sing through "unhappy consciousness" and find a redemptive pathway for reconstituting identity in this post-secular age.

This investigation of identity—through philosophy and song—reveals a set of shared concerns for the correlation of mind and matter, spirit and flesh, all in the context of modernity. What is the texture of identity that emerges from this relationship between the mind and the body, and what makes it uniquely modern? Interestingly, amid the search for an answer in the copious writings of philosophers spanning these past two centuries, it is the philosopher Charles Taylor, also from Montréal, who posits the thoroughly modern conviction that "a life spent in artistic creation or performance is eminently worthwhile,"[10] and that creative practice affects the contours of this "objective spirit." The worthwhileness of artistic creation, specifically in the lyrics of Leonard Cohen's song book, will serve as a pathway into the torn modern subject in search of spiritual sustenance.

However at the threshold of a more general philosophic investigation into the identity of the modern subject, it is imperative to first trace the contours of Jewish philosophy. If the primary purpose of Jewish philosophy, often referred to as "*Machshevet Yisrael*[,] is the never-ending attempt on the part of Jews to make some rational sense of the primary religious events that define their existence as Jews,"[11] then the nature of this attempt must be immutable and prone to objectivity and standardization. So goes the argument that has defined the field of Jewish philosophy for centuries. Letting go of the need to bridge the "significant gap between *Machshevet Yisrael* instruction and the students' world view is urgent and crucial in our post-secular age."[12] This gap exists precisely where, for German Jewish thinkers, such as Theodor Adorno (1903–1969), the sparks of insight from dialectical thinking reveal themselves. As a student of *Wissenschaft des Judentums* myself, I could not help but cringe at the delusion of objectivity that held sway over every aspect of our analysis of Jewish identity and praxis. But I bristled the whole way through, feeling that this approach no longer suffices in buttressing claims that, "[b]y returning the study of *Machshevet Yisrael* back to its natural location, as an outgrowth of the study of the facts of Judaism," the "relevance and impact"[13] of such thinking becomes apparent in its limitations.

Mere study of the facts of Judaism leads very quickly to reified thinking; there are of course some noble exceptions. These philosophies attempt to expand and interrogate the concepts that delimit *Machshevet Yisrael*—the conceptual triad of God-Torah-Israel[14]—each one with its own contribution to the possibility of furthering new pathways in Jewish thinking—especially in the works of Wolfson,[15] Green,[16] and Magid.[17] With the rebirth of Zionist fervor and proto-messianism in a post-1967 landscape, the category "Israel" now to eclipses God into a reified Torah.

This explains why, prior to 1967, according to one tragic yarn, if you wanted to join a synagogue the entry question was: "Do you believe in God?" but post-1967, if you want to join a synagogue the entry question remains: "Do you believe in Zionism?" Clearly Jewish philosophy remains in need of a serious negative dialectical propulsion. For how can new directions in Jewish philosophy emerge if the thinking itself is unable to transcend the stranglehold of the reified concept?

In struggling through the stranglehold of the reified concept, one finds solace in Taylor's philosophic investigation into the identity of the modern subject. For Taylor is unique amongst contemporary philosophers insofar as he intentionally aims to "put an end to the stifling of the spirit and to the atrophy of so many of our spiritual sources which is the bane of modern spiritual culture."[18] Overcoming this atrophy of the spirit requires the willingness and courage to confront one's self as a *disengaged subject.* This disengaged self is experienced through an exacerbated mind-body dualism, with an emphasis on self-mastery.[19] I extrapolate self-mastery here in Taylor to refer to any creative effort that affects selfhood. To realize any degree of such mastery of self, however, requires an openness to self-exploration, bordering on radical reflexivity, which Taylor juxtaposes alongside a necessarily deeper disengagement.[20]

The depth of the disengaged subject that Taylor presents is a natural outgrowth of Hegel's philosophy of mind, which Hegel began in earnest with his *Phenomenology of Spirit* (1806). What emerges in modernity is a concerted thinking around the capacity of the human subject to be conscious of things outside and distinct from itself. This kind of thinking requires the subject to have the capacity to be *self-conscious.* Moreover, the very act of recognizing other self-conscious subjects as subjects is what establishes a pattern of mutual recognition known as "objective spirit." This focus on "objective spirit" through mutual recognition allows for distinct patterns of interaction and community to emerge through the *Geist.* Such patterns lead to a tracking of "shapes of consciousness" that ultimately allow for recognition of the shapes of the spirit itself. The subject encounters "unhappy consciousness" [*unglückliches Bewusstsein*];[21] paradoxically, within the realm of self-consciousness, one would least expect to confront it—in *religious self-consciousness.* Institutionalized religious forms of meditation[22] serve to shatter the self and inflict suffering from disunion. It comes as little surprise then that what emerges within the disengaged subject of modernity is a distinct distrust and a disdain for any kind of intermediary between the self-conscious subject and their connection to divinity. Of Hegel's entire triadic structure of *subjective spirit, objective spirit* and *absolute spirit,* Taylor draws our attention to the "objective spirit," insofar as it allows for a recognition of the ways in which spirit is objectified into social interaction and religio-cultural institutions.[23] Poised in the post-secular context of North America, Taylor, as a post-Enlightenment philosopher, cannot make a wholesale endorsement here that would consider the human collective as a *corpus mysticum*; rather he wants to reconsider the value of "objective spirit" as it relates to the "spirit of the laws." Yet, Taylor's focus on the "spirit of laws" risks generating rather than overcoming the "unhappy consciousness" hovering within religious self-consciousness. How then can the shattered subject suffering from disunion of body and spirit continue in its search for a shared language and experience of meaning? It is precisely this disunion which Montréal bard, Leonard Cohen redresses through his "tangle of matter and ghost." That is, no matter how objective the spirit may be, it must always be tethered to an embodied situation.

But the difficulties the *disengaged subject* experiences with this "objective spirit" extend to the very idea of a social form of thought. Thinking then is a personal, if not solitary, affair, wherein someone's thought is always driving things through a personal, thinking subject. The collective is composed of thinking individuals, all *en route* to enlightenment, but by no means unified in this quest.[24] By interrogating whether there really is an "objective spirit" undergirding Taylor's philosophic project, Vincent

Descombes brings to light an important affinity between language and a sociological theory of spirit. Descombes builds on the work of Swiss linguist, Ferdinand de Saussure, specifically his distinction between *langue*, as "a socially shared set of abstract conventions" and *parole*, as "the particular choices made by a speaker deploying a language."[25] Descombes' reading of Taylor challenges the individual-society dualism implied in Saussure's *langue/parole* binary. To move beyond *langue* as a collective fact, and *parole* as a purely individual phenomenon, Descombes sees the act of *parole* as a necessarily social act, since it involves two people in conversation, yet *parole* is not a collective act, since it remains personal.[26] No matter how independent and alone the disengaged subject may be in Taylor's estimation, Descombes points to a bottom line of dyadic unity, wherein each individual is always taking part "in an activity [that] calls for a partner."[27] This leads Descombes to simultaneously see an *external* relation between the subject and her partner, while there is an *internal* relation between the activity that one undertakes (i.e. speaking to someone, writing a song) and the reciprocal element of that activity (i.e. responding to the conversation, listening to the song).[28] The general spirit of society, in Descombes's critical reading of Taylor, is therefore a metaphysical, if not a metapersonal one—privileging the *dyad* over the *monad*, interlocutors over hermits. The act of speaking, especially in Cohen's case of singing with one another, "presupposes the collective institution of a common *langue* realized outside the partners to the conversation."[29]

Beyond the question of privileging the *dyad* over the *monad*, there remains a much larger gap in the foundation of Taylor's metaphysical claims being carrying forward through Hegel's "objective spirit." Is it possible or necessary to come to know the *other* by knowing your own "objective spirit"? Or is it possible merely to know yourself as subject and object, and only then when the ego subsides, to move beyond the binding subject-object dualism? In attempting to establish a systematized "philosophy of spirit," Hegel constructs a grand metaphysical project through which *subjective* and *objective spirit* yearn to realize their apogee and reach *absolute spirit.* This apogee is the very point at which the eternal idea reveals itself and enjoys itself as absolute spirit. It was the audacity of such a claim by Hegel, that any system could reach for, and ultimately realize, an eternal idea, that really bothered his contemporaries, as it did Arthur Schopenhauer (1788-1860).[30] This "objective spirit" is "nothing more than a 'monstrous amplification' of the ontological proof for the existence of God, a proof that Kant had discredited long ago."[31] The problem that emerges from the Hegelian view of reason is that, for Schopenhauer, it claims "to reconcile the limited, finite, and putatively contradictory concepts upon which the sub-philosophical faculty of understanding shipwrecked itself."[32] When human agency itself is contingent upon the faculty of Reason alone, namely, Reason that thinks absolute objects of genuine philosophical thought, then the prospects of a more expansive understanding begin to fade from view. Schopenhauer understood the equivocation of being and nothing to be beyond the pale of Reason. Schopenhauer's metaphysics stand as a complete antithesis to Hegel, one that escapes any totalizing system and remains insatiable. It is indeed curious that Taylor seems to swerve what Schopenhauer saw as an obvious pandering in Hegel to both the State and Church through the actualization of the idea of freedom—spirit becoming conscious of itself. The rejection of Hegel's philosophy of history as well as his teleological view of history absolutely again is something which seems to elude Taylor's reading of the "objective spirit." How then can the aforementioned "unhappy consciousness" that emerges in pursuit of Hegel's "objective spirit" be remedied? It is necessary to consider this question which continues to, at once, plague and inspire the song book of Leonard Cohen through the lens of the philosopher who first dared to confront it—Schopenhauer.

The challenge arises: what are the kinds of changes in self-understanding that change us? How does this shift in self-understanding then affect the possibility of inward peace and quietness of spirit? In his late masterpiece, *The World as Will and Idea* (1883), Schopenhauer is willing to consider how Stoic philosophy traces the contours of happiness, which "can only be attained with certainty through inward peace and quietness of spirit, and that this again can only be reached through virtue; this is the whole meaning of the saying that virtue is the highest good."[33] But any system—whether Hegel's philosophy of history or Stoicism for that matter—inevitably succumbs to the totalizing nature of its own structure, as Schopenhauer is quick to notice in this tension between the idealist virtue and individual happiness:

> But if indeed by degrees the end is lost sight of in the means, and virtue is inculcated in a way which discloses an interest entirely different from that of one's own happiness, for it contradicts this too distinctly; this is just one of those inconsistencies by means of which, in every system, the immediately known, or, as it is called, felt truth leads us back to the right way in defiance of syllogistic reasoning.[34]

Part of the genius in this self-critique and critique of systematic thinking is how Schopenhauer turns to the power of music. While I have addressed more contemporary contributions to musical thinking elsewhere,[35] it is instructive that at the dawn of modernity, Schopenhauer has the vision to redress the Hegelian state of unhappy consciousness through the power of music, as the former writes:

> This is the origin of the song with words . . . the text of which should therefore never forsake that subordinate position in order to make itself the chief thing and the music a mere means of expressing it, which is a great misconception and a piece of utter perversity; for music always expresses only the quintessence of life and its events, never these themselves, and therefore their differences do not always affect it. It is precisely this universality, which belongs exclusively to it, together with the greatest determinateness, that gives music the high worth which it has as the panacea for all our woes. Thus, if music is too closely united

> to the words, and tries to form itself according to the events, it is striving to speak a language which is not its own.[36]

What is important here in exploring musical thinking is to appreciate how "music always expresses only the quintessence of life and its events," a perspective which will become evident in Leonard Cohen's lyrics, even though the Montréal bard ultimately inverts Schopenhauer's prescription. The elevation of music to a nearly transcendent medium, for Schopenhauer, is a music that speaks "its own language of its own so distinctly and purely that it requires no words, and produces its full effect when rendered by instruments alone."[37] What makes music unique in its capacity to elevate the external world is the degree that:

> Music, therefore, if regarded as an expression of the world, is in the highest degree a universal language, which is related indeed to the universality of concepts, much as they are related to the particular things. Its universality, however, is by no means that empty universality of abstraction, but quite of a different kind, and is united with thorough and distinct definiteness.[38]

Music, for Schopenhauer, provides a "universality . . . united with thorough and distinct definiteness," which allows for the most subtle of links between the transcendent and the immanent. Music serves to bridge "the universality of the concepts" as well as "the universality of the melodies."[39] It is no surprise then that Schopenhauer is highly attuned to the music of mysticism. Consider the arc of Schopenhauer's Christological *vision*, which contains within it a kind of musical aspiration. Specifically, he sees in the New Testament the first initiation into mystical *gnosis*. Following this, the arc curves to German mystics, such as Meister Eckhart, which marks an initiation into second mystical *gnosis*, one that confers a kind of lucidity on the New Testament initiation.[40] Within Schopenhauer's arc there is the sense of an emerging musical pathway of mystical *gnosis*. What emerges in this awareness is a newfound relationship, for Schopenhauer, with the will, insofar as "the deep unbroken solitude, spent in silent contemplation, with voluntary penance and terrible slow self-torture for the absolute mortification of the will."[41] Salient to our discussion, this raises the question: What remains of the will in the Jewish-Zen lyrical search of Leonard Cohen?

From this focus in Schopenhauer's musical thinking on the place of the will, two-tiered mystical *gnosis* and universality united with distinct definiteness, nothing could be more apt than to now make the turn from Schopenhauer's philosophy to Leonard Cohen's mystical music and prayerful poetry. Leonard Cohen's gift is an uncanny ability to navigate that simultaneous internal-external relation, and create lyrics from that palette of a "collective institution of a common *langue*" that resonates with almost every disengaged subject. The question then emerges: what are the kinds of changes in self-understanding that in turn change us through Cohen's songbook? It is this unique "tangle of matter and ghost"—what Cohen renders as a consciousness of "New Jerusalem glowing"—that is but an entanglement of all those dyads seeking enlightenment, alone together. There is no more apt moment, which begins with silence between the notes addressing these themes in Leonard Cohen's songbook, than the prayerful poetry of "If It Be Your Will":

> If it be your will
> That I speak no more
> And my voice be still
> As it was before
> I will speak no more
> I shall abide until
> I am spoken for
> If it be your will [42]

The silence that the singer enters into here is an intentional silence—to still the mind. This is a silence that grows out of a whirlwind of words in speech and the intensity of voice in song, transforming into no-thingness. There is a patience emerging here in the abiding time, between silence and word, between stillness and sound. In this space of patience, there is a shift in self-awareness, from speaking and singing, to being "spoken for" and singing for, from an active *willfulness* to a more quietist *willingness.*[43] This transformation of the will or *ratzous* is most directly articulated in the *mishnaic* teaching of Rabban Gamliel:

> Turn the Will of the One into your will,
> so that your will should be the Will of the One.
> Nullify your will before the Will of the One,
> so that the One should nullify
> the will of others before your will.[44]

This turning the will into the Will is really a process of truing from an active *willfulness* to a more quietist *willingness*. Nothing could be more urgent in this process of "truing"[45] than the moment when the prayer leader stands before the community to engage in leading song. The traditional liturgical moment within the High Holidays of *Hineini* is recited by the prayer leader as a way of monitoring that "truing" process, by reciting as a singular voice before those gathered:

> Here I am, utterly bereft, shuddering and afraid, in fear of the One who sits in judgment of the prayers of Israel. I have come to stand before You and plead on behalf of Your people, Israel, who have sent me, as unfit and unworthy as I am.[46]

The paradoxical nature of this prayerful poem and the urgent context of its delivery could not be more stark. Life and death are hovering in the balance—*will this prayer be heard? Will it be acceptable?* If so, then this singular moment of prayer has the power to exonerate all the sinners gathered at this holy convocation. And the one whose musical ability allows her to be qualified enough to serve as the communal representative as the leader of prayer and song, is precisely the one who must be most humbled in this devotional offering. The gift of song is the greatest burden, for how is this song of the soul to be delivered in a manner fitting to a more quietist *willingness,* rather than being confused for an active *willfulness*?!? Cohen continues to be at home riffing within the liturgical place of deepest spiritual urgency,[47] here again, with his own take on *Hineini*:

> If it be your will
> That a voice be true
> From this broken hill
> I will sing to you
> From this broken hill
> All your praises they shall ring
> If it be your will
> To let me sing
> From this broken hill
> All your praises they shall ring
> If it be your will
> To let me sing.[48]

The voice emerging from silence is only transformed once it has the capacity to experience its own limitations, namely, its brokenness. That is the *raison d'etre* of Atonement Day [*Yom haKippurim*] but the "unhappy consciousness" of religion has likely caused the singer to descend into silence. This is precisely what allows this selfsame singing subject to ascend and re-emerge from the limitations of the "objective spirit." The singer here has the courage to confront and experience Schopenhauer's description of the "the deep unbroken solitude," which for Cohen emerges in the years "spent in silent contemplation" on Mount Baldy Zen Center. From this stillness of *zazen* meditation, which allows for brokenness to emerge, the contemplative singer is coming to terms "with voluntary penance and terrible slow self-torture for the absolute mortification of the will":[49]

If it be your will
If there is a choice
Let the rivers fill
Let the hills rejoice
Let your mercy spill
On all these burning hearts in hell
If it be your will
To make us well.[50]

Once the will has been transformed through the mortification of its egocentricity, only then are songs of rejoicing able to emerge. This process of song coming to light in this unitive manner is one whereby the self merges with the world, from a place of separation where "burning hearts in hell" dwell within universality, united with distinct definiteness. Such a unification from the dual to the non-dual witnesses a transition from the self, to the collective, ultimately transformed into atomistic elements of this greater will.

And draw us near
And bind us tight
All your children here
In their rags of light
In our rags of light
All dressed to kill
And end this night
If it be your will (x2).[51]

The proximity amidst the merging of mortified will, through tiers of mystical *gnosis,* leads to a binding. This binding is an immersion that dissolves the distinctions between darkness and light, of matter and spirit. The shifting of orientation in "rags of light" from an externalized "their" to an internalizing collective "our," indicates this entry into non-dual consciousness. In evoking the subtle imagery in "rags of light," Cohen manages to bridge the division between matter and spirit by presenting a subtly embodied nexus. By reflecting on the scriptural verse that: "God made for Adam and for his wife garments of skins,"[52] Cohen is riffing on the legend that in the Torah scroll written by Rabbi Meir, this very verse was written as, "God made Adam and his wife *garments of light*."[53] Cohen's "rags of light" evokes the homophony of the Hebrew *'or* as both "light" and "skin." The lyric "rags of light" recalls how that blissful moment of Primordial Adam in the Garden of Eden enshrouded in *garments of light* continues to hover. It is only in falling into the human condition that these "garbs of light" are transformed into "rags of light" that are now seen as skin. But the resonance of light, no matter how muted, continues to concatenate through human skin back to its origin in light. What this kind of imagery in the song encapsulates reaches its apex in concluding that there is a universality of "light" united with distinct directness of "rags." The dark night of the disengaged, modern soul is coming to its end, as a new spiritual consciousness emerges in its wake.

Such recurrent markers of a thoroughly modern, disengaged subject, dancing alone together and struggling with mind-body dualism, emerge in many moments within the lyrics of Cohen. In dancing to the end of love that challenges any Hegelian "objective spirit," through a Jewish-Zen lens, Cohen's music attempts to hold the wobbling "position-less position." This dance of "not two" is a negation of all the divisive dualisms that define mundane existence, while "not one" designates the negation of monadism. This hybridity—so endemic to post-Zionism discussed elsewhere[54]— is precisely what allows for the realization of a *third* perspective dancing delicately between "not one" and "not two."[55] Reaching beyond the clutches of *dualism* ("not one") or *non-dualism* ("not two") is what marks the contours of this dance. It is this yearning to connect and channel "the universality of the melodies" that enables the proliferation of prayerful poetry to music that is unique to Cohen.

The resonance of "the universality of the melodies" could not be any louder as Leonard Cohen continues to sell out from Jerusalem's *Binyanai ha'Uma* to New York's Carnegie Hall to Dublin's 02 Arena. After a period of withdrawal into silence at the Mount Baldy Zen Center, Cohen descended back into the spoken world as a destitute poet, returning to sing the songs that were emerging from this intentional silence of retreat. This spiritual ascent from fiscal descent has been well documented recently.[56] The economy of words in the lyrics of Cohen's deftly crafted *Ten New Songs* is only sharpened by the austerity of the Zen setting in which they were composed. This non-dual perspective of the Soto school of Zen[57] versus the Rinzai Zen path teaches the practice of "just sitting" with reality as it emerges rather than relying on an elaborate *koan* system. The distinction between Soto and Rinzai Zen Buddhism is Soto's greater emphasis on having a "Buddha-nature" within every person, contrasted with Rinzai's greater emphasis on the practice to attain enlightenment.[58] The purging of one's evil nature to allow for the emergence of this pristine, innate nature is not effective through the usual intellectual understanding; there remains an overlooked, emotional approach. According to Cohen's master, Sasaki Roshi and his teaching on the matter, however, "both Rinzai and Soto put emphasis on [*koan* and *zazen*]—in actual practice."[59] How this American Zen Buddhism converged with the Leonard Cohen's mystical approach to his Judaism will be given further consideration.

This emerging brand of American Zen Buddhism—in the land of the religion of no-religion[60]—is what the Rinzai Zen Master, Sasaki Roshi, appears to have been teaching and modeling intensely for Cohen in his rigorous practice of *zazen* at Mount Baldy. Whereas the *koan* serves to crack through the confines of the rational mind that thinks dualistically so as to enter the Zen mind-stream, by contrast, the *zazen* practice of "just sitting" is a more integral approach that allows for an embodied mind-stream to flow, that opening to "find ourselves confronting an absolute affirmation quite beyond the ken of our discursive understanding."[61] Escaping the cage of intellectual dualism, where "yes" is an assertion and "no" is a negation, the redeemed subject comes to realize that there is no "freedom or unity in exclusion or in limitation."[62] While Cohen's commitment to the communal practice on retreat at Mount Baldy was to sit daily, his challenge remained to how to live with an emergent reality in the practice of "just sitting" in the throes of that quotidian, noble boredom known as "Boogie Street"—namely, traffic jams, laundry, shopping, cooking, and cleaning. What sets Cohen apart as a singer-songwriter is his uncanny ability to capture this tension with direct lyrics; for example, in "Boogie Street":

> A sip of wine, a cigarette,
> And then it's time to go.
> I tidied up the kitchenette;
> I tuned the old banjo.
> I'm wanted at the traffic-jam.
> They're saving me a seat.
> I'm what I am, and what I am,
> Is back on Boogie Street.[63]

The directness and forthrightness of the Jewish monk's entry back into the speaking world of commerce and *brouhaha* is remarkable. It shows just how much Cohen remains able to integrate his struggle to overcome the mind-body dualism and bring his non-dual clarity into the way he lives and engages with living in the material world.

To be ready to engage so directly with the world emerges through just sitting—*zazen*—a practice that Cohen and others on retreat at Mount Baldy (including co-writer, Sharon Robinson), would practice up to sixteen hours daily. Renowned for lyrical compositions that draw upon *eros* and its pursuit, the challenge of "just sitting" poses to the Montréal bard is the discipline with which it keeps returning one to a single-minded, diligent practice. The "just" of "just sitting" refers to the practice of meditation without being distracted, controlled, or coerced by any sort of ego-logical interest, concern, or most importantly, desire. The irony here is, of course, that it is precisely desire and its discontents which has continued to fuel so much of Cohen's lyrical output. What this path of meditation presumes is that the seeker engages in the practice *in the midst of* the original enlightenment, or as medieval master of Japanese Soto Zen, Eihei Dogen (1200-1253) described it "practice-realization."

This is a process of attempting to close the gap of dualism, between potentiality and actuality, between before and after, between love and death, between bliss and desire. There is then the need to collapse the distinction between "acquired enlightenment" [*shikaku*] and "original enlightenment," where the "acquired" enlightenment is realized through the practice of meditation. The collapsing points to a non-dual realization ("not two"). Upon reaching such a meditational state, one is then able to "see into one's nature" [*kensho*], an initial *satori* experience. "Not two" dissolves with the experience of "dropping off the body and the mind."[64] What meditational awareness provides as an elixir to this mind-body dualism is a dissolution, between the seeker's ego, the "I" and others, as well as nature. Once this dualism disappears, the Zen practitioner experiences a *practical* transcendence from the mundane dualism of either-or, whereby the ego controls the self.

Zen perspective is a response to the *dualistic* perspective that pervades modern consciousness. Zen provides a path upon which one can train consciousness at once to swerve around and with the appearances of outer and the inner worlds, thus collapsing the outer-inner distinction itself. This non-dualistic experience occurs in the very way we think about how we think, resulting in a kind of mystical epistemology. By collapsing how the mind thinks about what it is thinking as the meaning of "not two," there emerges a more holistic perspective. The bottomless ground that "sees" with non-dual perspective then allows the seeker to experience this very state of no-thing. Living with the dynamic oscillation of "coming-together" of "the two," whether this "two" happens to involve the "between-ness" of two individuals, individual and nature, or individual and trans-individual. What is important here is that, by living knowingly in the realm of the non-dualistic, the seeker occupies a non-ego-logical standpoint that allows for transcendence. How can a subject really be a trans-individual while retaining any form of individuality? It is here that one becomes carrier of freedom beyond the perspective of the unitary individual, whereby the individual *as* trans-individual is no longer ordinary, but extraordinary, all the while remaining ever so ordinary in appearance.[65]

So given the heights of self-transformation to which the Zen seeker can reach, what are the kinds of changes in self-understanding that in turn change us? Amidst its vigilant focus on direct experience as the doorway to self-transformation, Zen eschews any interest in God, the soul, and the potential encumbrances of any metaphysical speculation.[66] By contrast, Jewish Mysticism is engaged in the discourse of the soul and how it affects practice. The very struggle with dualism with which Cohen's lyrics have for decades continued to engage—that "tangle of matter and ghost"—emerges from the reality that the soul is a portion of its divine source [*helek eloha me'ma'al*].[67] *Nefesh* in Hebrew usually denotes "desire" or "inner drive,"[68] whereas *neshama* is a much later development that is post-biblical. Whereas *neshamah* comes to designate a soul in terms of its pristine roots that transcend the material, *nefesh* denotes the embodied soul, that very "tangle of matter and ghost" so close to Cohen's lyrical imagination.

What one encounters time and again in the lyrics of Cohen is an attempt to articulate, by riffing biblically and beyond, and one can see just how deeply the human being is an entanglement of what the Jewish mystics call "the bestial soul" or *nefesh ha'behemit* and "the divine soul" or *nefesh 'elohi*.[69] The living vitality of the *nefesh* serves much like the Freudian inner drive or I.D. As a Zen practitioner, Cohen seems to be uninterested in the more intricate soul-mappings that emerge with the flourishing of Lurianic Kabbalah in early Renaissance Safed.[70] Rather, the direct contemplation of this perennial entanglement in Cohen's lyrics demands a self-reflective interrogation: w*hat then is the nature of spirit embodied in my lived existence?* The struggle to clarify the pragmatic relationship between matter and spirit is real and in many ways is what scars the disengaged subject of modernity.

By succumbing to the compartmentalization of matter and spirit that tends to suppress the latter through a ruthless secularization, the spirit wobbles while the subject wanders. In this wandering, the subject becomes distanced from the spirit and disengaged in their very subjectivity.

Through this analysis of the prayerful poetry of Leonard Cohen in a post-secular context, one must confront the "unhappy consciousness" [*unglückliches Bewusstsein*][71] that resides within religious self-consciousness—yet it is precisely amid this malaise, devoid of the spirit, that his lyrics offer solace. It is Cohen's search for "the mysterious primordial unity" despite "the shattering of the individual and his fusion with primal being"[72] that allows his lyrics to shine with the *Dionysian* need to feel the "pain and contradiction" of a more "blissful ecstasy."[73] Amid this tension, Cohen's lyrics reveal a "truing" of Judaism along his quest, whereby he continues to overcome an absolute mortification of the will by his turning the Will of the One into his will through song. In sum, Cohen's prayerful poetry, through his Jewish-Zen practice, comes to reject the *Apollonian* model of artist as hero and learns to channel the *Dionysian* artist, whose dissolution into nature transforms him into a "primordial artist of the world."[74] The prayerful poetry of the primordial artist, Leonard Cohen, is what redeems moderns from the delusion of "objective spirit," tracing the contours of a non-dual reality that awaits an embodied Jewish-Zen spirituality hovering.

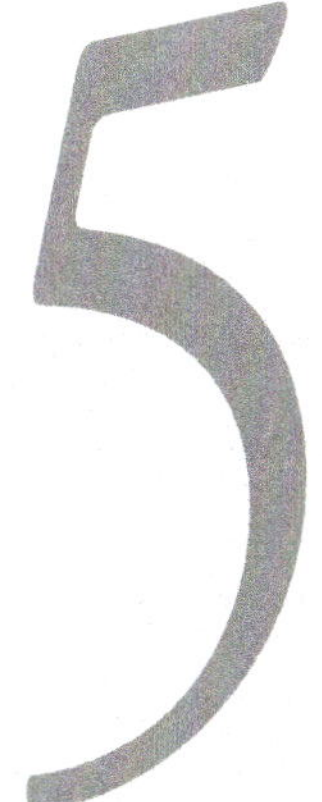

A Question of Pure Consciousness in the Priestly Blessing of Love

There are those moments we experience in life that remain etched in our hearts forever and the time of that etching stands still. Often those experiences can be transformative, to the point where we actually shift in our own awareness of the world and the role our consciousness plays in processing the "big picture." What I want to explore here is precisely that subtle shift in our awareness from the "thinking-I"—that bold declaration of modernity within philosopher, René Descartes's *cogito ergo sum,* "I think therefore I am"—which creates our perception of reality as moderns, to a pure consciousness of love, which permeates the entire constitution of self and universe. What I will argue here is that Judaism provides avenues for glimpsing such a transformation of consciousness through key liturgical moments like the Priestly Blessing. I will offer anecdotal encounters with remarkable poets reflecting upon their verse, teachings of spiritual masters and my own constructive approach to all these elements to address the question of the *(im)possibility* of pure consciousness in Judaism. To accomplish this, I will argue that it is possible to read the Montréal bard, Leonard Cohen, against R. Mordecai Yosef Leiner (1801-1854), known as the Ishbitzer Rebbe, to sense the beginning of an answer. In turn, I will fill out Cohen's path through Israeli poet, Yehuda Amichai (1924–

2000), and then turn to Sri Aurobindo (1872–1950), sage of Integral Yoga practice, to fill out my discussion of the Ishbitzer Rebbe. By taking this constructivist approach, I am searching for the experiences that inspired the poetic verse and homiletic teachings at hand. My juxtaposition of these "texts" will strike many readers as somewhat unconventional, but it is all part of an exploration to get behind the words of the Priestly Blessing so as to enter into the experience that powerful blessing points to—an experience largely remote to most moderns. If I have been successful, by the close of this exploration, you will never read the Ishbitzer's homilies the same way again, and you will never listen to Leonard Cohen's songbook the same way again—something in your relationship to Judaism and the pure consciousness of love transmitted through the Priestly Blessing will (hopefully) have shifted.

To appreciate just how effectively the songbook of Leonard Cohen serves to reveal this truth, it is necessary to take a step back to see the correlation between *art* and *edge*. For too long, the relationship of Jewish philosophy to aesthetics has remained asphyxiated by a misreading of aniconicism. This ban on imagery and iconography was upheld lest it lead to idolatry. This has begun to be redressed through the thinking of Elliot Wolfson on the central role of the *imaginal* realm in Jewish Mysticism.[1] Further sustained Jewish philosophical reflections on aesthetics focus upon medieval and modern periods in general by Kalman Bland, as well as Zachary Braiterman's analysis of Buber on the aesthetics of revelation.[2] Even more recently, there are journals, such as *Images* and *Ars Judaica,*[3] dedicated to more robust expansions of the historically neglected and maligned relationship of Jewish aesthetics and material culture with some inclination toward its philosophic roots.[4] Something is afoot indeed.

Recall that aesthetics as a subset of philosophy remains a longstanding tradition within Greek philosophy, in contrast with Jewish thinking, especially in delineating what is beautiful from what is ugly.[5] It is precisely with the modern turn in philosophy that we witness the rise of the "aesthetic" as a kind of object, judgment, attitude, experience, and value. Amid the diverse pathways of aesthetics, there remain a few pivotal points of interrogation, namely: (1) artworks as aesthetic objects; (2) the perceptual basis of aesthetic judgments; (3) the contrast between an aesthetic attitude and a practical one; (4) aesthetic experience as defined through phenomenological or representational content; (5) the correlation between aesthetic value and experience.[6] The contours of thinking that emerge in the wake of Existentialist Aesthetics, in general, remain as abiding influences upon the present investigation.[7] Reflections on *art* and *edge,* in particular, have been masterfully reformulated by distinguished professor of philosophy at Stony Brook University, Edward S. Casey (b. 1939), which provide further insight into my the present analysis of the songbook of Leonard Cohen.[8]

What is at stake with this juxtaposition of *art* and *edge?* To claim that "*art* is itself an *edge*," Casey envisions the *edge* of civilization as the place from which *art* eventually is able to peer forward.[9] How apt a lens for appreciating the ingenuity of Cohen's post-secular songbook that readily sees through the *edge* of our lives, soliciting "the imagination of new things, the renewed remembrance of past things, and the freely varied perception of existing things . . . [which] edges us out of the habitual patterns of experience."[10] There is something *unsaid* yet tangible that hovers around the *edges* of any artwork, and for Casey it is found in "possibilities other than those we thought we knew about before we dared to take these edges up: in short, virtualities in the penumbra of the possible."[11] What the outermost *edges* of artworks represent and play before us is the "transition from the invisible to the visible and back again, being the basis of the dialectic of the hidden and the unhidden, the known and the unknown—a dialectic that is at the crux, the hinge, of every work of art."[12] While there is convergence of *art* and *edge* in any given work of art, the *edges* are what afford the *art* to break out of the historical constrictions of convention and style.[13]

The *art* of Cohen's songbook, decade after decade, has not lost its dance near the *edge*, "its disruptive presence, its radical novelty, its challenge to our usual modes of classification."[14] Even though his early poetry may have dallied with the *avante garde*, Cohen's songbook has never been "cutting-edge," because these post-secular lyrics are not "so far out on the *edge* of our usual expectations that as listeners we cannot anticipate its inception or control its course once it has emerged."[15] Rather, through contemplative listening, one settles into the *edges* of the words, to join in the waltz intertwining singer, songwriter, and listener together on a journey towards meaning in a seemingly meaningless world. In such a convergence of *art* and its *edges* the songs of Leonard Cohen sing themselves. This is a nexus where both *art* and its *edges* are "necessary to being in a *place-world*, where things and people and happenings continually emerge from behind *edges*, thereby offering new openings from the heart of occlusion itself."[16] The purpose of my interrogation here is to witness what happens when I push against Cohen's *edge* between mysticisms Jewish and Buddhist. Moreover, I am exploring what happens in a post-secular context as I push against Yair Harel's *edge* of *piyyut* amidst its renaissance in Israel, as well as rubbing up against my own *edge* of an American songbook that traces the contours of diverse mysticisms.

To return to the investigation at hand, let us recall two remarkable encounters with poets of the pure consciousness of love. One is Montréal singer-songwriter Leonard Norman Cohen, and the other is an Israeli poet, the late Yehuda Amichai. Despite each of these encounters being distanced from me now by significant space and time, I can actually put my finger on what it was that touched me so in those encounters—an outpouring of pure love. It may sound strange, especially given that both Amichai and Cohen respectively were in their seventies, but these meetings with remarkable men touched me like no other. From these two encounters with Jewish poets, I will then turn to spiritual masters—first in the Hasidic tradition and then in comparison with the Integral Yoga tradition—to address the question of pure consciousness and its *(im)-possibility* within Judaism. All this is by way of really trying to get to the heart of the Priestly Blessing of love—which I am arguing is the closest Jewish expression there is to pure consciousness.

The Montréal bard Leonard Cohen had just returned to stage performances as a singer-songwriter again after over a decade of living as a reclusive Jewish monk, meditating on Mount Baldy on the outskirts of Los Angeles. The reasons for Cohen coming down the mountain were not that complex, even antithetical to his contemplative life—his longtime manager of decades had been embezzling the equivalent of millions from this cult folk singer. When he was ready to retire and turned to his savings, Leonard awoke to find out that he had been liquidated by his own manager. True, this bump in the road would only figure as one of many, as Cohen's life had been marked by bouts of depression and countered by his heartfelt attempts at alleviating them through various means, including spiritual practices. Sitting in a café with him, surrounded by a few fellow academics at an Association for Jewish Studies conference a few years ago, watching him interact with his daughter, Sasha, anyone in Cohen's presence could feel him emitting an energy that palpably shifted the vibe of the room. Years later, I invited a close friend of mine (who happens to be a cantor) to join me at Barclays Arena in Brooklyn to catch Leonard Cohen in what may be his last tour. This friend told me excitedly that, a few nights prior, he had seen Cohen at Madison Square Garden in Manhattan, and it was one of the most spiritual experiences he had had in quite a while. It sounded a bit hyperbolic, but I did not want to miss this finale. After three straight hours of performing music from his entire oeuvre, at times prostrating on his knees in prayerful positions, I had to agree with my friend—this was a truly transformational experience! Something palpable happened in that arena; Cohen was transmitting an energy of love that could only come from one place—pure consciousness.

Perhaps the ability to channel such pure consciousness emerged in Cohen after a close Jewish friend introduced him to Zen Buddhist master, Sasaki Roshi. Cohen was immediately drawn to follow this master because he claims there was something about this teacher that captivated him for decades. Although Cohen does not use the following language, it's quite likely that he experienced a common tantric phenomena known as *Shakti-pat* or an "energy-descent"—namely, a mind-to-mind release of pure consciousness transmitted by master to disciple.[17] Interestingly enough, the more Cohen advanced in his Zen studies and rigorous meditation, the deeper his anchoring to his Jewish identity. In part, this was a function of Sasaki Roshi wanting his student to be authentic to what the Zen *koan* describes as his "original face,"[18] and it was partly because Cohen remained aware of his own descent from a priestly lineage as indicated by his last name—*Cohen.*

Decades dedicated to Zen practice by Cohen can be seen as a commitment to redeeming the Jewish tradition including his priestly lineage through the rigor of a Buddhist lens, rather than succumbing to its betrayal through the frequently xenophobic, triumphalist content of Judaism. Ultimately Cohen comes to realize everyone is chosen to be loved and receive the love of pure consciousness! His master, Joshu Sasaki Roshi, instructed Cohen that there is ultimately no contradiction between the prayerful worship of Judaism and a/theistic practice of Zen. Notwithstanding his deep involvement with Buddhism, Leonard insisted to anyone who asked that he remained a Jew, more than satisfied in having a perfectly good religion, as he writes in his poem: "Anyone who says/I'm not a Jew/is not a Jew/I'm very sorry/but this decision/is final."[19] Cohen also points out that Roshi never made any attempt to give "this Jewish monk a new religion."[20]

What is most intriguing about the Montréal bard is his song-writing process. While Cohen appears to be a prolific songwriter, his craft goes through grueling stretches of agonizing rewrites until the song emerges complete. By contrast, as discussed already in chapter 2, this Yom Kippur War trip in 1973 to Israel remains one of the few times where Cohen was able to write a song so quickly. Leonard improvised the song "Lover Lover Lover" in front of the soldiers during his second performance with the band of Israeli musicians and the lyrics revealed to him the effects of war in Zion:

> May the spirit of this song/May it rise up pure and free/
> May it be a shield for you/A shield against the enemy.[21]

Clearly this ability to feel love and transmit such pure consciousness in the time of war stand as Cohen's own Priestly Blessing, even recalling its liturgical format. This is most evident once the Montréal bard actually returns again to Zion, despite his earlier post-Yom Kippur War poetic reflections on the impossibility of reaching Jerusalem: "I won't be going to Jerusalem after all. You will have to go to Jerusalem alone. It is yours. It was given to you by the angels of culture and time. But I can't go."[22] This feeling of love and ability to transmit such pure consciousness in the time of war through his own Priestly Blessing emerges anew in traveling to Israel three decades later, when Cohen reaches Israel at the end of his European Tour in 2009. Playing the finale of his concert in Tel Aviv, Cohen, wearing his signature black suit and fedora, gives this preamble to his invocation of the Priestly Benediction:

> I want to draw our attention to the Israeli and Palestinian member of the *Bereaved Parents For Peace* . . . and those other men and women, some of whom have been called foolish, irrelevant, defeatist, but no, no, not at all friends! They have achieved the victory, perhaps the only victory available—the victory of the heart over its own inclinations for despair, revenge, and hatred. So dear friends . . . [positioning his fingers into the Priestly formation bowing with his musicians on stage he begins reciting the benediction] *Yevarkekha Adonai* . . .

It is that same expansiveness intrinsic to the priestly blessing of the pure consciousness of love is something I also felt when I first met Israeli poet, Amichai, then in his seventies, a few years before he passed. Yet being in this poet's presence, one felt constantly embraced by unending love. He was visiting University of Toronto for a poetry reading, and we were involved in a deep conversation about translating his radio play, "The Day Martin Buber Was Buried,"[23] into a film script I was then planning on directing.

What was it that allowed this gentle septuagenarian soul to be so full of love? Born in Würzburg, Germany, to an Orthodox Jewish family, Amichai was raised speaking both Hebrew and German. Perhaps it was in part in response to a childhood trauma in Germany that caused him to dedicate his life to writing a poetry of pure love. Apparently, Amichai had an argument with a childhood friend of his, Ruth Hanover, that caused her to bike home angrily; she fell and as a result had to get her leg amputated. Several years later and due to her missing leg, she was unable to join the rest of her family, who fled the Nazi takeover; she ended up being killed in the *Shoah*. Amichai would write of that experience of love lost with his childhood friend in his poems, like "Little Ruth."[24] Premonitions of becoming a writer began for Amichai while stationed with the British army in Egypt on the underside of love facing death. As a soldier, he happened to find an anthology of modern British poetry, and the works of Dylan Thomas, T. S. Eliot, and W. H. Auden, each of whom inspired and confirmed his first serious thoughts about becoming a writer of love poetry. In 1956, Amichai served in the Sinai War, and in 1973 he served in the Yom Kippur War. He later became an advocate of peace and reconciliation in the region, working with Arab writers. How could a Hebrew poet steeped in the machinations of war and death be so open to pure love that suffuses all of his poetry? Such openness to pure love for Amichai finds its framework within his utter devotion to reading and writing the intricacy of the human condition.

Consider a few of his most powerful poetic expressions of this pure consciousness of love, as in the seventh stanza in his cycle, *Open, Closed, Open*:

> I believe with perfect faith that at this very moment
> millions of human beings are standing at crossroads
> and intersections, in jungles and deserts,
> showing each other where to turn, what the right way is,
> which direction. They explain exactly where to go,
> what is the quickest way to get there, when to stop
> and ask again. There, over there. The second
> turnoff, not the first, and from there left or right,
> near the white house, by the oak tree.
> They explain with excited voices, with a wave of the hand
> and a nod of the head:
> There, over there, not *that* there, the *other* there,
> as in some ancient rite. This too is a new religion.
> I believe with perfect faith that at this very moment.[25]

The poet's unstinting trust in the moment within which he stands and contemplates existence allows for an opening of his consciousness to a different experience of time. That experience is one that transcends his own subjective sense of self, allowing him to connect with millions of others facing crossroads and "showing each other where to turn, what the right way is." The consciousness of each individual involved in the search for "what the right way is" in life is guided by a process of continual turning to follow the directions of the moment. That pulsation of turning and returning throughout the universe is a pulse that precedes creation itself and continues guiding existence. This pulse of continual turning of *teshuva* within pure consciousness is something that fascinates the poet but also allows him to channel it as a universal force that abides within his view of existence.

It is precisely this pulse of continual turning of *teshuva* within pure consciousness that frees the poet from being trapped at intersections of binary thinking and getting entangled in the web of dualism. Amichai's non-dual view of the world is clear elsewhere in another poem, where he proclaims:

> A man needs to love and to hate at the same moment,
> to laugh and cry with the same eyes,
> with the same hands to throw stones and to gather them,
> to make love in war and war in love.
> And to hate and forgive and remember and forget,
> to arrange and confuse, to eat and to digest
> what history
> takes years and years to do.[26]

The poet here identifies with pure consciousness, where there is no longer any dualism separating loving from hating, remembering from forgetting. The poet conjures concluding verses here that open once again to a pure consciousness of eternal time within his experience of mundane temporality:

> . . . He will die as figs die in autumn,
> Shriveled and full of himself and sweet,
> the leaves growing dry on the ground,
> the bare branches pointing to the place
> where there's time for everything.[27]

These encounters with the remarkable Jewish poets, Leonard Cohen and Yehudah Amichai, may strike the reader as idiosyncratic, but I think they serve as helpful signposts along the path of the present investigation into the Priestly Blessing of love and the question of pure consciousness in Judaism. Truth be told, for most moderns, it is no small feat to scour through those mystical texts on the Jewish bookshelf that convey such experiences of pure consciousness. That is not to say states of pure consciousness have not been experienced by adepts and mystics in the Jewish tradition; rather, the issue is whether these experiences have been considered worthy or even safe enough to transmit through a textual record. If these experiences do exist in Judaism, then certainly the most we will find in our search is a delicious hinting, always more concealed than revealed.[28]

Even with a cursory search of Jewish liturgy, one will find that the only term which repeats with as much frequency as "with love" [*b'ahavah*] is probably "with peace" [*b'shalom*]—*why is that?* Regarding our specific question for this essay, we can sharpen things by asking: why is that priests to this day during prayer services recite at appointed times the benediction "Blessed are You, Eternal One, Master of the Cosmos, who has sanctified us through the holiness of Aaron, and commanded us to bless His people Israel with love [*b'ahavah*]"? There are many layers to this question, so let us first outline the contextual meaning [*peshat*] through translation, of the Priestly Blessing itself, which is found in Numbers 6:24-27 as follows:

> May YHVH bless you and protect you!/May YHVH deal kindly and graciously with you!/May YHVH bestow favor upon you and grant you peace!/Thus they shall link My name with the people of Israel, and I will bless them.

To understand the power of this blessing, one can benefit from seeing these words in their historical context relative to recent archaeological discoveries at *Ketef Hinnom* (Hebrew for "shoulder of *Hinnom*"), a hill overlooking the Hinnom Valley, southwest of the Old City of Jerusalem. These silver plaques contain benediction formulas in paleo-Hebrew script. The major discovery of the *Ketef Hinnom* excavations were several rock-hewn burial caves dating from the end of the First Temple period (seventh century BCE). One of the larger tombs, which probably belonged to a wealthy family, was found almost intact, with over a thousand objects in it. The most important are two small silver scrolls placed in the tomb. In light of these archaeological discoveries at *Ketef Hinnom*, consider Milgrom's insightful reading here of Numbers 6:27 as follows:

> Literally, "And they (the priests) shall place My Name on." In light of the *Ketef Hinnom* silver plaques, which demonstrate that in the seventh (or sixth)-century Jerusalem the Priestly Benediction was worn on the body in the form of amulets, the possibility exists that the literal meaning of this phrase is the correct one, that is, that the Priestly Benediction delivered by the priests in the sanctuary was also to be placed on the Israelites as prophylactics. The usual interpretation, adopted in translation, is that God's Name is figuratively "placed" by the priests on the Israelites through the medium of benediction. Alternatively, God's name is *nikra'*, "called" upon Israel (Deut. 28:10). Both verbs imply ownership (Deut. 12: 5; Jer. 7:10).[29]

This description of the historical reality surrounding the way this Priestly blessing was actually used is instructive, insofar as the words were worn and embodied by each person constituting the tribal people of Israel. The assumption of course is that not only do "clothes make the man [*sic*]" but that these kinds of amulets do more than protect you—they bring the divine presence into your life. So what happens when we do not live up to that call to live in the pure consciousness of love? The prophet Malakhi (1:8-10; 1: 6-7, 11-14; 2:2-9) hurls this blessing against the hypocritical priests by decrying:

> . . . will he lift your countenance [*ha yissa' panekha*] . . . that He may be gracious to us [*vi-hannenu*] . . . will He lift His countenance [*ha-yissa' panim*]? Would that you not light [*ta'iru*] my altar in vain [*hinnam*]?!?

Undoubtedly, this stands as a scathing prophetic critique of priestly corruption of their powerful blessing. One could argue, however, that both the priest and the prophet—each in their own way and time—attempted to link the divine name to their own being and in so doing embody pure consciousness.

Pure Priestly Consciousness "Soft Antinomianism" in Ishbitzer/Radzin Hasidism

If the language of the Priestly Blessing necessarily must first invoke the formula "Blessing your People with Love . . ." then one is left with questions: *Is the priest the only channel of transmission for such a blessing? What/who is the source of that blessing? If this transmission leads to a state of pure consciousness imbued with love, then what does this suggest about the constitution of the divine? Do emotions like anger and jealousy exist within a God that stands as the very source of this flow of Love?* We now turn to one of the most creative and radical schools of Hasidic thought in Judaism, known as Ishbitzer Rebbe/Radzin, to explore some answers.

The original thinker in this Ishbitzer Rebbe/Radzin lineage was R. Mordecai Yosef Leiner (1800-1854). Also known as the Ishbitzer Rebbe, after the town of Ishbitza, where the rebbe taught and wrote his homiletical commentaries to Scripture and Talmud known as *Mai haShiloah*, which translates roughly as "The Waters of Release." The Ishbitza dynasty is an offshoot of the Pryzsucha school (lead by R. Jacob Isaac ben Asher Rabinowitz, filtered through the dynasty of Kotzk (lead by R. Menachem Mendel).[30] That the Ishbitzer Rebbe's Hasidic dynasty flourished the way it did during such a tumultuous time in Polish history is a reminder of how Jewish ingenuity survived and, at times, was even inspired in the face of tragedy. This tumultuous moment in Polish history occurred within a cultural and political world of a rapid period of modernization, tolerance, and emancipation, facilitated by Pope Pius IX's ascendancy to the Vatican in 1846, as well as the coronation of Alexandar II as Czar of Russia in 1855.[31] Hasidic communities in Congress Poland, like that of the Ishbitzer Rebbe, did not necessarily participate fully in Polish culture and politics, and remained disenchanted with access to Enlightenment thinking, which had become virtually inescapable. This modernization brought with it the advantages of technological advances, travel and increased availability of printed books and manuscripts. But it also posed challenges to these staunchly conservative Hasidic communities, in the form of military service and secularism. What is important to note here is the degree to which messianic overtones imbue the teachings of the Ishbitzer Rebbe, beginning with a contentious split between R. Menachem and R. Mordecai Yosef during the years 1839-1840.

What is the nature of this messianism and how does it relate to pure consciousness? Firstly, one needs to recall that messianism in Judaism is often a yearning to redeem the world in the final *eschaton* through a cycle of redeemers, beginning with the Messiah son of David, followed by the Messiah son of Joseph.[32] The general way of understanding the roles of these redeemers has been to see them as part of a narrative that culminates with the apocalyptic vision of Armageddon's final battle, lead by Messiah son of David. Following his death in battle, a new *eschaton* of peace ensues, ruled by the ensuing Messiah son of Joseph. Some Jewish thinkers, like the Ishbitzer Rebbe, have sought to bring that yearning to redeem the world in the final *eschaton* closer to the here and now, in what we might term the proto-messianic era.

Secondly, one must keep in mind that the messianic era in general is considered to be a time where the commands no longer obtain and are thus nullified.[33] Thus, the messianic era becomes intertwined with an antinomianism whereby the law itself is suspended and no longer practiced, as it has been fulfilled. The system of *mitzvoth* or commands assume free will, whereby one has the freedom to choose between good and evil, thus reinforcing values and consequences that make its adherence worthwhile. Once the human and divine will are unified through messianism, the *mitzvoth* as a system no longer obtain, given that free human will itself has dissolved into a unified will.[34] Both R. Mordecai Yosef and his grandson, R. Gershon Henokh, articulate a "tension between illumined experience and the authority of *halakha*."[35] That tension arises once human and divine wills have been unified because *halakha* is a system meant to legislate submission to the divine will through human will and agency. Once the tension within competing wills has been resolved through unification, then what remains is a life completely and utterly free of any yoke of *mitzvoth* "as it will become clear that God is directing" the individual.[36] Rather than producing an outright transgression of Jewish law, what emerges, according to Shaul Magid in his investigation of Ishbitzer Rebbe/Radzin Hasidism, is a "soft antinomianism"—that is, by redefining "piety as acting in accordance with divine will," it thus "can extend beyond the law."[37] Such a "soft antinomianism" is "capable of living with *halakha* while challenging its basic tenet—that is, its exclusive right to divine will."[38]

There is a blurring of the boundaries between the messianic era and the (individual) person in Ishbitzer/Radzin Hasidism whereby the one who has refined the self through humility and piety becomes the messianic archetype acting outside the confines of *halakha* in a pre-messianic world.[39] This kind of soft antinomianism is a sanctified transgression in the law, whereby the communal experience of revelation at Sinai gives way to individual illumination as a guiding force. *What then is the purpose of following the commands if one is guided by the unified will of illumination rather than human free will yoked to the divine law?* The devotional way of life then serves as a touchstone for piety—"the submission to the over-arching principle of *mitzvot*—[which is] to occupy oneself with God, even as the specific *mitzvah* may no longer serve any constructive function."[40] What Magid concludes in his study of Ishbitzer/Radzin Hasidism is that—

> …personal illumination generally shares the same basic values with the *halakhic* system and, in most cases, enhances rather than opposes *halakhic* norms . . . Therefore, acting outside (and against) the system "for the sake of heaven" (i.e. to oblige the divine will) is built into the system and is always possible. Therefore, it seems that *mitzvoth* function best when performed by someone who no longer needs them.[41]

With this approach to "soft antinomianism" now in mind, the question remains: *how does living a life guided by such personal illumination then manifest the love of pure consciousness?* To answer this question, we now return to our opening concern with the Priestly Blessing of Love as a manifestation of living with pure consciousness. Commenting on the eight components of the priestly garbing[42] and its mystical symbolism, the *Mai haShiloah* notes a parallel between these dressings and the eight spiritual modalities in the blessing preceding the *Shema* prayer.[43] The unspoken link to be unpacked here is that of love. In this symbolic matrix, the Breastplate of Judgment or *Hoshen Mishpat* aligns with "discernment." As the *Mai haShiloah* teaches:

> . . . every human needs to contemplate in order to realize that within divine consciousness anger against the Israelites is non-existent, "for He is angry but a moment,/and when He is pleased there is life." (Psalms 30:6)[44]

Love is the natural spiritual state of reality, and anything other than love—especially anger—is non-existent. What is remarkable in this comment is the degree to which the Ishbitzer Rebbe is willing to recast the cosmos as a manifestation of pure consciousness—that is, love. The Priestly Blessing then serves as a perpetual witness beyond its liturgical invocation, speaking to this spiritual reality of love that courses through the cosmos. The necessary re-alignment of dual consciousness into non-dual unity is catalyzed by this Priestly Blessing and, in a sense, unveils the larger purpose of the contemplative process of prayer in Judaism.

A further look into the language of the Priestly Blessing in its component parts invites the Ishbitzer Rebbe to reflect on the numerology of the divine names as a matrix of the cosmos. This granular look at the letters within the words of the Priestly Blessing allows the Ishbitzer Rebbe to make the following nuanced comment on the invocation in Numbers 6:26 as follows:

> "*May YHVH bestow favor upon you*"—where the language of "bestowal" [*yissa*] implies that the divine should supply you with a "spiritual elevation" [*hitnassut*]; "*and grant you peace*!"—namely, you will have an even greater "spiritual elevation" [*hitnassut*], even in the midst of dialectical opposition have no fear from the opposition because God is with you. So this is the meaning of "[*grant*] *you*"—namely, within yourself.[45]

In this hyper-literal reading of the Priestly Blessing, the Ishbitzer Rebbe is spiritualizing the blessing. This is a process whereby the one invoking the blessing is engaged in an act of turning the *outward* blessing of the Priest exoterically directed to the Israelites toward an *inward* esoteric blessing of the one invoking the blessing within oneself. Through this inner transformation of the body as a "temple in miniature" [*miqdash me'at*], the contemplative gesture allows for the pure love channeled through Priestly Blessing to expand throughout the macrocosmic structure of the individual rather than the collective. As one becomes imbued with pure consciousness by this self-reflexive energy transmission, the very constitution of subjectivity shifts from its previous dichotomy of human will and divine will to a unified will of love. Through the dissolution of human free will into nothing but divine will, the Ishbitzer Rebbe is making a compelling case for the possible reconciliation between the pre-messianic consciousness of exile and a proto-messianic consciousness of redeemed living in the here and now.[46] To gain a better understanding of the very texture of this pure consciousness, we will have to turn outside of Judaism in order to understand the Priestly Blessing more deeply.

Embodying Pure Consciousness in Sri Aurobindo

What the Jewish mystic experiences in the state of *devekut*, or merging of the human mind state with that of the divine, is not that dissimilar to what the Integral Yogi, Sri Aurobindo, might have experienced in the *nirvana* state. What both states of *unio mystica* or mystical union do certainly share is the cessation of ego-consciousness in the all-pervading peace of what, for the former, is the *Ein Sof* or Without End, while for the latter is the silent *Brahman*. Upon the disappearance of the ego in this state of unitive consciousness, what the mystic must grapple with then is the sense of unreality of the external world. Putting aside the nuances in stages and states of consciousness within each spiritual path, what these mystics share is the reality that this experience of unitive consciousness generally lasts only a short while—*and then what?* Jewish mystics tend to be highly attuned to the ebb and flow of unitive consciousness inherent in this state of cleaving, called *devekut*, while an Integral Yogi, like Aurobindo, notices how the transient experience of unitive consciousness is replaced by more integral experiences of an "immense Divine Reality" *behind, above,* and *within* everything that had initially appeared illusory.[47] This is a realization that consciousness is the ultimate reality in the universe of which all existence itself is but a manifestation. Further, consciousness operates beyond any final qualification. Pure consciousness, while unqualifiable, is nevertheless real, as Aurobindo describes it:

> In the state of pure consciousness and pure being we are aware of that only simple, immutable, self-existent, without form or object, and we feel that to be alone [is] true and real. In the other or dynamic state we feel its dynamism, to be perfectly true and natural and are even capable of thinking that no such experience as that of pure consciousness is possible. Yet it is now that to the Infinite Consciousness both the static and the dynamic are possible; these are two of its statuses and both can be present simultaneously in the universal awareness. . . .[48]

It is precisely here in this state—where the ultimate ontological category and the material cause of all that exists—that Judaism appears to rub up against the *(im)possibility* of pure consciousness. The challenge that such a state of integral consciousness poses for Judaism is how to relate to the distinct categories of Creator–creation–creature. It is precisely this challenge that emerges within the *devekut* state that I have been exploring within a Hasidic re-reading of the Priestly Blessing. While the Jewish mystic yearns to reach and remain in the *devekut* state, the Jewish conception of consciousness would seem to dictate that a return to dual consciousness is necessary to maintain its distinct categories of Creator and creature.

With this understanding in mind, consider now the re-reading of the Priestly Blessing by the Ishbitzer Rebbe. Recall how the Ishbitzer Rebbe stands as one of the rare mystical voices in Judaism that advocates for cultivating and remaining in a state of pure consciousness. According to the Ishbitzer Rebbe, a perpetual *devekut* state is cultivated by entering into a single commanded act of a *mitzvah* with deeper consciousness. This very immersion leads to a cessation of all further commandments. There is no longer a need for commanded acts in such a state of pure consciousness, as there no longer exist distinct categories of Creator–creation–creature. While the Ishbitzer Rebbe may be the most radical exponent of this antinomian tendency in Judaism, one could argue that this direction really drives the broader Hasidic movement in Judaism. Recall how Hasidism, the spiritual renaissance movement that swept through Eastern Europe in the mid-1700s, posited that one could serve the divine either through the "613 commands" [*taryag mitzvoth*] or "integral immersion" [*messirat nefesh*]. Given the ban on Hasidism and its wild mystical spirituality thwarted by the Gaon of Vilna in 1772, one can only speculate as to whether Jewish mystics after Hasidism would have eventually followed the path of integral immersion in consciousness.

Conclusion

In considering the challenge as to whether Judaism makes space for the cultivation of a state of the pure consciousness of love, we have encountered some remarkable, if not disorienting teachings. Our investigation began with anecdotal encounters with two remarkable Jewish poets, Leonard Cohen and Yehuda Amichai. We explored how it is possible for such seekers so embroiled in the darkness of depression and death to continue writing and singing love poems. From these encounters, which confirm experiences of pure consciousness in Judaism, we then attempted to respond to the curious repetition in Jewish liturgy of the phrase "with love" [*b'ahavah*], which is recurs frequently within Jewish liturgy. It turns out that there are many layers of meaning, but that the deepest layer appears to abide in the most unexpected of places—within the Priestly Blessing. By examining the contextual meaning of this blessing found in Numbers 6:24-27, we then turned to a hyper-literal reading found in the homiletical commentaries of the Ishbitzer Rebbe, known as *Mai haShiloah*. In the process of unpacking commentaries to Numbers 6:24-27 in *Mai haShiloah*, we discovered that an over-arching "soft antinomianism" emerges, whereby the illuminated personality allows for a unification of the human will with the divine and in the process changes the praxis of *halakha*. The change takes place in a twofold manner, as Magid explains:

> First, it keeps the messianic personality rooted in the proto-messianic world, preventing him from moving beyond the boundaries of legitimate Judaism until the world catches up to him. Second, by living in tension inside the *halakha*, the messianic personality destabilizes the law, thereby extending the elasticity of the *halakhic* tradition.[49]

From this vantage point straddling pure consciousness of the illuminated personality within Judaism, we then turned to a comparison of the Ishbitzer Rebbe's teachings with the tradition of Integral Yoga formulated by Sri Aurobindo. The comparison yielded a point of contrast. This point of contrast was instructive insofar as it set into relief the degree to which Judaism must struggle to maintain the "straddling of pure consciousness" as a proto-messianic posture. Integral Yoga appeared less fraught, since it provides a state of pure consciousness that is never lost once cultivated. Whereas pure consciousness allows the mystic to remain tuned in with clear reception to a channel constantly broadcasting love, the *halakhic* system of *mitzvoth* in Judaism serves as both an anchor and a prophylactic against losing one's self within pure consciousness.[50] For Leonard Cohen, Yehuda Amichai and others like them, poets who have by and large transcended the *halakhic* system of *mitzvoth* of Judaism while remaining creative Jews, are able to manifest and create poetry of pure love. More than the Hasidic mystic, it is the Jewish poet—as seen in Amichai's transformation of Hebrew liturgical language and Cohen's invocation of the Priestly Blessing—who truly embodies the messianic personality rooted in the proto-messianic world yet catching the world up to live continually in that state of love emanating from pure consciousness.

Amen to American Agnosticism

Your faith was strong but you needed proof
...Now maybe there's a god above...[1]

"I am *spiritual*, but not *religious*"—so goes the standard quip that countless clergy serving in synagogues, churches, and mosques across North America might hear when a seeker crosses the threshold of such sacred institutions in search of meaning in their lives. Recently, I shared a table at a book signing with a respected senior theologian who reminded me of the wittiest response to this fallacy.

Spirituality is what you *feel*; *religion* is what you *do*; and *theology* is what you *think*. As we both awaited customers to consume our theological wares, I wondered if something was not quite right with that response. If you don't *feel, do*, or *think* along these lines, then what happens to your relationship to the infinite? After all, about half of Americans say that the growing number of "people who are not religious" is "bad" for American society.

Yet in the face of such nay sayers, there is no one who captures the cracks in our theology like Leonard Cohen, as these succinct verses from Hallelujah attest. Faith can be challenged, and the existence of a divine power can hover in a "maybe" state of mind. I will return to Cohen after a momentary digression. But there are just as many who say either that this trend is good or that it does not make much difference. No matter whom you ask, there appears to be evidence of "a gradual decline in religious commitment" in the US public as a whole. Not the nuns, but the "*nones*"—those who proudly proclaim "no affiliation" or simply unaffiliated—is the fastest growing demographic: about one-fifth of the public overall. One-third of adults under thirty are religiously unaffiliated as of 2012; one-third of US adults say they do not consider themselves a "religious person"; and two-thirds of Americans—affiliated and unaffiliated alike—say religion is losing its influence in Americans' lives. As is always the case, the younger cohorts are less concerned than the older cohorts about the negative impact of the non-religious upon American society.[2]

If religion is losing its influence in our lives, then Jewish philosophy needs to recover its self-critical *edge*. Through this process, an embrace of *un*knowing is necessary to open space for newer modalities of knowing. By taking this deeper dialectical turn through the negative, its resurfacing through the *imaginal* allows for a more immediate reflection in thinking that gives rise to a more vibrant language of Jewish philosophy. Crucial for the dialectical process to allow thinking to emerge and evolve is a harnessing of the radical imaginary. For Adorno, as philosopher and pianist, much of that radical imaginary is embedded in the music he was playing and thinking through. Recall Adorno's demand for *second reflection* that continues the mediations of thinking to *second immediacy* and ultimately constructs a *second language*.[3] If indeed, for Adorno, "metaphysics stands convicted of the crime of transfiguration, which can no more be atoned and made amends for than the misery and suffering of the past,"[4] then how is it possible for a language of the first imagination itself as well as its enacted works remain ineffable and inexplicable? Hovering beyond all ontologization and identity-thinking is what leaves the door open for that very "scandal of the imagination" that nourishes the radical imaginary.[5] Adorno is committed to rediscovering that very instant when rationality transcends its existent discourse from within through music.[6]

When thinking does not allow for the negative dialectical turn, ontologization and identity-thinking set in. Case in point is the aforementioned problem with the post-1967 elision of Israel as a substitute for God, of metaphysics as the new Zionism. The possibility of self-transcendence, which avoids ontologization and identity-thinking, is only possible ironically when the dualistic nature of the Greek imagination is released and opened to the Hebrew imagination. Within the Hebrew language there is a deeper difference at play, which then affects thinking. The Hebrew imagination is integrally embodied in the doubling of language, expressed by *H̲oSHeV maH̲aSHaVot*. That doubling of the same upon itself, leads to the very self-transcendence Adorno needs in thinking. Hebrew thinking is intrinsically *imaginal*, as expressed in its root verb, *h̲sv*. What the Hebrew imagination then facilitates is an integral relationship between the inceptual roots of the imagination that spread forth into its conceptual branches. From the path of these inceptual roots, there is the experience of a deeper poetics: *the musicality of imagination*.

Musicality is embodied in song. The diaphanous word *shir* in Hebrew is at once both song and poem. Yet the song in its beginning [*bereishith*] is always "a song of desire" [*shir ta'av*].[7] This desire dwelling within the song emanates from the world of creatures yearning to reunite with their Creator through the singing of poems. Through an awareness of this diaphanous word, *shir*, recurrent motifs and archetypes can further reveal this *imaginal* realm within the designatory word itself.[8] Words, however, may not be enough to convey the power of this experience of the inter-world that nourishes the radical imaginary. Rather, an image or a sound oftentimes contains a more direct experience of this *imaginal* realm. The archetype of the *imaginal* is the angel, oscillating between poetry and song. Like notes and musical phrases, angels are constantly fluttering to and fro, but their only recognizable form is the guise of their own temporality. By exploring this realm as part and parcel of the negative dialectical process, what emerges is a powerful temporality of music, or what Adorno recovers as the metaphysics of musical time.[9]

The challenge in recovering the metaphysics of musical time requires accessing the *imaginal* realm. Modern Jewish philosophy continues to struggle with an unspoken privileging of the intellect over the imagination on the road to prophecy, and so one must confront and transform the scandal of the imagination from that lingering perception of immaturity and irrationality.[10] The act of recovering the *imaginal*, then, is that necessary recovery of a sublimated *imaginality*, a kind of "second naïveté"[11] back into the realm of the thinking subject. Adorno reflects on this loss of the "extremely tender and subtle layer of inner subjectivity, of the spontaneous, and of the instinctive,"[12] and so his thinking is thus able to display a yearning to engage in its recovery and application to thinking. Continuing to cultivate this lost tenderness, as embodied in music or epistemic concerns, evinces an abiding conviction that such remnants of the *imaginal* "can become 'a center of power that stands against' its own societal and historical conditions of possibility."[13] These missed notes are in desperate need of recovery if the metaphysics of musical temporality are to be heard thinking once again.[14]

It is through the lens of Adorno's keen philosophical eye that we turn to the *noumenal* side of musical thinking. Returning to Adorno, one encounters an insightful way through the thicket obscuring Jewish Thinking, an urgent call for musical thinking:

> Of course, it is no objection to new music to point out that in the dialectic of the general and the particular, it is always bumping up against the limits of the particular. Only, it must have the power to carry this dialectic through to its end. All of this revolves around the concept of internal musical tension and its enfeeblement, a phenomenon that forces itself on our attention today and yet obstinately resists identification. The process is objectively determined. The concretization

> of musical idiom whose whole impulse rebels against concretization is enforced by its language-like nature, even though it is in conflict with its own underlying ideal.[15]

It is this very musical tension—"the dialectic of the general and the particular"—that allows for the resistance of identification with and closure from the concept to over-ride it. By remaining "in conflict with its own underlying ideal," the texture of that internal tension within Jewish Thinking shines with brilliant inspiration. Without that internal tension that Adorno time and again refers to as the negative dialectic, there is no possibility of encountering the sparks of the imagination nesting in the *noumenal* realm. Moreover, through the ages when Jewish Thinking has slipped into complete identification with either universalism or particularity, it has *de facto* loosened that internal tension, desecrating any of its musical depth, or what will be referred to as musicality.

With a loss of the will to truly think anymore, and then for those whose thinking is enfeebled by an inability to resist identification with the particularity of concepts, the least constructive elements continue to be carried forward. Turning back to Adorno to see forward once again, thinking can take its cue from music:

> By negating both the general and the particular, new music presses forward to absolute identity, and in so doing, it aspires to the voice of the non-identical—of everything that refuses to be submerged.[16]

Amid the context of negation within such musical thinking, the answer for so many seekers today would have to be"losing my religion," as Michael Stipe of R.E.M. Paradoxically, the "nones" are ready, willing and able to sing along to the line: "every waking hour/I'm choosing my confessions." The need for confession as a part of the process of self-transformation still abides, just not inside the confessional! Despite their negation, "nones" today are "trying to keep an eye on you/Like a hurt, lost and blinded fool. . ."[17] Revelation of sorts took place when R.E.M. guitarist, Peter Buck, started trying to learn how to play the mandolin for "Losing my Religion," claiming:

> I started it on mandolin and came up with the riff and chorus. The verses are the kinds of things R.E.M. uses a lot, going from one minor to another, kind of like those "Driver 8" songs. You can't really say anything bad about E minor, A minor, D, and G—I mean, they're just good chords.

Indeed, those good minor chords—the epitome of negation—that Buck appears to be just wrapping his mandolin have sympathetic resonance with the "minor fall and major lift" to which Leonard Cohen seems forever attuned to—that "secret chord/that David played to please the Lord."[18]

One way to approach this conundrum of losing one's religion through negation is the chameleon's path, which claims that: "If you can sidestep the problem of belief—and the related politics, which can be so distracting—it is easier to see . . . God is good. The world is good. Things will be good, even if they don't seem good now. That's what draws people to church."[19] The point Tanya Luhrman is making here is that living a religious life with all of its doubts and uncertainties is possible once the dogma of belief is bracketed from the larger playing field of faith. This requires being like a chameleon, such that I pray "as-if" and garb myself accordingly around fellow pray-ers who do believe, even though my belief is bracketed and faith concealed. *(Of course, like Raskolnikov, I cannot stand that F-word, faith so we'll have to return to redress that shortly!)*

Another way to approach this conundrum is the iconoclastic path of J. K. Carter, who advocates for the need to take atheism seriously, not "the atheism of the likes of Richard Dawkins, Daniel Dennett or the late Christopher Hitchens. The atheism I'm talking about entails social, political and intellectual struggle, not against some god-in-the-abstract, but rather against a specific or particular god: the 'American god.'"[20] Such audacious iconoclasm smashes the idols of a racist god that Carter sees as having enveloped so much of America. Like the patriarch Abraham tending to his father's idol shop, Carter is advocating we do not lock up our social, political, and intellectual struggles, but bring them to bear on a living relationship with a particular god in a given time and circumstance.

But Carter's demands may be too much for a large swath of seekers today, turning away from spirituality, religion, and theology—today's Raskolnikovs through and through. Raskolnikov, the anti-hero of Dostoevsky's *Crime and Punishment*, challenges the unexamined piety of his sister, Dounia. In turn, Dounia fears her brother has nothing left to hold onto in the hour of his greatest trial, save fear if he confesses to murder: "I haven't faith, but I have just been weeping in mother's arms; I haven't faith, but I have just asked her to pray for me. I don't know how it is, Dounia, I don't understand it."[21] How might today's Raskolnikovs hold this paradox of remaining steadfastly faithless within their prayers? *To have no faith*, but weep in your mother's arms; *to have no faith*, but ask her to pray for you. . . .

What I am suggesting is the need for another category—a kind of mystical *agnosis*—as with our opening discussion between two theologians sharing a table at their book signings. The generational divide between the younger and older theologians track their disagreement on whether being nonreligious is bad for America. This divide also inheres in their assumptions concerning, first, what we *do* in prayer (religion) and second, how we *think* (theology) we can or should grapple with the grip atheism has on this generation. That is why I decided to start my session on prayer following the book signing with the following statement, which shocked most of the participants:

> Prayer today is broken. If we do not take this seriously, then there is no God. For prayer is not *about* God—prayer *is* God!

Related to this conundrum but in a different context entirely, while participating in a think-tank over the future of Jewish theology, participants were exposed to different guest theologians at some point during each day of the gathering. Amid all the masterful thinking about God that came from accomplished Jewish theologians, I was utterly dumbfounded by one young emerging church theologian, Peter Rollins, who stayed with the group throughout the conference. When it came his turn to present on the theology he was formulating to reach this generation, he spoke passionately about his new book, *How (Not) to Speak about God*. My cynical inner voice said, "Oh here comes another Christian reformulation of Maimonidean 'negative theology' and Rosenzweig's 'A/Theistic Theology'!" Yet Peter's sensitivity to the Christian theology, coupled with a nuanced understanding of postmodern thought, allowed him to offer an unprecedented message of transformation that has the potential to revolutionize the theological architecture of theology, through what he later came to call "Pyrotheology."[22]

This feisty, Irish theologian of the emerging church movement showed all the Jewish theologians in the room how to explore the theory and praxis of this contemporary expression of faithle or faith. He began with theory and then unpacked his book, which is divided into two parts: the first half is entitled, "Heretical Orthodoxy: From Right Belief to Believing in the Right Way," while the second half is entitled, "Towards Orthopraxis: Bringing Theory to Church." In discussing how he applies his critical theory to ritual, as a fellow theologian who also engages in creative ritual, I was most moved by his ritual for a/theism. In *Service 4: A/theism*, the plethora of images affixed earlier is removed from the wall of his itinerant parish—the local pub, *Ikon*—and transformed through their erasure, as someone intones over the microphone on the stage: "Many of us have lost sight of the fact that a deeply religious form of atheism lies at the heart of Christianity. This atheism is not one that rejects the idea that there is a source to the universe, nor is it simply the rejection of gods different from our own.

Rather, this faith-filled atheism is one which understands that the God we worship is bigger than all our imaginings."[23] I began to wonder in earnest: could Rollin's "faith-filled atheism" speak to *today's Raskolnikovs?* Would the nonreligious dare to drift back to institutions that until then had offered nothing but platitudes, hypocrisy, and inauthenticity?

This last critique of inauthenticity seemed to strike a deeper chord inside my soul. While my recent book *A New Physiognomy of Jewish Thinking*[24] was being translated from English to Hebrew, an argument ensued between me and my gifted but impetuous Israeli translator, Guy Elgort. A philosopher studying for his doctorate in Nietzsche at a prestigious university in the northeast, Guy argued for the all-too-common one-to-one relationship between "authenticity" and its correlate in Hebrew, "*authentiyut*." I opposed this borrowing tendency and suggested the more spiritual expression from Hasidism of "*emet l'amitah*" (literally, the *truest truth*). The translator's argument hinged on the reality that secular Hebrew readers of theology and critical theory in Israel were becoming very used to this tendency to borrow terms from languages like English and then (shamelessly) import them into Israeli Hebrew, rather than grappling with and succumbing to an indigenous Hebrew idiom. Even a literate society like Israel, rife with secularists ruled by the Ultra-Orthodox, can at times cringe and recoil from the hold a hegemonic religious discourse has upon their lives and their lexicon. The same can be said about our theological gateways, and the urgent need to open those gates further to embrace atheism and the non-religious.

We urgently need to expand the theological conversation. Imagine the following scenario: a young person, an affiliated "none," in seeking her authenticity, challenges a theologian with the line: "I am *spiritual*, but not *religious*." The theologian dares to respond with: "*Spirituality* is what you *feel*; *religion* is what you *do*; and *theology* is what you *think*." Imagine instead that this seeker is offered a fourth category, one of "faith-filled atheism" that will speak to today's Raskolnikovs, to today's "nones." The non-religious need to know that there is space to challenge their atheism and imbue it with a depth that reveals a concealed "faith-filled atheism." Only then will today's Raskolnikovs—the fastest growing demographic of nonreligious in America—dare to drift back into institutions open to doubt, integrity, and authenticity.

* * *

What exactly defines and unites today's Raskolnikovs—the fastest growing demographic of nonreligious people in America? Atheism or agnosticism? These questions are by no means new, nor is the underlying phenomenon. At the heart of the matter, I am suggesting that Leonard Cohen's song *Amen* inclines, "leaning in love" toward an American agnosticism rather than a dogmatic atheism, but in this discussion, semantics matters little. But the agnostic is more at home as an iconoclast within a religious stream, waiting to be convinced, a seeker in a mind-space of relentless pursuit. This brings me to the iconoclastic rabbi, Menachem Mendel of Kotzk (1787-1859), who grappled with these questions as part of his own relentless search.[25] A young seeker once came to Menachem Mendel of Kotzk to complain:

> "Rebbe, I can no longer believe in God."
>
> "Why is that?" the Rebbe inquired.
>
> "I cannot believe in God because the world is so filled with pain, with suffering, with ugliness and with evil.
>
> How could there be a God in such a world?!" the young man answered.
>
> "Why do you care?" asked the Rebbe.
>
> "What do you mean, why do I care?" the frustrated young man explained.
>
> "How could a person not care?! Innocent people suffer, the world is ruled by the cruel and the heartless, its beauty is drowning in evil.

I care because it hurts me so and I can't understand why a God would let it be this way!"

Again, the Rebbe inquired,

"But why do you care?"

The young seeker grew even more exasperated—

"Someone has to care! Someone has to witness the pain of the world and cry.

If not, then all the suffering is meaningless.

If no one cares, then the universe is a dark, lifeless place.

I care because I want with all my heart to see a better world for my children and for theirs. I owe it to them to care!"

And again, the Rebbe asked,

"But why do you care?"

At this point, the young seeker lost his composure altogether and wept.

"I care. I have to care. I must. It's what and who I am."

"Well then," the Rebbe responded, "if you care that much, then God exists."

You see, Menachem Mendel of Kotzk appreciated this thinking Jew whom some would label "atheist," so much so you can almost hear the rebbe saying to himself—

"I would rather have *shtarker mitnaggdim* than *pareve Hasidim*!"[26]

[I would rather be surrounded by those who doubt with strong convictions than be surrounded weak disciples!]

This story has much to offer us as we ponder the place of today's Raskolnikovs—the fastest growing demographic of nonreligious people in America. Why do I share it? I share this story because it is real. Real in our lives. It is not about an atheist versus a believer, or good faith versus bad faith; rather it is about the importance of *safek* in relation to *'emunah* of doubt in relation to conviction. First things first, enough of the F-word—"faith."

Rather than translating the Hebrew word *'emunah* as the F-word, it would be more accurate to render it closer to its biblical roots—like "trust." Just take a cursory look at the Hebrew Bible, and you will see that it points in the very direction from where we have arrived at the F-word in western culture thanks to Paul. Consider Exodus 17:12:

> But Moses' hands were heavy; so they took a stone, put it underneath him, and he sat thereon; and Aaron and Hur stayed up his hands, the one on the one side, and the other on the other side; and *his hands were steady* until the going down of the sun.

The interesting turn of phrase here is at the close, the response to the challenge. Moses is able to withstand the travail before him because of his interconnection with Aaron and Hur. "His hands were steady" [וַיְהִי יָדָיו אֱמוּנָה] precisely because of that human interconnection. Paul, also known as Saul of Tarsus, revises the covenantal relationship inscribed through circumcision in the flesh, radically changing the human interconnection that steadies Moses. With this Pauline revision, human interconnection is superceded by a universal "faith" inscribed in the heart.[27] In my mind, and the minds of many of today's Rashkolnikovs, this should already be enough to swerve away from such a weak misreading of *'emunah* as the F-word.

But does this make room for doubt? Through the Hebrew word *safek*, I hope readers will understand why I chose to translate it as "sacred doubt." Surely if quantum physicists already know and "trust" that the universes (or *mulitverses*) we are slowly becoming aware of are filled with indeterminacies, then why cannot religion also embrace such "trust" in a kind of space for "sacred doubt"? What we are just learning now in religion—what quantum physicists have been excited and sleepless about for some time—is a different way of seeing reality. What we are just relearning in religion is something very important about how we know what we think we know.

To *truly know* something in our religious lives implies something more than mere data; knowledge in our spiritual lives has the power to affect the cosmos. For that to happen, we have to see ourselves as part of larger framework. When what is going in our world of consciousness becomes integrated with a "cosmic consciousness," then all possibilities need to arise and be seen.

What this new awareness of reality suggests is that even though there may be mutual contradiction, infinite possibilities all exist.[28] I am suggesting here that without *safek* as "sacred doubt," rather than "uncertainty," and *'emunah* as "trust"—a vibrant Judaism has not much of a future.

* * *

What then is the problem with most religious Americans? Simply put, the F-word requires dogmatic belief in the certainty of a metaphysics of reality. What separates Judaism and Christianity, as Heschel once quipped, is that while the latter requires "a leap of faith," the former demands "a leap of action."[29] Fewer and fewer of today's *Rashkolnikovs* are willing to countenance swallowing that *credo quia absurdum* pill that requires blind faith.[30] Furthermore, the F-word in America is perceived as a mental acceptance lacking any doubt. But honestly, for Judaism that begins its journey from the Hebrew Bible, authentic *'emunah* requires a relentless confrontation with the difficult questions, which life inevitably raises. And, as a result, when those questions do arise—as indeed they must—while the foundations of the F-word are often destroyed in its wake, it is *'emunah* that allows the seeker to press forward in the search for a deeper truth.

Whether we take the case of Moses or even of Abraham for that matter, what emerges is a radically different kind of *'emunah* experience. Recall how Abraham comes to understand that *'emunah* is not the passive or blind acquiescence to an idea, nor does it require obediently stifling a doubt. *'Emunah* is a willingness to trust, in spite of doubts and uncertainties.

Think about it. Why would God reckon Abraham's *'emunah*, that is, trust, to his merit? This sounds completely absurd. Recall the scenario—at a ripe old age, Abraham gets the divine call for an heir. This child will inherit not only Abraham's property, but also his ancestral covenant. Surely such a late night divine call would strain the credulity of even the most devoted follower!?! The incredulity of Abraham's *'emunah* is tersely but eloquently captured by Bob Dylan in his "Highway 61 Revisited" with his own Americana inflections to boot:

Oh God said to Abraham, "Kill me a son."
Abe says, "Man, you must be puttin' me on."
God say, "No."
Abe say, "What?"
God say, "You can do what you want Abe, but
The next time you see me comin' you better run."
Well Abe says, "Where do you want this killin' done?"
God says, "Out on Highway 61."[31]

Despite the impossibility of childbearing looming large, and despite even Sarah herself testifying beyond herself—that her husband was far too old to father children—we, as readers of the Hebrew Bible, *trust* that somehow the inevitable sacrifice will turn out all right—somehow!?! In the face of this seeming impossibility, God tells Abraham to trust that he will have a child, to trust that his descendants will outnumber the stars in the sky, and eventually to trust that every trial will work out. The astounding promise of Torah simply states in Genesis 15:6 that:

Since he put his trust in YHVH [וְהֶאֱמִן בַּיה-וָה],
he reckoned it to his credit [וַיַּחְשְׁבֶהָ לּוֹ צְדָקָה].

The beauty of the poetics at play lies in its very ambiguity. In this one ambiguous sentence, the Torah contrasts the rich complexity of biblical *'emunah* and the flaccid, superficiality of the contemporary F-word.

Take note here: amidst this very ambiguity, eleventh century French commentator, *RaSh"I*, teaches that God is actually crediting Abraham's trust to his *tzedakah* (righteousness) because Abram "did not ask God for a sign." Or read the verse otherwise: Abraham trusted God and considered this very divine promise as evincing God's righteousness.[32] Yet another way to read the verse is to recognize Abraham's willingness to trust in the divine—trusting in the search for the journey is itself the destination. True, such a route is far from predictable. Despite the reality of setbacks and suffering, what strikes me here is just how much Abraham and God present *'emunah* as a willingness to trust each other.

So at the risk of being impolite, if not outright invasive, I'm willing to bet that you have asked yourself (more than once) in private late at night: *Can I really believe in God?*

As I continue to ask myself these questions as a rabbi serving in a traditional egalitarian community devoted to Torah study and daily liturgical Tefillah, I have found meaning and solace with a few teachers who molded my responses these questions to my *'emunah*: (1) the Kotzker Rebbe; (2) a bookstore owner in Berkeley; (3) Rabbi Shapiro, *o.b.m.*, from the Jewish Theological Seminary in New York; (4) Rabbi Israel Salanter, founder of the *Mussar* movement in Judaism.

First, the night the Kotzker Rebbe lost his religion. . . .[33] What exactly happened that fateful night of his withdrawal, no one knows with certainty any longer. The likelihood is that in the moment when Menachem Mendel of Kotzk, known simply as the Kotzker Rebbe, was expected to recite the blessing of *Kiddush* to sanctify the wine for Sabbath, he uttered these words, with all their existential angst:

> *Leyt din v'leyt dayan!*
> There is no judgment, and there is no Judge!

True to his relentless quest for authenticity, for being present to the moment, at that moment in his journey, Menachem Mendel then put down the goblet, proceeded to withdraw, and spent the last twenty years of his life in seclusion (from 1830-1859). So relentless was this quest for authenticity, he could no longer handle living surrounded by the hypocrisy of this world—so he had no choice but to withdraw.

Once withdrawn, much like the divine Creator in the process of *tzimzum*, the Kotzker saw the world unfolding before him. The hypocrisy that was apparent while he was fully in the world now became completely overwhelming. Even more devastating is the degree to which this relentless quest for authenticity is actually hindered by false disciples and fraudulent fellow travelers. Neither of these frauds is truly interested in delving deeper. Rather, each one is only self-interested. The greatest obstacle to belief, and for that matter, to redemption, is the ego. Until the ego can be controlled, there is no way to make space for the divine—so why even consider the possibility of belief?!?

I thought I could still *believe* until an encounter with a remarkable teacher, Rabbi Morris Shapiro, *of blessed memory,* a distant disciple of the Kotzker. It happened while everyone else in the Study House/*Beit Midrash* was waxing thick over some minor details in a super-commentary of the *Tosafot* to the Talmud we were learning that year in rabbinical school. As was his way, Rabbi Shapiro volunteered to always be there sunrise to sunset, to bail out anyone who was lost, perturbed, or perplexed by the Talmud being studied that year. But I was stuck on a problem no super-commentary of the *Tosafot* could answer, a quandary I would never *dared to ask.*

So I had to muster up my courage to ask, waiting until the Study House/*Beit Midrash* was slowly beginning to retreat after a long day, students leaving exhausted after the setting of the sun. Sometimes I'd just look at him. Here's a man who has gone through the horrors of the *Shoah*, whose entire family perished in the camps. While the other students would ask him for a tutorial on the renowned rabbinic argumentation of the *Gemarah*, I never had the nerve to ask him, until that one time when I finally mustered up enough courage, and I asked Rabbi Shapiro:

> "Please don't be offended, but I have this burning question! Rabbi Shapiro, how can you believe?"
>
> He looked up from his *Gemarah*, a tear and a smile intermingled, and he said,
>
> "I DO NOT BELIEVE; I have CONVICTIONS!"

He then explained: belief is like an opinion because it can change from week to week. I believe it will rain tomorrow. I believe that the Toronto Maple Leafs will win the Stanley Cup. *Beliefs* are predictions that may or may not come to pass. (At least not since 1967 for a die-hard Leafs fan!?!) But *convictions* are central to your soul! That day he told me everything I needed to know; it changed my life.

He still had convictions about God—*anger, frustration, despair, longing*, but these were deep convictions that caused him to act and dedicate his life to teaching Torah from morning till night and praying thrice daily. Years later, I recall bumping into Rabbi Shapiro in the streets of Jerusalem. It was a sweltering afternoon. I had just crouched down beneath a tree to grab some shade, waiting for the bus after a great book sale. The sun was streaming right through him as he approached. I was not even sure it was him, as all those years I'd never seen him stand up and walk—he was always seated with the *Gemarah* in front of him at a desk. As he approached me, immediately we recognized each other, like long-lost friends on a desert island. He started retelling me, with tears in his eyes, this story of the rebbe Kotzker being visited in seclusion by an old friend:

> Once, Once [Rabbi Yitzchak of Vorki] visited Kotzk after a long absence, knocked, entered Rabbi Mendel's room and said in greeting:
>
> "Peace be with you, Rabbi!"
>
> "Why do you say rabbi to me," grumbled the rabbi of Kotzk. "I am no rabbi! "Don't you recognize me? I'm the goat! I am the 'sacred goat.' Don't you remember the story?"

> An old Jew once lost his snuff box made of the horn of a goat on his way to the House of Study.
>
> He wailed: 'Just as if the dreadful exile weren't enough, this must happen to me! Oh me, oh my! I've lost my dear snuff box.'
>
> And then the old Jew came upon a sacred goat that was pacing the earth and the tips of his black horns touched the stars. When the goat heard the old Jew lamenting, he leaned down to him and said,
>
> 'Cut a piece from my horns—whatever you need to make a new snuff box.'
>
> The old Jew did this, made a new snuffbox and filled it with tobacco. When he returned to the House of Study, he offered everyone a pinch of tobacco. Everyone was awed by the scent:
>
> 'What a wonderful tobacco! It must be because of the box. Where did you get it?'
>
> And the old man told them about the sacred goat. Then one after the other, they went out onto the street and looked for the sacred goat. The sacred goat was pacing the earth and the tips of his black horns touched the stars. One after the other they went up to him and begged permission to cut off a bit of his horns. And time after time the sacred goat leaned down to grant the request. Box after box was made, and the fame of the boxes spread far and wide. Now the sacred goat still paces the earth—but he has no horns."[34]

While Rabbi Shapiro never withdrew into complete seclusion, he did withdraw from congregational life. He also withdrew himself from part of a given equation in Jewish Thinking. Once, in response to my growing curiosity as to how he could still believe after Auschwitz, he told me, "Well, 66 percent isn't bad!"

I had no idea what he meant. In those early years of study I poured through as many equations and as much numerology as I had access to and remained stumped, but still curious. The next week, I shared my frustration over his elliptic 66 percent, to which he replied:

> *Kedusha Brikh Hu, Yisroel, V'Orayyta—chad ninhu!*
> The blessed Holy One, Torah and Israel—are all one![35]

What was Rabbi Shapiro saying in his unsaying response? Did he really dare to admit that his authenticity would no longer allow him the space or self-respect to believe in a God that allowed Auschwitz to decimate his family and six million others? True to his path, Rabbi Shapiro gave me permission to respect a deep interconnection with two-thirds of Judaism's core while remaining free to think through my own convictions about the remaining third. If he could uphold his piety by teaching Torah to us and serving the people Israel, so could I! I'll never forget that moment.

Having recently relocated to San Francisco, I had the pleasure of wandering around in Berkeley, which some cynics call "Bezerkeley." As I'm wandering around Martin Luther King Jr. Way, I stumbled upon Angel Light Bookstore—how remarkable to still find a spiritual bookshop standing! Inside the window was a huge sign with an inverted pyramid. The top line read, in large block letters:

SCIENTOLOGY DOESN'T WORK.

Beneath it in slightly smaller letters, it said:

YOGA DOESN'T WORK.

Then again, even slightly smaller, it said:

T. M. DOESN'T WORK.

After going through six or seven more would-be spiritual paths, the sign concluded, again in large letters:

YOU HAVE TO WORK!

Which means quite simply,

NO THING AND NO-*ISM* WORKS;

YOU MUST MAKE THE EFFORT!

As Kotzker rebbe says, the essence of religion is—

Arbetn oif zikh—To work on yourself!

IT doesn't work, YOU have to work! There is no substitute

for your work; and what does Judaism demand you to work on?—YOURSELF![36]

After we've worked on our convictions, we need to figure out how to rebalance things; otherwise we appear to be hypocrites. Now let me tell you what Rabbi Israel Salanter taught me:

A hypocrite is someone who asks about everyone else's *neshama* [soul], and worries about his own *guf* [body]. If we are honest, then we can admit that at some time or another all of us have rubbed up against the mirror of authenticity. I had a classmate at seminary who would pat me on the back and "feel me up" to see if I was wearing *tzitzit* or not, or he would ask, did you *davenn minha* yet? See, he worried about my *neshamah*. A caring, righteous person, known as a *tzaddik*, is someone who asks about every else's material needs and then worries about his own *neshama*. A *tzaddik* is not a missionary like my classmate; he cares if you've eaten.

Do you see the difference? When it comes to ourselves, we should each be more concerned with spiritual rather than with material matters; another person's material welfare is *my own spiritual concern*. When I struggle over my convictions it takes place inside, it's heartfelt, but when I see you are hungry, homeless, then that is my real concern.

Every morning as I rise before the sun here in San Francisco, I ascend to pray in a quorum. In that process of ascent, I have to maneuver my way over a handful of bodies still sleeping in front of my synagogue stoop. As I don my morning *phylacteries*, I make sure that I am in view of each waking body, sheltered in overhang of the synagogue. It reminds how little separates me from the street, yet I still hope to ascend.

I learned something else from my teacher and friend Shaul Magid. As the rabbinic alarm clock would ring each summer in *Elul*, the month before the Jewish High Holidays, we would each be pondering the meaning of it all. We spent many wonderful walks following the ebb and flow of those Fire Island shorelines with his dog, Shlomo, trying to make some modicum of sense of it all. Nothing escaped this relentless questioning, nothing. Everything, right down to the holidays greetings, like *Hatima tova*, deserved deeper questioning and could prompt further self-examination. I felt that power from the moment he interviewed to teach as a professor of Jewish Mysticism at the Jewish Theological Seminary. Everyone seated at this faculty lecture was afraid not only to listen to his talk on Lurianic Kabbalah, but even to look at him.

So there we were on the Fire Island shoreline, waiting for the Ferry with Shlomo, wondering, after all, what is a seal *good for*? Shaul and I shared just how much we had been struggling with this for some time. Recently, it dawned upon me what this seal is good for.[37] It happened one afternoon back in the day. I remember so clearly that one unremarkable afternoon and how it changed my life. I was studying in the *Beit Midrash* at JTSA. We were breaking for afternoon services before returning to more Talmud study. After the repetition of the *Amidah* "the prayer of silent devotion," we were reciting *tahanun* (the prayers of supplication that include the confessional centerpiece of the Days of Awe liturgy). As we began to recite the confession—

> *Ashamu, bagadnu, gazalnu . . .*
> We are guilty, we have transgressed, we have stolen . . .

. . . lightly beating our chests as we were taught, someone walked up to me from behind and whispered in my ear—

"*Nu*, Aubrey, you never *really* stole anything?!?" then he quickly turned around and walked away.

This moment was made all the more macabre because of who it was that whispered into my ear—*it was Rabbi Shapiro!* That great Talmudic scholar, considered a genius by age twelve in the Volozhin *yeshiva*, surviving Auschwitz to begin again in America, Rabbi Shapiro was a pleasant yet serious man—but the last thing he was known for was being a joker!

Rabbi Shapiro never mentioned that incident at prayer ever again; and I never worked up the courage to confront him—until years later.

Upon reflection, Rabbi Shapiro may have been saying something quiet deliberate. In my youthful pious fervor, I was too easily drawn to every small detail of what I was doing and at the same time not really reflecting on my actions. *Was I really guilty of the things we were confessing? Did I even think about it? In short, was I telling the truth?* Not surprisingly, Rabbi Shapiro didn't whisper to me, "*Nu*, you never really *lied*?!?" The reason is obvious.

Of course I lied—I'm human! I probably lied between the time I went to pray that morning and when it came time to *davenn* that very afternoon. We all lie, all the time, in all kinds of ways. And we almost always justify, and excuse, lying. We are so evolved as human beings, that we've even come up with a category talmudic for legitimating the lie—we call it the "white lie." So while we may confess "we have lied"— as if to say "and we will lie no more"—we are *already lying*. The confession is a lie. Not only will we lie, but we lie *in the very act of saying that we won't*. So what are we to do about lying?

I remember while studying as a rabbinical student and then later teaching rabbinical students at JTSA, I used to attend the morning *minyan* in the Women's League sanctuary there. The back window looks out onto the 1/9 train as it ascends from underground to travel above ground through Harlem. I used to put my *tefillin* (prayer phylacteries) on in that spot overlooking the brick wall where the train comes over ground, setting them on the ledge of the window. One day as I was tying my *tefillin* around my arm something caught my eye. I happened to notice some graffiti on the stone wall surrounding the tracks. The graffiti was a simple five word phrase: "the truth is a lie." *Well*—I thought as I adjusted my *tefillin—that's a humbling thing to think about as one wears words of the Torah on one's arm!* I made sure every morning that I put my *tefillin* on in that very spot so I could be reminded of those words—"the truth is a lie."[38]

As one who studied to be a rabbi and then trained rabbis to heed their calling in that very seminary, ostensibly teaching "the truth"—a tradition that regularly declares, "Moses is truth and his Torah is truth,"—it was a welcome, if somewhat painful, reminder for me.

We tell lies to get at the truth. We tell lies to save our people, to exonerate our story, to justify our existence. We tell lies to protect our children, our parents, and even ourselves.

"Remember, it's not a lie . . . if you believe it!"

Can we really trust these words that George Costanza says to Jerry Seinfeld? After all, as Plato once remarked, the greatest poets, and by extension artists, are liars. So Rabbi Shapiro, *of blessed memory*, while you are no longer walking this earth, maybe sometimes you think of us and wonder—"Whatever became of those naïve, young rabbinical students who didn't speak *Yiddish* but went to the pray and study every day at the *Beit Midrash*?" You always admired that. When we recited the confession *Ashamnu* you never said to us, "Boys, come on, you never *lie.*"

You knew somehow, Rabbi Shapiro, that in our fervent prayer we were *lying right there* even as we were *seeking the truth.* But there are private moments when we can let the truth seep in. And the truth is, as Shaul Magid continues to remind me, that *we are liars.*[39] Maybe that is what *Yom Kippur* is about. Why else would the rabbis bother teaching us that "truth is a seal" [hotmoshel ha'Kadosh Baruch Hu—Emet!]? What is the "seal" we wish each other good for anyway? What exactly does it keep us from? *Ourselves? Our lies?* If for one moment we can tell the difference between them, we have come farther than most. And that perhaps is what a seal is good for—חתימה טובה *Hatima tova*!

It seems that once we reach the seal, we really have reached the end of this analysis—*but have we?* Reaching the seal is an admission that we must now go on living with the seal's difference, which beckons for more support. That support is derived from the *'emunah* of being able to conclude the encounter of a trial by saying, *Amen.* How do we carry this brokenness with us? In his inimitably paradoxical way, when Leonard Cohen sings "Amen," he touches upon precisely this kind of truth as a lie that has become stitched into the fabric of our broken being:

> Tell me again
> When I've been to the river
> And I've taken the edge off my thirst
> Tell me again
> We're alone and I'm listening
> I'm listening so hard that it hurts
> Tell me again
> When I'm clean and I'm sober
> Tell me again
> When I've seen through the horror
> Tell me again
> Tell me over and over
> Tell me you want me then
> Amen
> Tell me again
> When the victims are singing
> And Laws of Remorse are restored
> Tell me again
> That you know what I'm thinking
> But vengeance belongs to the lord
> Tell me again . . .
> Tell me again
> When the day has been ransomed
> & night has no right to begin
> Try me again
> When the angels are panting
> And scratching the door to come in
> Tell me again
> When I'm clean and I'm sober
> Tell me again . . .
> Tell me again
> When the filth of the butcher
> Is washed in the blood of the lamb

Tell me again
When the rest of the culture
Has passed through the Eye of the Camp
Tell me again. . . .[40]

What Leonard Cohen's "Amen" demands is our confrontation with the truth that is a lie in our lives and in our times after Auschwitz and each and every human-made horror of the twentieth century. How is prayer even possible in the face of such horror? Forget about "no atheists in foxholes"; why are there agnostics "standing on this place where there used to be a street"? In mustering the courage to say *Amen* to a prayer that feels like a lie in trying times, I am connecting to the *'EMuNah* that supports this quest, contrary to some current misunderstandings about *'emunah* as "blind faith" in the teachings of the Hasidic master from Tiberias, R. Menachem Mendel of Vitebsk.[41] I will conclude here with a retranslation and rereading of one of the Vitebsker's core teachings on *'emunah*, found in his commentary on the Binding of Isaac.

Oppositional forces, like doubt and uncertainty within the self, are the natural setting of the human mind. So for the Vitebsker, the deeper a person speculates about existence, the greater their oppositional inner impulse. Furthermore, this inner impulse is constantly attempting to derail a person from their path, so without a support system, like 'EmuNah the natural mind-state would be completely overwhelmed. By suggesting that every spiritual apperception requires an equal and opposite force, the Vitebsker makes room for doubt and uncertainty:

This is the operative principle regarding spiritual apperception and devotion—its grandeur depends on its oppositional force. *'Emunah* is what allows the mind to re-set the pendulum, seeing how the subject stands outside the continuum of the dialectic we see that:

> The more one grows in spiritual apperception and devotion, the more oppositional energy emerges as a counterbalance. When opposition

> befalls you, then fortify yourself as intensely as possible by holding onto this simple, powerful *'emunah*. *'Emunah* is the act of grasping onto the Holy One outside that reality system of opposition. Complete support is possible through such *'emunah.*[42]

If one's relation to the absolute is based solely upon intellectual argument or dogma, it is vulnerable, for it can always be undermined by a better argument. Here lies the brilliant vigilance of the agnostic throws his/her hands up in uncertainty, waiting for proof. *'Emunah* is an ability to realize that what one believes in is not contingent upon the way one explains it. Rather, the human heart and mind have a direct and clear relationship with that which cannot ever be fully apperceived. The mind is not the absolute arbiter of the spiritual relationship, for the purpose of knowing is *unknowing*. This is not "blind faith," rather it is a knowing that is *not-knowing*, a kind of enlightened *agnosis*, which is key for *'emunah.*

Since *'emunah* is simple and not complex, there is nothing that can oppose it, and in this sense it is beyond reason. For whenever one's mind is operating through intellectual constructions, at some point, it will collapse. It is necessary to return to the undifferentiated oneness of *'emunah*, knowing that is not-knowing, an enlightened *agnosis*, so sublime. The power of this *'emunah* is in its form of *gnosis,* the unknowability of what you are knowing, a *gnosis* that never produces an intellectual apprehension, one whose "purpose of knowing is unknowing."[43] It is pure wonder and radical amazement. This is the greatest help that there is, for nothing can defeat it. One's daily connection with the divine can then withstand the fall of any paradigm or construct.[44] And to this surely every agnostic can say *Amen!*

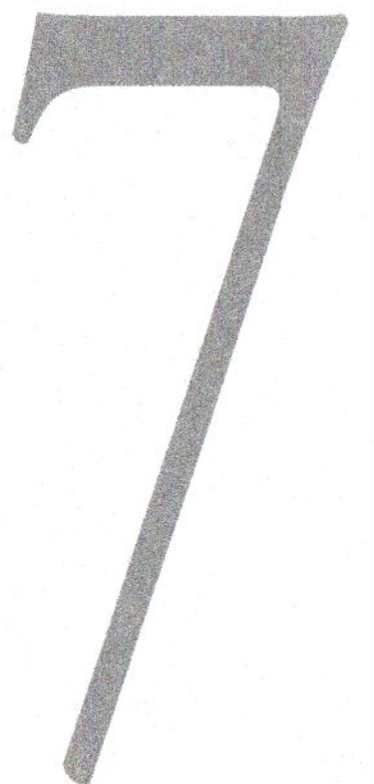

Nothing as Whole as a Broken Middle *Matzah*

This cold and broken world can be repaired,
or I will have to sell my pretty mouth.
signed: The Mechanic.[1]

When the majority of Jewish America find themselves at a Passover seder, something sticks! Given what a ubiquitous marker of identity the celebration of Passover remains upon Diaspora Jewry,[2] it is small wonder that every year another *vade mecum* through the liberation from Egypt is necessary in North America—a.k.a. the season of the latest *haggadah*![3] If indeed Jews have always eaten according to the norms of their host cultures, then the North American *seder* should also serve to reflect its host identity![4] It should come as little surprise, then, that since 1932, the American coffee company, Maxwell House, has dominated the scene of the corporate sponsored *haggadah,* although there were many other prior iterations. From the 1919 *haggadah,* sponsored by the West Side National Bank in Chicago, to the 1920s *haggadah*, sponsored by the American National Bank in Newark, surprisingly, no corporate-sponsored *haggadah* emerged north of the Canadian border! Perhaps this was a function of the nuances in the religo-cultural imperatives: whereas American Jewry embraced the "melting pot" theory of culture, Canadian Jewry held to "multiculturalism"—these differences come through in the nature of the *haggadot* favored in each religious culture. Most of the American *haggadot* were flanked with illustrations of the Israeli and American flags. From Maxwell House coffee to Manischewitz wine and Hebrew National meat, corporate sponsorship really dominated the proliferation of printed *haggadot* for Passover and impacted the textures of spirituality that permeated the journey to liberation as recounted in North America. One can sense the danger at hand—with each corporate sponsorship, the journey of liberation becomes ensnared more deeply in the fetishisms of the culture industry. The retelling and publication of the journey to liberation through the *haggadah* has always attempted to navigate the manifold realms of the mind, the spirit, and the stomach. So, adapting Adorno's warning, the *haggadah* is also a product of how the culture industry has transformed the commodity character of its original art to *haggadot* with advertisements, its promise of freedom from societal usage, and its genuine use value that people can enjoy in its ritual context. As a product, the *haggadah* remains inevitably mediated by the culture industry so that often its use value is *replaced* by exchange value.[5] Alas, in ashes of Auschwitz, by 1945, a *haggadah* emerges that is sponsored by *Striets*, the makers of the most elemental piece of every *seder*—*matzah*!

To appreciate just how the "cold and broken world can be repaired" requires a momentary reflection on what it means to be *(dis)placed.* To be *nowhere* is the opposite of belonging *somewhere.* To be in *place* is to be situated in the world. To be *(dis)placed* is to experience rupture and exile, which in turn cultivates a yearning for return and redemption. Much of the rupture of modernity has been marked by the alienating and violent manifestations of *(dis)placement.*[6] In order to come to terms with the unmoored texture of postmodernity, Casey privileges the primacy of *imagination, memory*, and *place* in much of his thinking.[7] This symbiotic triad plots the pathways of his thinking through new ground after postmodernity:

> Just as imagination takes us forward into the realm of the purely possible—into what *might be*—so *memory* brings us back into the domain of the actual and the already elapsed: to what *has been*. Place ushers us into what *already is:* namely, the environing subsoil of our embodiment, the bedrock of our being-in-the-world. If imagination projects us out beyond ourselves while memory takes us back behind ourselves, place subtends and enfolds us, lying perpetually under and around us. In imagining and remembering, we go into the ethereal and the thick respectively. By being in place, we find ourselves in what is subsistent and enveloping.[8]

The impact of *(dis)placement* on the self after postmodernity requires a reconsideration of the idea that to be *nowhere* is the opposite of the belonging *somewhere*—a state of navigating *indirection*. "'*Nowhere*'. . . *does not signify nothing*:" according to a German philosopher to whom Nazism was not foreign, Martin Heidegger, rather, "*this is where any region lies, and there too lies any disclosedness of the world for essentially spatial Being-in.*"[9] In contrast to the belonging *somewhere,* a region is itself actually located *nowhere.*[10] By contrast, *Being* (*Dasein* in Heidegger's lexicon) has a distinctive place of its own by "being there as such [is] a place for the disclosure of Being."[11] There is a tendency to read early Heideggerean thinking as primarily concerned with temporality. However, more recently, discoveries within this philosopher's *Black Notebooks* [*Schwarzen Hefte*] expose different facets of place that have concerns beyond time.[12] The rootlessness of the Jew in space emerges amidst these personal notes to his philosophy, leading Heidegger to situate Jews as leaders in international conspiracies like capitalism and communism. If the Jew is a Semitic nomad to whom the nature of German spatiality will never be revealed, then how does any such *indirection* assist the Jewish thinker out of a real dead-end?

It is along this path, from *indirection* to the "subsistent and enveloping" within oneself, that allows for this experiential category of *place* to emerge in thinking. It becomes evident that *(dis)placement* is a combination of being alienated "*from* (a given) place and the violence that has been done *to* (some) place, and not only in places."[13] Thus the emergence of a distinct motif of yearning to return to place, according to Casey, recurs often in postmodern thinking.[14]

Furthermore, the impact of *(dis)placement* is felt within the dissolution of the postmodern self. Building upon testimony of the Navajo Indian's *(dis)placement,* Casey's thinking shows how the place of the Greater Self is an identity that "depends upon the continuation of a devotional connectedness to earth, ground, community, and ancestral place." What this suggests is that "the system of sacred places was deeply internalized by the Navajo and became essential to their self-identities."[15] The tragedy of *(dis)placement*–whether for the Navajo or for the Zionist—is "not to be in place [*which*] is not only to be nowhere; it is not to exist."[16] Place matters, and taking leave of place leaves its mark.

What happens when one is separate, distanced, or exiled from such a place? What then emerges is a process of mourning the very loss of place, what Casey calls a form of *decathexis* from place.[17] For Jewish philosophy after postmodernity, there is a need to encounter the self as impacted by *(dis)placement,* insofar as this "triple-place bind" affects thinking: namely, the isolation from *other*, from *place*, and *from myself in place*.[18] The guiding questions here as Casey are important in understanding the place of *(dis) placement* in Leonard Cohen's post-secular songbook, namely: "Is it possible that the reconciled self holds within itself a precipitate of abandoned *place*-cathexes; indeed, that it also contains the history of those *place*-choices?"[19] What emerges in this symbiotic triad for thinking is an internalization of place as a way of coping with the desolating loss of place brought about by all forms of peremptory displacement; this internalization ultimately commemorates "abandoned places within the place-bereft psyche."[20] Thinking through this symbiotic triad of *imagination, memory*, and *place* allows *(dis)placement* to give way to *re-implacement.* What emerges is a kind of "authentic consolation that no longer leaves us isolated from others, from place, or from our own divided selves."[21]

(Dis)placement also inspires much of Adorno's critical thinking. Some of Adorno's most important writing and thinking was inspired by his own dream life in exile, notwithstanding his critique of the reliance on intuition as a source of knowledge.[22] While displaced in the exile of New York and Santa Monica, where he thought and wrote *Minima Moralia*,[23] Adorno "claimed that he always noted down his dreams immediately after waking" and then "later selected a certain number of them for publication."[24] Drawing on the *imaginal* as a doorway into the depths of subjective desire allows the search for objective truth to be more clarified. Such clarification of homecoming then guides one's thinking. Voyaging into the unchartered realms of *(dis)placement* so as to expand thinking leads to a shift from rational to *supra*rational, all through the process of negative dialectics. What the negative turn in dialectics allows for is a necessary "decentering" of the knowing subject.[25] The emergent tension in decentering implies that the subject no longer grasps itself as the center of reality regarding its conceptual constitution. At the same time, this very loss allows for a new self-understanding from the outside in. Seeing the world this way means that there is a new clarity no longer obscured by the closed systematization mired in the mediation of concepts.[26] In this negative turn within dialectics, *un*knowing emerges as a decentering of the subject, no longer capable of rationally penetrating reality. It is this *un*knowing that makes way for the subject's liberation from the compulsive need to unify all its knowledge. Such supra-rational knowing stems from "all the stirrings of its senses triggered by the uncontrollable world of objects and events in an open and undifferentiated way."[27] It is in *(dis)placement* that an anchor for new thinking is possible through this inter-world between imagination and reality, known as the *imaginal*. Here the rationalist tendency that often stultifies Jewish philosophy lets go to take hold of the insight of the *supra*rational to illumine the pre-intellectual, thus enabling thinking to evolve.

If indeed there is something called "Canadian Jewish Mysticism," as I have argued in chapter two, then surely there must be room for a trilingual, Canadian *haggadah*! After all, given the reception of the recent *New American Haggadah* by millennial authors Jonathan Safran Foer and Nathan Englander, surely friends and family north of the border must be yearning for their own take on the *seder*—the *Canadian Haggadah Canadienne*![28] One's take on the *seder*, of course, has a lot to do with language, not merely spelling differences but the art of translation. In ruminating on the art of translation, Walter Benjamin famously noted: "It is the task of the translator to release in his own language that pure language which is exiled among alien tongues, to liberate the language imprisoned in a work in his re-creation of that work."[29] I argue that the language yearning to be liberated and too often being neutralized is, at its core, a mystical language. This will become evident in the section of the Passover *haggadah* called *Yahatz* and how the rendering of this breaking of the middle *matzah* in a handful of *haggadot* reveals a deeper truth about Canadian Jewish Mysticism.

To appreciate what is at stake with the recent publication and reception of the *Canadian Haggadah Canadienne*, it is helpful to compare it to the reception of the language in the *New American Haggadah*. One could not imagine a finer dream team of American authors than Jonathan Safran Foer and Nathan Englander to spearhead this project to reach millennials. On the one hand, "the best part of this new Haggadah," Englander's liturgical translation, "stills us, and allows us to hear again the austere beauty of the original Hebrew."[30] Millennial literary critic, Sasha Weiss, clearly appreciates the thoughtfulness of these authors trying to "de-familiarize a familiar text" and their firm conviction "in the capacity of language to spur readers to empathic acts," leading to results that are "startling" and hopefully inspiring and "performative."[31] On the other hand, boomer literary critic, Leon Wieseltier, excoriates Englander for his "infelicitous locution for all the blessings," primarily in regard to rendering the Tetragram as a fused "Lord God-of-Us," or *Barukh ha-makom, barukh hu*, as "Blessed is the One that is Space and the Source of Space, the One that is the World but Whom the World Cannot Contain, blessed is He" that is "ridiculously cumbersome, and could not be more unlike the original."[32] For Wieseltier, this latter translation is a sin; insofar as it reaches the point of ultimate hubris or even *hutzpah d'meshikha*, Wieseltier claims, "Englander has taken it upon himself to eliminate the mystery, as if this is an improvement."[33] I will return to this idea of "skirting the mystery" in what follows, but Wieseltier's concluding criticism of the *New American Haggadah* must be heeded, especially since the volume's editor makes the limpid claim that "[t]his Haggadah makes no attempt to redefine what a Haggadah is." In response, Wieseltier beckons: "Why not? I would have thought that a redefining, a rethinking, a retelling, a reimagining, would have been the greatest adventure of all."[34]

How then have the authors of *Canadian Haggadah Canadienne* come together, as self-proclaimed "bridge" figures,[35] to redefine a third solitude *seder*? Rabbi Adam Scheier is an American serving in Montréal at Congregation Shaar Hashomayim, who came north eleven years ago. Richard Marceau is a Québecois who converted to Judaism in 2004. What these two share is a similar cultural awareness, having been raised "on the border" between English-speaking and Francophone Canada. Neither has the need to reference this unique cultural situatedness, what Tom Marshall classically called the Canadian Jew's "third solitude."[36] What has united the Rochester native to Marceau (who is general counsel and political adviser at the Ottawa-based Centre for Israel and Jewish Affairs), is a common yearning "to deepen the Canadian Jewish identity by presenting something that's uniquely Canadian. . . . It's never been done."[37]

So what exactly is path-breaking about this Canadian/*Canadienne* retelling of the Passover story? A coterie of photographic images, including over one hundred rarely seen, archival pictures of Jewish life from every region of the country: William Goldbloom in front of his fur-and-hide store in Prince Rupert, British Columbia (1921); Marco Zimmerman, Jewish prospector, planting a stake in the Yukon Territory (1920); an immigrant boy from Lisbon just before Passover (1944); children munching on *matzah* at the opening of a matzah factory in Montréal (1948). In contrast to "Jewish life," there is the real "religion of the Jews" that must include photos of Montréal Habs goalie legend Ken Dryden at Israel's only skating rink, and current Prime Minister Stephen Harper hoisting a Team Israel jersey on his visit there last year. As its co-authors joyfully remark: "There is so much flavor and so much that should start a conversation about what it means to live as a Jew in Canada and how deep our roots are," Scheier said.[38] The roots of Canadian Jewry, however, seem to run only so deep. The greatest adventure of any experience, especially the mystical, or the mystery as Wieseltier renders it, remains in the retelling and reimagining. Returning to Walter Benjamin, we are reminded that, concerning Holy Scripture: "Where the literal quality of the text takes part directly, without any mediating sense, in true language, in the Truth, or in doctrine, this text is untranslatable . . . all great texts contain their potential translation between the lines; this is true above all of sacred writings."[39] The task of reimagining and retelling the primarily mystical layers of the experience of Passover's liberation may indeed remain "untranslatable" but the *haggadot* continue to appear. Whereas Wieseltier ultimately laments the rising illiteracy of Diaspora Jewry and its inability to feel nestled in the original Hebrew text, assimilated German-Jewish philosopher Benjamin embraced the project of translation amid its ineffability. With this "potential translation between the lines," I now turn to a few key sources in Canadian Jewish Mysticism that should be part of any Passover rumination, especially the breaking of the middle *matzah*, known as *Yahatz*.

The unanswered question that hovers on Passover night remains: How could a *Canadian Haggadah Canadienne* that features commentaries from twenty rabbis from across the Great White North and the denominational spectrum (including an ordained female clergy in modern Orthodoxy, known as *maharat*)—how could such a *haggadah* be missing teachings from arguably two of the most influential Canadian Jewish mystics we already met in chapter two—Leonard Cohen and the Tosher Rebbe? In poring over this reasonably designed but not overly inspiring *Canadian Haggadah Canadienne*, the most glaring absence of these Canadian Jewish mystics is felt in the act of witnessing the brokenness of the middle *matzah*, called, *Yahatz* as well as the seeking of that hidden, broken *matzah*, known as *Tzafun*.

The treatment of these pivotal moments in the journey of the Passover *seder* could not be more wanting. In the French translation of *Yahatz*, Marceau's choice to render it as "*Partage en deux de la matzah du milieu*" (to break the middle matzah in two) is pedestrian, at best.[40] The performative act here is not limited to "dividing" or merely "splitting" the middle *matzah* in two; rather it is more of a rupturing, conveyed more sensitively by "*découpage*," "*rupture*," *fissuration*," etc. More to the point, it remains baffling what could have inspired Rabbi Aaron Flanzraich, who, in his comment on *Yahatz*, swerves Canadian Jewish mystics to cite Turkish scholar Yaakov Culi to say that *Yahatz* points to "our most breaking moments."[41] Surely if the *Canadian Haggadah Canadienne* editors saw fit to include Rabbi Ron Aigen's commentary to *Pesah, Matzah*, and *Maror*, then they might have considered consulting with the very editor of *Wellsprings of Freedom* who unabashedly incorporates Canadian Jewish Mysticism into his *haggadah*, as we shall see shortly.[42] There is no shortage of apt excerpts of great rabbinic thinkers, from Rabbi Naftali Yehudah Berlin[43] to "the Rav," Joseph Soloveitchik,[44] all wonderfully processed by a pantheon of well-intentioned Canadian rabbis. But the glaring absence of any real Canadian Jewish rabbis, thinkers, or mystics seems completely counter to the stated project of this *haggadah*. Finally, as the *haggadah* reaches its climax with the return of the repressed, of finding what has been hidden in *Tzafun*, the reader seeking any crumb of spiritual sustenance is left dry with Rabbi Philip Bergman's suggestion that: "The *Tzafun* section has no prayers associated with it and yet it is the most significant part of the *seder,* not only because it has previously engaged the children in a treasure hunt, but also because it reminds us that there are many things in life that remain concealed from view or hidden from our understanding."[45] What could possibly be so significant that it defies any spiritual reflection, unless of course it is, after Benjamin, "untranslatable"?[46] What a profound missed opportunity!

Previously, I argued in the second chapter for the ubiquitous influence of both Leonard Cohen and the Tosher Rebbe on Canadian Jewish Mysticism. In light of this, it strikes me that the *Canadian Haggadah Canadienne* remains stuck in a myopic political narrative, rather than being open to the expansive spiritual journey that underlies a more expansive and mysterious rendering of the story. To my knowledge, it is only in another Montréal *haggadah, Wellsprings of Freedom* by the late, great Rabbi Aigen, that offers any attempt at encountering the Canadian Jewish Mysticism of Cohen's oeuvre. Specifically Aigen dares to evoke Cohen's iconic verse on brokenness as spiritual direction for *Yahatz.* In breaking the middle *matzah, Wellsprings of Freedom* suggests that one recites: "There is a crack in everything./That's how the light gets in."[47] I want to complicate Aigen's usage of Cohen's lyric a bit further, to show just how much the Montréal bard is pushing for the spiritual direction for *Yahatz* to come through in our lives more expansively.

Part of Leonard Cohen's lyrical magic consists precisely in his ability to translate the esoteric into the everyday. Consider how the brokenness of life emerges as a site of revelation regarding equality, as "Democracy is coming to the U.S.A":

> It's coming through a crack in the wall;
> on a visionary flood of alcohol;
> from the staggering account
> of the Sermon on the Mount
> which I don't pretend to understand at all . . .[48]

As a Canadian Jewish mystic writing from the place of his "third solitude," Leonard Cohen at once throws up his arms at lost mystical project of Christian universalism in Jesus Sermon on the Mount, and expresses frustration with the triumphalism that accompanies most nationalisms. As a Canadian ex-pat living between Los Angeles, the Mount Baldy Zen Monastery, and his villa in Hydra, Cohen is forever sensitized to the suffering that emerges from inequality around him. The crack in everything—*Yahatz*—is everywhere, as he sings from the wounds of the Rodney King police beatings in Los Angeles:

> It's coming from the sorrow in the street,
> the holy places where the races meet;
> from the homicidal bitchin'
> that goes down in every kitchen
> to determine who will serve and who will eat.[49]

Cohen's glance of prophetic ire is unflinching, one that dares to aim at the place of his exile—America. This is the one country that has never fully understood or embraced Cohen's music, and yet, the USA is where he resides most at ease. While in exile from Canada, Cohen clearly sees the cracks in the veneer of American culture of democracy as he warns:

> It's coming to America first,
> the cradle of the best and of the worst.
> It's here they got the range
> and the machinery for change
> and it's here they got the spiritual thirst.[50]

To understand Aigen's extrapolation of Cohen's iconic verse on brokenness as spiritual direction for *Yahatz* in *Wellsprings of Freedom,* it is worthwhile seeing the context of the song's refrain. It serves as part of the larger lyric of the song "Anthem":

The birds they sang
at the break of day
Start again
I heard them say
Don't dwell on what
has passed away
or what is yet to be.

Ah the wars they will
be fought again
The holy dove
She will be caught again
bought and sold
and bought again
the dove is never free.

Ring the bells that still can ring
Forget your perfect offering
There is a crack in everything
That's how the light gets in.[51]

The pendulum of the apocalypse swings *to and fro*, but the brokenness that is incurred is meant to be a teacher. That brokenness can only serve as a guide through the vagaries of life if one learns to truly live in the present: "Don't dwell on what/has passed away/or what is yet to be."[52] By seeing within the cracks of life the revelation of the Tetragram—"I will be that which I will be"—Cohen's lyrics once again make the mystical meaningful and render it in a uniquely Canadian manner—disarming and deep.

Now to the other glaring absence in Canadian Jewish Mysticism—the devotional teachings of the Tosher Rebbe.[53] In turning to R. Segal-Loewy's Passover *haggadah, 'Avodat haLevi*, one is immediately brought to the heart of the matter abiding in the station of *Yahatz* as he teaches:

In order to [performatively] speak the *haggadah*, it is all a matter of *Yahatz*, which is articulated by our Blessed Saints regarding the Talmudic teaching: "*Lehem Oni*—bread that must be responded to through many speech performances" (b*Pesahim* 116b). This means that we receive responses from the divine totality on many matters. This is the real spiritual power of this night, that the Israelites receive responses to their prayers, which is only possible through a "broken heart." This is known from the teaching of the Holy Zohar (Zohar III: 195a, etc.) where prayer for "the downtrodden" is [the fabric from which] all prayer is woven, so that what one pray in an utterly downtrodden state, when the heart is truly broken, taking oneself to be downtrodden and needy for Torah and sacral deeds, bereft of true intuition as the Blessed Sages teach that being spiritually bereft only applies to "*da'at*" (b*Nedarim* 41a), [that state of intuitive consciousness] whereby one knows that one has not even begun to delve into devotional duties, that sense of feeling that the only aid and assistance in this process is the divine totality—[it is the state of downtrodden consciousness] that makes prayer most acceptable. This is analogous to the children of Israel in Egypt, knowing that they were in a state of consciousness naked and negligent of any sacral deeds, and so they were deeply broken-hearted in the core of their being over their distance from serving the divine totality, and it is precisely in this feeling of broken-heartedness where redemption emerges. This then relates to the [Passover as *Peh-Sakh*, namely] that many matters are answered, for through downtrodden and broken-hearted prayer, one is able to answer and pray to the divine totality over many matters, for prayer that emerges from this place of downtroddenness and broken-heartedness is immediately received by the divine totality. This explains why the Blessed Sages [suggest that the *seder* should] begin with in downtroddenness and end with praise, namely, that one should begin through the downtrodden place within one's self, to crack open one's heart before the divine totality. In so doing, know that one has still done next to nothing relative to the devotional service required to serve the divine totality. Know that from a personal perspective one is basically worthless. Only in overflowing compassion and grace is one granted one the opportunity to stand and serve this divine totality. This then

> leads one to be overcome with joy and jubilation, granting permission to fulfill devotional service and sacral deeds, and to approach the divine totality, which is this sense of culminating in joy. [If one is to culminate the journey of liberation with such joy, therefore] it must really begin in downtrodden consciousness, surely leading to overwhelming joy in the divine totality and its teaching [path of] Torah. All of this is alluded to in *Yahatz*, by breaking the middle *matzah* of emptiness into two, to allude to the matter of the broken heart, which is the bread of emptiness. Through this shall we merit being redeemed from all our heart's yearnings on this night.[54]

Brokenness as experience is the necessary opening to spiritual growth that is central to the Tosher Rebbe's reading of *Yahatz* within the *seder*. Correlating both mystical sources as well as uniquely hyperliteral mystical readings of Talmudic sources, the Tosher Rebbe is laying claim to a devotional pathway that necessitates a deeper self-reflection and contemplation of one's most vulnerable locatedness within every step of the journey to liberation. But the journey to spiritual liberation itself, paradoxically, comes with the realization of emptiness, and the willingness to become devoted to sacral deeds. This commitment is the acknowledgement of work still to be done. From this awareness and acknowledgement, it is possible for truely heartfelt prayer to emerge and transform the aspirant from a state of spiritual downtroddenness to joy and jubilation. Echoing the earlier dictum of the Kotzker Rebbe, that there is indeed nothing as whole as a broken heart, the Tosher Rebbe effectively extends the spiritual probing further. He would have us focus on just how much the wholeness of the devotional life and yearning depends on the willingness to begin each step within our spiritual downtroddenness. In so doing, a deeper joy and jubilation within that brokenness is revealed.

In analyzing and correlating Leonard Cohen and the Tosher Rebbe's thinking through one station of *Yahatz* in the long journey of the Passover *haggadah*, what I have argued for here is the need for a greater awareness and openness to the variegated spiritual landscape of Canadian Jewish Mysticism. From the prophetic post-secular songs of Leonard Cohen to the Hasidic devotionality of the Tosher Rebbe, this analysis coupled with the second chapter make the case that there is much to explore in Canadian Jewish Mysticism that would only enrich any so-called Canadian *haggadah*. The danger that inheres in the mystical quest remains its ultimate "untranslatability." Further, the quest's challenge does not free us from confronting those performative texts that enact traces of the ineffable within mundane ritual and existence—especially those nestled away in the Great White North!

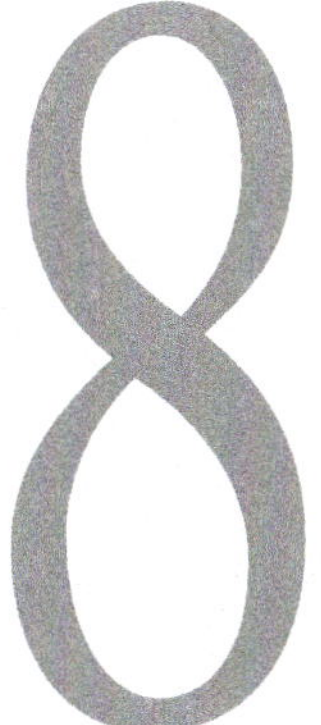

Falling with Our Angels, So Human

> Since we grow up, we fall, or, more simply, are fallen.
>
> —Harold Bloom[1]

> . . . Falling angel, angel . . .
>
> —Leonard Cohen[2]

Capturing all of existence, in his inimitable way, critic Harold Bloom manages, to pinpoint the predicament of the distanced, disengaged modern subject—to be human is to be wrought in the Adamic condition. Like no other—except, as we shall soon see, Leonard Cohen! In Bloom's estimation: "The angel Adam was a fallen angel as soon as he could be distinguished from God. As a latter day Gnostic I cheerfully affirm that we are all fallen angels. . . ."[3] Existence itself is a marker of that separation from a lost, primordial unity.

Song, then, is an elixir for our being fallen angels. Song is a bridge back to the celestial spheres from the infernal present moment. Song is the stairway to heaven that lines its towers. The angels keep vigil to their divine source by continuously singing from the "Tower of Song" [*heikhal d'negunah*]. It is this image of the "Tower of Song," so lusciously imagined in the Zohar that I will focus on in a future-oriented reflection through the post-secular mystical songbook of Leonard Cohen. Let us open with this ancient image, aptly re-imagined anew into a troubadour-esque *migdal* in Cohen's unique rendering as the "Tower of Song":

> I was born like this, I had no choice
> I was born with the gift of a golden voice
> And twenty-seven angels from the Great Beyond
> They tied me to this table right here
> In the Tower of Song.[4]

The palette from which Leonard Cohen draws his inspiration strongly echoes albeit intuitively the imagery in *Tiqqunai Zohar* in this evocative way:

> There is a tower which is forbidden to enter unless by way of tears, and there is a Tower of Song which is forbidden to enter unless by way of song. And so David encroached this tower through song. . . .[5]

King David is the singer-songwriter *par excellence* for Cohen, not only as author of the broken-hearted 150 psalms, but also as the one who shall bring on redemption through song as Messiah, again evoked in the Zohar:

> As soon as King Messiah reads in the Torah scroll, the two eagles will rise, on either side, the dove lowering herself. King Messiah descends [from high in the tower to its bottom level] with the crown on his head to the last level, and the two eagles fly above his head.[6]

Nothing is incidental in this portrait, not even the chirping of the birds, which points to the most heavenly song adorning the tower, as the Zohar imagines that:

> When this tower returns to its place, it shines like the radiance of the eye of the sun . . . at the top of this tower are birds of fire, who chirp as morning arises—a lovely chirping, who loveliness is unmatched by any melody.[7]

These singing angels appear to pulsate in and out of existence as birds of fire, for as the Talmud already imagines them:

> . . . every single day, ministering angels are created from a river of fire, chant song, and then cease to be. . . .[8]

This fleeting image is expanded by the Zohar, as it adds another layer to their ephemeral song of the angels, to suggest that "all those angels who denounce their Master above and are burned, consumed by fire; and all those others who vanish, unenduring, devoured by fire!" So it is precisely those angels created on the second day of Creation from nothing but Judgment, the side of *Gevurah*, which do not have the capacity to survive.[9] God's burning the angels who opposed human creation is envisioned as the *Shekhinah*, "fire consuming fire."[10]

"Tower of Song" captures the ephemerality of all songs, building upon quandaries that deal with creation and its spiritual support, known as *'emunah* in its peculiar rendering of Lamentations 3:23: "They are new every morning; Great is Your trust [in us]." The Tower of Song finds a loose blueprint in the rabbinic exegesis upon this verse from laymen tuitions realizing this mesmerizing passage:

> R. Helbo said: "Every day the Holy Blessed One creates a new band of angels who utter a new song before the divine and then pass away." R. Berekiah said: "I replied to R. Helbo by quoting, 'And he said: Let me go, for the day is breaking' (Genesis 32: 27) [and my time has arrived to utter a song before the Holy Blessed One!] But he answered me, 'You strangler, do you think to strangle me [with such a specious argument]? The angels [concerned in the incident with Jacob] were Gabriel and Michael who were celestial princes, and while the others pass away [daily], they do not pass away!'"[11]

While those angels intertwined with Jacob sing on, all other angels fade from the score.

The only interruption of the forever-flowing songs recited by the angels in the tower is when the divine intercedes, demanding the angels take a moment to acknowledge the suffering of God's creation as the Egyptians are drowning at the Reed Sea. Judgement ultimately consumes the angels along with their songs. The opportunity for transformation in the eternal world strikes us as counterintuitive, if after all, the divine is perfect. But the transformation possible through *teshuvah* is embedded in the very brick and mortar of the "Tower of Song," as later Hasidic master Reb Naftali Zvi of Ropshitz (1760-1827) teaches:

> ". . . the Heavenly Palace of Melody [*Heikhal haNegina*] was adjacent to the Heavenly Palace of Return [*Heikhal haTeshuva*]."
>
> So a person who did not leap from the former [*Heikhal haNegina*] to the latter [*Heikhal haTeshuva*] was an absolute fool because both palatial doorways are interconnected.
>
> Regarding the teaching of the *Divrai Yisrael* [of Modzitz], we learn this additional insight:
>
> ". . . everybody claims that Heavenly Palace of Melody [*Heikhal haNegina*] is adjacent to the Heavenly Palace of Return [*Heikhal haTeshuva*]."
>
> But I say that Heavenly Palace of Melody itself [*Heikhal haNegina*] is the Heavenly Palace of Return [*Heikhal haTeshuva*].[12]

This kaleidoscope of towers folding in on themselves as envisioned by the Ropshitzer is imagined as emanating music within human reach, later according to R. Arele Roth (1894–1947) that:

> . . . of all the heavenly palaces, it is the Tower of Song that is closest to us, extending in its ascent [from the lowest places on earth] right up until the celestial realm. As a result [of such direct accessibility] one is able to open the celestial channels to enable the flow of holy blessing [into the lowest places on earth].[13]

Existence itself is then a marker of that separation from a lost, primordial frequency still playing in the Tower of Song.

The closest trace of such a loss that scars existence is the glimmer from the ever-turning fiery sword guarded by the angels at the gates of Eden. Bloom reminds us that indeed the Hebrew Bible knows of no fallen angels *per se*. Recall Job's opposing attorney, Satan, or Jacob's wrestling partner at the midnight encounter at the River Yabok—neither are fallen, but each protagonist encounters their angel, ascending and descending while intertwined with them. The human being, no matter how fallen, is never alone in that fallenness. Angelology has an illustrious history in its ebbs and flows within Judaism as early as the Second Temple period, especially in *Heikhalot* literature and magical texts.[14] Yet, as moderns we abide in the shadow of the medieval philosophical swerve from embodiment and imagination, and our minds are directed in vein a strongly apophatic. We can thank Maimonides (1135-1204) for this turn toward the apophatic. Indeed, his influence and his vigilance to rid Judaism of all inner idolatry through ascent and conjunction with the tool of the active intellect, continues to run deep.[15] What we are witnessing as moderns in a post-secular context is how the angels have morphed into that struggle for primacy of the mind over the heart. At the same time, we are witnessing how the angels continue to lose their currency in exoteric Judaism. In short, angels are being relegated to cursory encounters with Cupid *et al.*

There is a tendency for Jewish mystics after Maimonides to correlate the union of the human consciousness with the active intellect to the union, with "an angel of the Most High"—namely, the "union of Enoch with *Metatron*."[16] While the scant mention of Enoch's life in the Hebrew Bible would suggest a nasty, brutish, and short existence, mystics have continued to see and project into Enoch the heights of a spiritual avatar, emblematic of apotheosis. The transformation of Enoch from human prophet to angelic being through a merging experience of apotheosis is a function of his righteousness—what we have here is a full-fledged ascent without any suspicion of descent.[17] So when we reach the prophetic medieval Kabbalah of Abraham Abulafia (1240–ca. 1291), for example, what we find is an articulation of the Enoch experience as a physical sensation of anointing that enables a spiritual transformation into an angelic presence.[18] This ecstatic embodiment of angelic presence becomes, for Abulafia, the entire purpose of the Torah. But how much of this spiritual ideal enters into the mainstream of Judaism as a religion?

Just how much esotericism remains in exoteric Judaism is a doubly perplexing query when turning to octogenarian singer-songwriter, Leonard Cohen. Much his rebellion against the Montréal Judaism forefathers (exotericism) remains a point of departure for his discovery of his primordial ancestors (esotericism). What draws listeners deeper and deeper into the seemingly facile lyrical landscape of Cohen's popular musical songbook is the feeling that, indeed, something has fallen through the cracks between the exoteric and esoteric positions. This allows for his lyrical path to remain committed, after all these decades, to rediscovering what it means to be human through the fallen angels that continue to accompany his journey. The most enriching pathway to a redemption song for Cohen is in confronting the reality of living a fallen life whose very descent is its ascent. "[A] fallen angel and a human being," as Bloom aptly describes it, "are two terms for the same entity or condition."[19] This singular condition of being a fallen human angel between the absorption of ascent into apotheosis and the encounter of descent into theophany[20] provides Cohen a kind of compass that continues to guide his lyrical journey, both through his music and, recurringly, in his *koans*. For example:

> We had high/hopes for you—/we thought/you would/fly apart—/and now we/find you/adhering—/signed: the paraclete.[21]

This rhythm of the angelic pathway for Leonard Cohen is what allows for a creative interweaving of ascent and descent, a recurrent motif in his lyrics. The following lyrics from "The Window" articulates this rhythm:

Oh chosen love, Oh frozen love
Oh tangle of matter and ghost
Oh darling of angels, demons and saints
And the whole broken-hearted host
Gentle this soul

And come forth from the cloud of unknowing
And kiss the cheek of the moon
The New Jerusalem glowing
Why tarry all night in the ruin
And leave no word of discomfort
And leave no observer to mourn
But climb on your tears and be silent
Like a rose on its ladder of thorns

Oh chosen love, Oh frozen love . . .[22]

This image of the rose and its thorns that Cohen plucks from the garden of mystical symbols guides this journey of ascent through descent. What sets apart this recurring motif of the rose and its thorns in Zoharic Kabbalah,[23] for example, is the degree to which its dualism prevails in the journey of ascent. In order to reach the beloved, the lover continues its attempt to ascend, likely through Jacob's ladder [*Sulam Ya'akov*], albeit strewn with thorns. The ascent is riddled with moments of descent, while not ultimately detracting the lover. Extrapolating from the classic image in the *Song*, "Like a rose in a field of thorns,"[24] Cohen continues the journey to the beloved, painting from the palette of thorns in Zoharic Kabbalah, further applying other colors from Jewish residues in Rosicrucianism[25] as well as incarnational theology, to create a uniquely modern canvas, as the lyrics continue:

Then lay your rose on the fire
The fire give up to the sun

The sun give over to splendour
In the arms of the high holy one
For the holy one dreams of a letter
Dreams of a letter's death
Oh bless thee continuous stutter
Of the word being made into flesh
Oh chosen love, Oh frozen love . . .
Gentle this soul.[26]

The intertwined symbols of embodiment evoked in this lyric—whether the rose enmeshed with its thorns or the "continuous stutter/ Of the word being made into flesh"—blurs the incarnational language between the theophanic stuttering of Moses and Isaiah, with the incarnational apotheosis of saints and *tzaddikim* from Jesus of Nazerath to the Ba'al Shem Tov. However, such blurring is more on the order of a Chagall painting than an example of Cohen's putative but (mis)attributed doctrinal Catholicism.[27] As a lyricist, Cohen deftly navigates the nuances of "Oh chosen love, Oh frozen love" to reveal the dynamism of imagery hovering over a continuum from which he draws inspiration without being tied to it in any doctrinal fashion. The genius of his lyrics emerges in what Cohen is able to craft from the "cracks in everything" between religion and spirituality—for indeed that "is where the light gets in" for this Montréal bard. After all, in wanderings of fallen angels, it is the modern human subject that is best situated to discover the angelic resonances in Cohen's songs.

Part of the reason why Cohen's lyrics strike such chord in the hearts and minds of modern listeners is the accessibility of the lyrics. There is something familiar in the condition of missing the mark *as part of* the quest for the holy that makes the journey of the spirit so relevant, realistic, and urgent. All those human yearnings to find love, sustain it, and remain in it even while falling are what draws the heart to feel tethered to its expression in Cohen's lyrics. That blurring of incarnational language between the theophanic stuttering requires the human subject to overcome that sense of forgetfulness of an incarnational apotheosis of merging with the divine that began the whole story:

> Well you know that I love to live with you,
> but you make me forget so very much.
> I forget to pray for the angels
> and then the angels forget to pray for us.[28]

Forgetting angels, and by extension God in our lives is much more manageable when it does not come with a heavy dose of Catholic guilt, but rather with a realistic sense of empathy from fellow travelers, especially fallen Jews. The human subject can experience a catharsis in being fallen, once s/he knows that they are not alone. No matter how far one falls, if indeed the angels are falling with us, then humanity is not alone. The subtlety of such fallenness that has generally marked Cohen's songbook is what gives listeners through the decades the assurance of never being alone. Even in those moments, sometimes quite debased, when the human heart appears to be in descent, no matter how seemingly out of control, it is still in the course of a larger ascent:

> And I can't wait to tell you to your face
> And I can't wait for you to take my place
> You are The Naked Angel In My Heart
> You are The Woman With Her Legs Apart
> It's written on the walls of this hotel
> You go to heaven once you've been to hell
> A heavy burden lifted from my soul
> I heard that love was out of my control.[29]

The struggle that catches the human being with its angelic counterpart occurs here in the midst of an erotic encounter, akin to Jacob's struggle at Yabok River, transposed from an open landscape of nature into the gritty interiors of a hotel room. But even in such confines, the bard finds a way to render the erotic encounter as a struggle with the angelic that precipitates a fallenness together—never alone. Even if "I don't claim to be guilty/Guilty's too grand," the bard is still able to articulate an awareness that "there's a Law, there's an Arm, there's a Hand" of a Judge and Justice. Just exactly how justice is adjudicated and rendered becomes another story entirely, but in the meantime, the bard admits he is not alone: "I fell with my angel/Down the chain of command."[30]

The "glorious pain of our existence as fallen angels," as Bloom paints it is a paradoxical celebration of "angelicism that so profoundly contemplates the paradox that love engenders death."[31] This sense pulsates in the paradoxical lyrics composed by Cohen in that very "painful glory" of "Closing Time":

> Ah we're drinking and we're dancing
> and the band is really happening
> and the Johnny Walker wisdom running high
> And my very sweet companion
> she's the Angel of Compassion
> she's rubbing half the world against her thigh
> And every drinker every dancer
> lifts a happy face to thank her
> the fiddler fiddles something so sublime
> all the women tear their blouses off
> and the men they dance on the polka-dots
> and it's partner found, it's partner lost
> and it's hell to pay when the fiddler stops:
> it's CLOSING TIME.[32]

Cohen's shift from Judgment [*Din*] to Compassion [*Hesed*] is noteworthy in the angelic sphere. Notice the shift here away from the Zoharic image of God's burning the angels who opposed human creation through the *Shekhinah* as "fire consuming fire" to "the Angel of Compassion [who's] . . . rubbing half the world against her thigh." Yet another ironic riff on liturgy of this very "painful glory" of "Closing Time" echoes the conclusion of the holiest day on the Jewish calendar, *Yom Kippur,* whose final moment is known as *Neilah*. Cohen continues in his pursuit of an angelic face within human fallenness. What these paradoxical images suggest is a fallenness that rises up, or a descent for the sake of ascent. This scenario is a distorted refraction of that very yearning of religion for the sacred. Sacredness is set up within a dualism that includes and is in opposition with the profane. Is there a way to maintain an end of closing time when the beginning and middle of such sacred myths no longer resonate? What this "painful glory" of "Closing Time" betrays is just how much the profane *is sacred* in a post-secular world.

Reaching such an awareness of that "painful glory" amid post-secularism requires a shift in perspective as well as an elixir for the pain in making such a shift. The elixir which serves as a salve to the incessant dualism is love. So, for the lyrics of Leonard Cohen, then, falling in love is an opportunity to transcend the dualism and dwell in the unification that love provides:

> There ain't no cure for love
> There ain't no cure for love
> All the rocket ships are climbing through the sky
> The holy books are open wide
> The doctors working day and night
> But they'll never ever find that cure for love
> There ain't no drink no drug
> (Ah tell them, angels)
> There's nothing pure enough to be a cure for love . . .
> I walked into this empty church, I had no place else to go
> When the sweetest voice I ever heard, whispered to my soul
> I don't need to be forgiven for loving you so much
> It's written in the scriptures
> It's written there in blood
> I even heard the angels declare it from above

There ain't no cure,
There ain't no cure,
There ain't no cure for love.[33]

As love continues to afflict spiritual seekers with an unquenched yearning, the singer appeals to the magnetism of *eros* in scriptures: the Song of Songs; the blood of embodiment, incarnation, and sacrifice; and finally by appealing to the celestial chorus, decrying: "I even heard the angels declare it from above." When this opium for the masses is most effective in any religion, it assuages an ongoing affliction to return to that shot of love that continues to draw the seeker on the journey. The more the spiritual seeker is aware of the desire that drives her quest, the more such a person is ascending in descent with fellow fallen angels.

Angels are not necessarily cherubic children, enshrouded in innocence. There is a more raucous rendition of this fallen journey, a kind of country version. This version, featuring members of what later becomes the Charlie Daniels Band, includes these two additional (excised) verses at the end of the song:

> I've looked into the mirrors in numberless places;/They all smile back at me with their troublesome faces./In the cards that they dealt me there weren't any aces./And the horses never listened to me at the races.
> There are still one or two of us walking the streets,/No arrows of direction painted under our feet,/No angels to warn us away from the heat,/And no honey to keep us where it is sweet.[34]

Angels here function as psycho-pomps, as those needed guides who can navigate every wanderer through the infernal heats of passion and love that too often lead astray.

Opening anew the possibility for blessing to flow in a post-secular context is at once liberating and terrifying. Liberating, in that the human subject once again can own remorse and shame in the prospect of fallenness, even though vengeance is restored to a Judge and his judgment that the human subject must now trust:

Tell me again
When the victims are singing
And Laws of Remorse are restored
Tell me again
That you know what I'm thinking
But vengeance belongs to the lord
Tell me again . . .

While sometimes it seems safer to keep angels at a distance, Bloom reminds us wisely that "fallen angels can be uncomfortably close, in whole and in part."[35] Brushing up against the catastrophe of the *Shoah*, Cohen re-primes the canvas after Auschwitz to allow for painting with a more expansive color palette, even if it is darker:

Tell me again
When the day has been ransomed
& night has no right to begin
Try me again
When the angels are panting
And scratching the door to come in
Tell me again
When I'm clean and I'm sober
Tell me again . . .
Tell me again
When the filth of the butcher
Is washed in the blood of the lamb
Tell me again
When the rest of the culture
Has passed thru' the Eye of the Camp
Tell me again. . . .[36]

Here is a powerful moment when incarnation, so commonly syphoned away into Catholic theology, is actually engaged as a living theologoumenon that allows for a new layer of meaning to emerge. Rather than seeing the angels as passive, cherubic figures operating under the ultimate volition of the divine, here, in a post-*Shoah* cultural landscape, now even the angels of yore "must pass thru' the Eye of the Camp." Just as angels can serve to test human souls as they pass from one world to the next, what Cohen's lyric is challenging here is for an inversion—namely, how does the post-*Shoah* landscape cause fallen humanity to recast its notion of the angelic facet within each and every one of us? Are we fallen angels or demons on the rise? The closer one is to the fallen angel, the closer one is to death, for as Bloom again reminds us: "In relation to death, we once were the immortal Adam, but as soon as we became subject to death we became the fallen angel, for that is what the metaphor of fallen angel means: the overwhelming awareness of one's mortality."[37] Bloom further articulates the precise nexus point: "[T]he dilemma of being open to transcendental longings even as we are trapped inside a dying animal is the precise predicament of the fallen angel, that is to say, of a fully conscious human being."[38] Cohen's songbook shows how, in a post-secular, post-*Shoah* context, key lyrics pinpoint and then caress a void within the listener, and in so doing enable a deeper listening that leads to self-exploration of transformation. The impact of such transformation of the subject's existence itself is then a marker of that a separation from a lost, primordial unity. In this realm, angels are scarred, orphaned companions in search of their song, in the words of the Zohar:

> Those ascending, playing a melody—what melody do they play? An orphaned song: *A Psalm. Sing to YHVH a new song, for He has worked wonders . . .* (Psalms 98:1). A new song—now, is there such a thing as an ancient song? However, a song that until now the holy angels did not offer in praise; for it is new, and may it be new. Why is it new? Because the one who renews youth offers it in praise.[39]

It is from this intimate place of lost unity, no matter the pain nor the price, that Leonard Cohen's lyrics ascend in descent with every fallen angel, so human.

"An Appetite for Something Like Religion": *Un*binding the Binding of Isaac, Jesus Christ & Joan of Arc through Zen

"Even though we have *no religion*, we have an appetite for something that is *like religion*."[1] It is precisely by listening to those "deep feelings" and "irrepressible appetites" in the post-secular songbook of Leonard Cohen that more nuanced attunement can be cultivated regarding mysticism after modernity.

How and what does post-secularism have to do with Leonard Cohen? Or as Cohen sings recently, he's "got a little secret"—so readers and listeners continue to wonder just what is the nature of that secret embedded in his songbook? Is this secret one entangled in those "deep feelings" and "irrepressible appetites" of the post-secular that can be told? Yet if it is true, as scholar of religion Jeffrey Kripal claims, that "the religion of America is no religion,"[2] then there is no reason "to promise not to tell."[3] The secret of Cohen's post-secular songbook is how he continues to unite heaven and earth as he sings: "I've made a date in heaven but I've been keeping it in hell."[4] This unrelenting search for an expansion of the sacred in a post-secular context remains an abiding inspiration for Montréal bard and singer-songwriter, Leonard Cohen.

A deeper appreciation of what is meant by this current post-secular age is necessary in addressing the opening question about the textures of enlightenment. But skepticism abounds when it comes to analyzing the emergence of contemporary spirituality, especially from the heart of disenchantment to re-enchantment where I'm writing this book, on the West Coast, as I return to the inimitable critique of the post-secular context by second generation critical theorist, Jürgen Habermas (b. 1929):

> The Californian syncretism of pseudo-scientific and esoteric doctrines and religious fundamentalism are thoroughly modern phenomena which may even express social pathologies of modernity, but which certainly do not offer any resistance to them. The missionary successes of a literal, but liturgically extravagant spiritualism are certainly also interesting from the sociological points of view. However, I cannot see what importance religious movements, which cut themselves off from the cognitive achievements of modernity could have for the secular self-understanding of modernity.[5]

While I argue that the songs of Leonard Cohen sit squarely outside the "literal, but liturgically extravagant spiritualism" Habermas is pointing to, there is a larger context of post-secular critique emerging amid these seemingly dismissive remarks. What disturbs Habermas is the withdrawal of the cognitive in favor of the emotional (read *spiritual*). Habermas shows a reticence for seeing the importance of religious movements that are intentionally swerving away from the head-centered, cognitive approach and are choosing to hover in a more heart-centered, emotional realm of the spirit that typifies the religion of no-religion that is America. Habermas is right about some aspects of fundamentalist America, but off the mark when it comes to the heart-mind at the center of most Judaisms.

If, indeed, in this post-secular context one can claim that "we have no religion," then is mysticism possible or even necessary? What then is Cohen's real concern, inspiration, and drive as poet and bard? Here, Canadian critic Pierre Burton, already in 1965, interrogates Leonard Cohen while interviewing him only to discover that for this Montréal bard: "The real concern is whether I am in a state of grace."[6] I will argue that in the post-secular songbook of Leonard Cohen, there remains a consistent engagement with experiential forms of mystical *gnosis* from Judaism, Christianity, and Rinzai Buddhism. That is, when he makes such an early comment about his daily search for grace, or decades later while on extended retreat at Mount Baldy, when the ongoing spiritual work of liberating the heart from its enslavement to suffering through the technique of *zazen*, Cohen remains on a consistent path, as he reflects:

> . . . when you get out of the way of your own love, it becomes true, it is not fixed, it is not solidified and when it is not focused rigidly on another object, then it broadcasts in front of you and in back of you, to the right of you, to the left of you, above you and beneath you, and you are in the center of a force field that includes everything, but has no inside and no outside at all, that doesn't look at anything, nor does it need to be looked at . . . it's like the taste of honey when you're young, . . . or chocolate when you eat something sweet, you know and every cell of your body says "thank you"—that's what [meditation] is like.[7]

Between these oscillating impulses, of getting "out of the way of your own love" and opening to grace, Cohen's songbook leads to what Wolfson in his pioneering study has already analyzed as "untimely prayer" which is the very "time of *poesis*."[8] If the prayer that comes to replace sacrifice is considered to be "a yearning to call upon the transcendent,"[9] then an emerging guiding question is whether unique mystical syncretism of Cohen's songbook implants itself in the boundedness of the Abrahamic religions, including its deity, or whether such songs transcends that path altogether, venturing beyond into "something that is *like religion*."[10]

What exactly holds such a dissimilitude to religion without being trapped by its pinions and limitations? That sense of feeling torn, as an artist yearning to create something new with ancient resonances, is echoed in Franz Kafka's desire for his writings to become a Kabbalah:

> I can also say, assault on the last earthly frontier, an assault, moreover, launched from below, from mankind, and since this too is a metaphor, I can replace it by the metaphor of an assault from above, aimed at me from above.[11]

I am not concerned with Cohen's indebtedness to Kafka; rather, what interests me is the degree to which both of these Jewish artists share a subversive yearning expressed through their own contemporary mysticism from below as an assault from above. This post-secular mysticism yearns at once to express the human assault from below as a co-mingled divine assault from above that inextricably marks the inspiration behind creative works nestled within and beyond the clutches of modernity. The mystic cannot escape the calling of being assaulted in all embodied spaces from the head of the thinker, to the heart of the poet, to the mouth of the bard.

Building upon Wolfson's path-breaking analysis of Cohen's mystical *oeuvre* through the lens of an Americanized Rinzai Zen practice, one could ask whether or not Cohen's post-secular songbook is just another "mode of subversion," namely, remaining "consistent with Zen to affirm that path that is not Zen as an expression of Zen." As Wolfson remarks elsewhere on "untimely prayer":[12]

> . . . so we are bound to pray by not-praying, praying the prayer before and after there is any prayer, praying for the possibility to pray. In this precarious moment of spiritual impoverishment, that alone should suffice.[13]

After Auschwitz and Hiroshima, and closer to home, Black Lives Matter, to pray for the possibility to pray remains an authentic stance of the seeker after modernity. Through the sands of time and its collective catastrophes, religion necessarily shifts. While that "good ol' time religion" remains a favorite hobby of the Montréal bard, often one yearns for the solace that religion from time immemorial has been a form of binding and re-binding the finite to the infinite, revelation to reason, that remains forever in the offing. At its root, religion "functions as an aggregate signifier for the 're-binding' (*re-ligio*) together of previously profuse and dissociated particularities of faith and devotion with their own indigenous, or 'territorial,' characteristics into a grand ideology of 'unity in diversity,' where the principle of integration is the divinization of the political—'emperor worship.'"[14] While the current "war of religion" echoes age-old tensions between revelation and reason, its new garb is no longer entangled between doctrine and revelations that are irreconcilable with philosophy. Rather, what emerges now is a tension between the Enlightenment forces of globalization and "tele-mediatization" pit against the reactive force of faith with its own place of truth.[15] In this landscape after postmodernism, as French Jewish thinker Jacques Derrida once quipped, a "religion without religion" is a strange religiosity that is "obliged to ally the reactivity of the primitive and archaic . . . both to obscurantist dogmatism and to hypercritical vigilance . . . they can displace the traditional structures of national citizenship, they tend to efface both the borders of the state and the distinctive properties of languages."[16] The return of the repressed need to *sacrifice to* rather than holding in the more evolved place of making *sacrifice for* is a return of the primitive and archaic urge in religion,[17] whether it is inspired by a yearning for *eros, thanatos*, or redemption from both.

Arguably, there is no stranger tale of this "war of religion" than within the battle between revelation and reason as *re-bound* in the story of (un) binding in Genesis 22 known as the *Akeidah.* It is important to dwell for a moment on Derrida's interpretation of this archetypal narrative and how it brings to light the nuances of sacrifice in *self* and *other.*[18] The double bind of religion is at once incommunicable and felt directly.

By focusing on the paradigm of the sacrifice of *self* and *other* through the biblical narrative of the Binding of Isaac, a kind of intertextuality opens in Cohen's songbook, intertwining the prophetic call, along with what Wolfson identifies as Christ's passion, Zen awakening, and ascetic yearning.[19] If *Akeidat Yitzhak* continues on as the baffling story of Genesis 22 forever inscribed in our hearts—why then does this puzzling story so capture Cohen? Existing with "the *hunters,* hungry and shrewd, and with the *hunted* quick, soft and nude,"[20] living with the one offering the sacrifice and the sacrifice itself is what allows Cohen to return to these "ashes of experience"[21] embedded within this story of the binding of Isaac from many different angles throughout his songbook. Is it a story of fear or one of love? Of sacrifice from the place of fear or from the place of love? Of sacrificing the *other* or the self? What happens when one internalizes this narrative and contemplates it? Is the contemplation of such a rich interpretative narrative singular or collective?[22]

It behooves us to return to Cohen's primary engagements with this binding narrative within his songbook, starting in 1969 with:

> The door it opened slowly,
> My father he came in,
> I was nine years old.
> And he stood so tall above me,
> His blue eyes they were shining
> And his voice was very cold.
> He said, "I've had a vision
> And you know I'm strong and holy,
> I must do what I've been told."
> So he started up the mountain,
> I was running, he was walking,
> And his axe was made of gold.[23]

In contrast to Dylan's "Highway 61," the retelling of *Akeidat Yitzhak* by here Cohen absorbs that narrative and melds into a personal journey of the singer's youth, decades younger than the consensual, thirty-something Isaac, participating in his imminent sacrifice by father, Abraham. The tension between the warmth of his luminescent "blue eyes" and his cold voice is disconcerting. The difference in pacing, between the lumbering father and the racing son, emerges as the golden axe hovers above. This iteration of the binding serves as part of Cohen's searing critique of Montréal Jewry's materialism and conservatism, which echoes from Cohen's neglected speech reconstructed here from notes in the Leonard Cohen Archive, called, "Loneliness and History." This talk delivered at the Jewish library a few days after Christmas 1964 marks Cohen's shift from poet to singer.[24] In this watershed speech, Cohen dons his prophetic mantle and reflects on what he has learned from reading the priestly laments of fellow Montréal bard, journalist, novelist, short story writer, and lawyer, A. M. Klein, by describing his fellow poet's journey as a failed *psychopomp*, one that is:

> . . . sometimes his nostalgia for a warm, rich past, becomes more than nostalgia, becomes rather, an impossible longing, an absolute ruthless longing for the presence of the divine, for the evidence of holiness. Then he is alone and I believe in him.[25]

From this reflection on Klein's lament falling upon deaf ears in the Montréal Jewish community, Cohen's own rebellion in turning away from his priestly lineage becomes more lucid, when he states categorically: "An artist should become one of two things: a priest or a prophet."[26] Klein, for Cohen, is the failed priest: "He became their clown. He spoke to men who despised the activity he loved most. He raised money. He chose to be a priest and protect the dead ritual. And now we have his silence. The priest kept the community intact. And the community was 'like an old lady whose canary has escaped in a storm, but who continues to furnish the cage with food and water in the convinced hope that the canary will come back. The priest tries to persuade her that *this optimism is religion.*'"[27]

I want to complicate the analyses of both Liebowitz, who privileges the prophetic within Cohen to conform with his rock and roll rebel biography, and Wolfson, whose analysis at time privileges

Cohen's priesthood, evidently inscribed in his family namesake. While both analyses are invaluable, what interests me here is the degree of Cohen's oscillation between his prophetic and priestly calling in a post-secular context that can be felt through the decades. So, for example, when Cohen reaches Tel Aviv, Israel at the end of his European Tour in 2009, wearing his signature black suit and fedora, as we have already noted in chapter five he gave this preamble to his invocation of the Priestly Blessing to the *Bereaved Parents For Peace*.

And yet, decades earlier, Cohen is reading Montréal Jewish religious history from this perspective of the prophet, castigating Klein for having *sacrificed himself to* the needs of the community as its priest, whereas now Cohen in the guise of prophet will *sacrifice himself for* a greater ideal and not be consumed by the community:

> Well, the trees they got much smaller,
> The lake a lady's mirror,
> We stopped to drink some wine.[28]

The shift in the landscape here as it appears to be withdrawing is jarring, pointing to the child's shift in vision, in seeing the world through different eyes. As the child shares wine with his father, a feminine presence emerges, mirroring their intimacy.

> Then he threw the bottle over.
> Broke a minute later
> And he put his hand on mine.
> Thought I saw an eagle
> But it might have been a vulture,
> I never could decide.[29]

This moment of intimacy is interrupted by a cataclysmic outburst, shattering their connection. But this rupture is then restored by the assurance of the father putting "his hand on mine."

Then my father built an altar,
He looked once behind his shoulder,
He knew I would not hide.
You who build these altars now
To sacrifice these children,
You must not do it anymore.
A scheme is not a vision
And you never have been tempted
By a demon or a god.[30]

The shift from the interpersonal to the price to be paid for collective sacrifices *to* the community rather than sacrifices *for* a higher ideal here comes into relief.

You who stand above them now,
Your hatchets blunt and bloody,
You were not there before,
When I lay upon a mountain
And my father's hand was trembling
With the beauty of the word.[31]

This focus on "beauty of the word," with its Christological resonances of incarnation, to be explored shortly in his song, "The Window," remain an intriguing juxtaposition between "trembling" and "beauty." Most often the juxtaposition in Jewish Mysticism is between fear and love, as the bard continues:

And if you call me brother now,
Forgive me if I inquire,
"just according to whose plan?"
When it all comes down to dust
I will kill you if I must,
I will help you if I can.
When it all comes down to dust
I will help you if I must,

I will kill you if I can.
And mercy on our uniform,
Man of peace or man of war,
The peacock spreads his fan.[32]

This surreal "binding" of Isaac by Cohen riffs on recounting God's command to Abraham to offer his thirty-something son, Isaac, as a sacrifice. Obedient Abraham takes docile Isaac to the place of sacrifice and binds him. The angel interrupts this *near* sacrifice, bidding Abraham to stay his hand. And a ram is offered in Isaac's stead. So exactly where does this *Akeidah take place*? What can *place* teach us about the post-secular journey? How can we know where we are meant to go on this journey if we cannot see the *place*? Cohen captures this yearning for *place* when he sings:

"Show me the place
Help me roll away the stone
Show me the place
I can't move this thing alone.[33]

Abraham "can't move this thing alone," so he enlists his servants to get him as far as he can before the place emerges. While Abraham is leading this journey, it takes some time before he has an inkling of the *place* to which they are going. Seeing the *place* from afar, means that even after verse 4 details the duration of three day's journeying in Genesis 22, that *place* still remains in the offing [הַמָּקוֹם—מֵרָחֹק]—perhaps only the contours are emerging. Sometimes in life, we embark on journeys or projects with intuition as our guard, the contours of that *place* not yet having fully emerged, but still we take that leap of action.[34]

So in arriving by verse 9 at the *place* [וַיָּבֹאוּ, אֶל-הַמָּקוֹם] detailed in Abraham's deep listening [אֲשֶׁר אָמַר-לוֹ הָאֱלֹהִים], this moment then lets him feel assured in stopping, setting up camp, building the altar, and preparing the kindling upon which he is about to sacrifice his son, Isaac. As soon as they arrive at what feels like the designated *place* to begin with the formulaic ritual of sacrifice—that is the moment when everything shifts. Just as Abraham begins feeling as though he has arrived in his *place*, the ground of his being shakes, as he is challenged by a new element that disrupts his relationship to this *place*. When what he sees *above* and *behind* him in verse 13 is disrupted, something deep within Abraham's own sense of *place* shifts. Just as his inner *place* is now "caught in the thicket by his horns" [נֶאֱחַז בַּסְּבַךְ בְּקַרְנָיו] mirrored by the ram, so the ritual sacrifice that typifies Ancient Near Eastern religion of his time and place also shifts. Now the ram takes the *place* of Isaac, so a father now sees his son differently than when they embarked on this journey.

It is only in the moment of *displacement*, perched high upon the mountains of our dearest moments in life, that such divine disruption can be experienced. That experience is often a *place* of disruption, a *displacement*, a shift in what we expect to see. That is why verse 14 explains the motivation for the naming of "that *place Adonai-Yireh*" [יְה-וָה יִרְאֶה]—the *place* where Abraham is able to truly see the divine—[בְּהַר יְה-וָה יֵרָאֶה]—right in the midst of the disruptions in his life, especially in relationship to Isaac, does the divine appear.

After angelic interruptions, Abraham is able to see the place of his relationship with Isaac with new eyes. The ram in place of his son allows Abraham to now see his need as Cohen sings: "Show me the place/Where the suffering began."[35] The *place* of this relationship has changed. Coming down the mountain, something has clearly changed. Even though in verse 19 "they walked on as one" [וַיֵּלְכוּ יַחְדָּו], father and son are not speaking. And they are not going home together either. "Abraham dwelt at Beersheba," while we are still awaiting confirmation of where Isaac is dwelling—where is his place now that this displacement has occurred? Both father and son must make this journey back home, but in the process the place of their relationship has changed, matured. Again this journey down the mountain as one is wonderfully captured by Cohen, who sings about this transformation:

Going home
Without my burden
Going home
Behind the curtain
Going home
Without the costume
That I wore.[36]

What burdens are unloaded and what costumes are unveiled between father and son, between every parent and child, between every master and disciple here at this *place of displacement*? Every loving relationship must undergo its trial, sometimes even the betrayal of its core assumptions, in order to grow and transform. This process of letting down in order to carry one's suffering forward into transformation is duly noted by Hillman: "Perhaps this tells us something about why betrayal is such a strong theme in our religions. [Betrayal] is perhaps the human gate to such higher religious experiences as forgiveness and reconciliation with this silent labyrinth, the creation."[37] *Displacement* is part of such critical growth.

The love that bound father and son together was so deep that only once the "burden" of expectations was unloaded and the "costume" of assumptions shed, could their relationship move into a new *place*. We cannot always control our lives, especially the ones we love. If we truly love someone, we must set them free, as Abraham eventually lets go of Isaac.

Now that the assumptions and projections have been displaced, a new *place* of relation between father and son, between every parent and child, between every master and disciple, can emerge. Even, and especially, when a new *place* emerges from brokenness, only we are able to see each other more "complete." This sense of completion that emerges from both sides of the father-son relationship is articulated in a classic mystical interpretation of Genesis 22 the Zohar:

> But Abraham, precisely! For he had to be encompassed by judgement, since previously Abraham had contained no judgement at all. Now water was embraced by fire. Abraham had been incomplete until now, when he was crowned to execute judgment, arraying it in its realm. His whole life long he had been incomplete until now when water was completed by fire, fire by water.[38]

This incompletion on earth mirrors an incompletion in the godhead. As father and son complete each other at the moment when Abraham was able to manifest severe judgment while Isaac submitted lovingly, so too the spheres of divine consciousness needed a rebalancing from being too one-sided. Abraham symbolizes the sphere of Love or *Hesed*, while devoid of its complementary opposite sphere of Judgment or *Din*, symbolized by Isaac.[39] The free-flowing love of Abraham's *Hesed* was encompassed by the fervid power of *Din* in Isaac,[40] thus allowing a veritable "binding" of the spheres of father and son archetypes together. This depth of connection was only possible once the "burden" of expectations was unloaded and the "costume" of assumptions shed, only then could their relationship move into a new *place*.

This urgent yearning for liberation in relationships was precisely what Leonard Cohen sang about in his "Story of Isaac":

> You who build these altars now
> To sacrifice these children,
> You must not do it anymore.

Rather than coming down the mountain with "a love song" or "an anthem of forgiving," what appears after that "cry above the suffering" that catalyzes the unloading and the shedding is simply "a manual for living with defeat." As father and son walk back down the mountain going home again, there is "a sacrifice recovering" that is now "complete."

From the father-son archetypal paradigm of sacrifice, we turn to another motif of *sacrifice to* in Cohen's songbook regarding the feminine martyr. It is intriguing that this Jewish prophetic bard turns to the French heroine and Roman Catholic saint Joan of Arc (1412-1431) for further inspiration. Joan was born in obscurity to a peasant family, travelled to the uncrowned Dauphin of France, advising him to reclaim his French throne and defeat the English. Joan of Arc was sent alongside French troops at the siege of Orleans and rose to prominence after the siege was lifted after nine days. Later Joan was captured and burned (perhaps sacrificed) at the stake for heresy. However, as she predicted, seven years after her sacrifice, France was reunited with the defeated English and Charles crowned King. Joan of Arc remarked that: "One life is all we have and we live it as we believe in living it. But to *sacrifice what you are* and to live without belief, that is a fate more terrible than dying."[41] Notice the emerging tension within her prophetic calling and its attempted conjunctive resolution between the feminine and the masculine:

> Now the flames they followed Joan of Arc
> as she came riding through the dark;
> no moon to keep her armor bright,
> no man to get her though this very smoky night.
> She said, "I'm tired of the war,
> I want the kind of work I had before,
> a wedding dress or something white
> to wear upon my swollen appetite."
> Well, I'm glad to hear you talk this way,
> you know I've watched you riding every day
> and something in me yearns to win
> such a cold and lonesome heroine.
> "And who are you?" she sternly spoke
> to the one beneath the smoke.
> "Why, I'm fire," he replied,
> "And I love your solitude, I love your pride."[42]

Any real sense of agency in the sacrifice of Joan of Arc is eclipsed here by the power of the fire. Rendered here as a masculine, all-consuming presence, it is the fire devours the passive saint. Although Cohen comes to Jewish Mysticism unwittingly,[43] still his reading is in line with the thrust of Wolfson's critical analysis of the recurring phallocentrism of Kabbalah, whereby the feminine is absorbed into the masculine.[44] This nexus of eroticism and asceticism is subtly intertwined with martyrdom in the life experience of Joan of Arc,[45] for example:

> "Then fire, make your body cold,
> I'm going to give you mine to hold."
> Saying this she climbed inside
> to be his one, to be his only bride.
> And deep into his fiery heart
> he took the dust of Joan of Arc,
> and high above the wedding guests
> he hung the ashes of her wedding dress.[46]

Akin to the fusion of fire and water in the earlier Zoharic reading of the Binding of Isaac, here the completion takes places through another *unio oppositorium* of opposing alchemical elements, between fire and water, ether and ash. This fusion between the fiery desire and cold embodiment leads to absorption of the body as dust into the fiery heart:

> It was deep into his fiery heart
> he took the dust of Joan of Arc,
> and then she clearly understood
> if he was fire, oh then she must be wood.
> I saw her wince, I saw her cry,
> I saw the glory in her eye.
> Myself I long for love and light,
> but must it come so cruel, and oh so bright.[47]

Bringing together the insights of the masculine and feminine sacrifice, it is now possible to appreciate the vision of ascent to that *place* as recounted in Cohen's "The Window." This next song correlates with the "beauty of the word" above in the "Story of Isaac," which makes the sacrifice itself so enticing and erotic:

Why do you stand by the window
Abandoned to beauty and pride?
The thorn of the night in your bosom,
The spear of the age in your side;
Lost in the rages of fragrance,
Lost in the rags of remorse,
Lost in the waves of a sickness
That loosens the high silver nerves.
Oh chosen love, Oh frozen love
Oh tangle of matter and ghost.
Oh darling of angels, demons and saints
And the whole broken-hearted host—
Gentle this soul.
And come forth from the cloud of unknowing
And kiss the cheek of the moon;
The New Jerusalem glowing,
Why tarry all night in the ruin?
And leave no word of discomfort,
And leave no observer to mourn,
But climb on your tears and be silent
Like a rose on its ladder of thorns.
Then lay your rose on the fire;
The fire give up to the sun;
The sun give over to splendour
In the arms of the High Holy one;
For the holy one dreams of a letter
Dreams of a letter's death—
Oh bless thee continuous stutter
Of the word being made into flesh.
Oh chosen love, Oh frozen love
Gentle this soul.[48]

In reaching that *place* by ascending into immolation, what happens to the self? Is the self sacrificed and lost or is something new gained in the process? While this brings to the fore the common typological reading of Genesis 22 as a prefiguration for the crucifixion of the Christ, the question to now be explored in the wake of Isaac in Leonard Cohen's songbook is how the bard reads and sings about the sacrifice. From Joan of Arc to Jesus, listen to what emerges in his popular song, "Suzanne":

> And Jesus was a sailor
> when he walked upon the water
> and he spent a long time watching
> from his lonely wooden tower
> and when he knew for certain
> only drowning men could see him
> he said, "all men will be sailors then
> until the sea shall free them . . ."

Witnessing other human beings suffer "from his lonely wooden tower," either as a lifeguard at the beach or a soldier in a death camp, is what gives this oscillating archetype of the Christ its continuous perspective of the human condition. Liberation from suffering appears possible so long as others who are suffering see their interconnection so to overcome this tribulation alone. Only then does the singular brokenness emerge as part of a larger collective:

> but he himself was broken
> long before the sky would open
> forsaken, almost human
> he sank beneath your wisdom like a stone.[49]

That stone needs to be moved later on in his song, "Show Me the Place." The muse hiding behind the stone of many a Montréal beat poet in the 1960s, Suzanne (Verdal McCallister) became the inspiration for

Leonard Cohen's spiritual folk song. As the lover and dance partner of Armand, Suzanne recalls being introduced to Leonard at the place called, Le Vieux Molin and their synchronous connection in the summer of 1965:

> It was just a spiritual moment that I had with the lightening [*sic*] of the candle. And I may or may not have spoke to Leonard about, you know I did pray to Christ, to Jesus Christ and to St. Joan at the time, and still do.[50]

So Leonard conflates his love for Suzanne with her love for Jesus and Joan of Arc. He wants to travel this path of part his own spiritual conviction, but remains in the agnostic realm:

> And you want to travel with him
> And you want to travel blind
> And you think maybe you'll trust him
> For he's touched your perfect body with his mind.[51]

These star-crossed lovers never consummate their love, remaining forever platonic friends. And yet, as irony would have it, when Cohen began down his path of Zen Buddhism, his retreat on Mount Baldy Zen Monastery was but a few miles down the road from where Suzanne was living with her seven cats, working as a dance instructor and massage therapist.[52] Cohen's "celibate piety," as Wolfson has astutely analyzed, is a mixture of Christ's passion, Zen awakening, and ascetic yearning.[53] The capacity of Cohen to travel christlike through his songbook oscillates from the romantic spirituality of "Suzanne" to the fragmented absurdity and suspicion over any and all religion, in "Jazz Police":

> Jesus taken serious by the many
> Jesus taken joyous by a few
> Jazz police are paid by J. Paul Getty
> Jazzers paid by J. Paul Getty II.[54]

The absurdist juxtaposition of Jesus to J. Paul Getty is an intriguing return to the tension intrinsic to the aforementioned sacrifice of Isaac by Abraham. The challenge of re-binding religion cannot be appreciated apart from the father-son dynamic. Here the archetypal dynamic is the lens through which the religion and spirituality of Jesus is experienced.[55] The religion of Jesus could be "taken serious by the many" and practiced by a wealthy materialist like J. Paul Getty, while the spirituality of Jesus was "taken joyous by a few," like his son, J. Paul Getty II, a radical hippie who remained hostile to taking over his father's business.[56] Recall this motif in the father wielding "the golden axe" of his materialism over his son seeking a different kind of spirituality in the "Story of Isaac." This generational divide, evident in the father-son dynamic emerges in the tension between the religion-spirituality dynamic surrounding Jesus. The son's spiritual critique of his father's religion continues for Cohen once again via the Christ archetype:

> Well, if you look at the Sermon on the Mount, no one has really carried that out . . . I mean "Blessed are the poor, the downtrodden . . ." I tried to say that, "there's a crack in everything, that's how the light gets in."[57]

But the inversion that results from the child spiritual critique of their father's religion has staying power, as Cohen reflects on how his own children react to criticisms against his own Zen Buddhist practice as a Jew:

> They understand their father. I'm so lucky to have kids [Adam and Lorca] who understand what I do—better than I do. They're tolerant, supportive of what I do here [at Mount Baldy Zen Center]. I heard that my daughter [Lorca] defended me in a conversation with some of my friends who were putting down this experience of what I'm doing here, saying "you don't know what this means to my father." I'm very lucky.[58]

Cohen's songbook, as well as his own progeny, serve here as an elixir to the dichotomy between the discipline of religion and the joyful play of spirituality he seeks—the place is discovered in his post-secular songbook.

The sacrifice motif moves from the father-son dynamic and shifts into the collective, embracing and transforming classic Judeo-Christian motifs of the apocalypse. By invoking the anger of the apocalypse, Cohen calls for the return of the repressed through a series of the archetypal symbols of tyranny[59] that repeat almost as a refrain, the second time with these additions:

> Give me back the Berlin wall
> Give me Stalin and Saint Paul
> Give me Christ or give me Hiroshima . . .
> I've seen the future brother: it is murder.[60]

Most intriguing of this list of the archetypal symbols of tyranny is the juxtaposition of Saint Paul with Stalin. Cohen seems to be suggesting a tyranny of misinterpretation here: just as Stalin misread Marx, so did Saint Paul misread Jesus.[61] The vision of "The Future" begins in an apocalyptic Judeo-Christian tone where "things are gonna slide in all directions,"[62] where God and Satan, good and evil appear to become inverted, where the binaries dissolve into non-dual consciousness (as discussed in Chapter Five already).

The image of Jesus being crucified on the cross right side up to redeem humanity from sin is evoked and inverted into a "woman hanging upside down." While this woman's features "are veiled by her fall gown,"[63] this inverted sacrificial image suggests another possible redeemer in unexpected places and positions. Yet by the song's close, a complete dissolution of these binaries takes place, shifting closer a vision of Buddhist *Nirvana*. As a blowing out of self and its boundaries, the redeemer is also blown apart, akin to a nuclear blast. The dissolution of self and other, God and man, good and evil points to a greater non-dual view of existence.

Notwithstanding the movement toward the dissolution into a non-dual view of existence that *Nirvana* provides, Cohen cannot so easily let go of the Jesus archetype, as he explains:

> I like the character of Jesus and I like his role as well but the Old Testament is really the Testament of the victory of experience—it's history, it's men, dealing with the Absolute and who have to deal with other men as well as and who also have to deal what is relative and the absolute. This kind of [*Zen*] training is very important for looking into that tension.[64]

Cohen is able to fashion an idiosyncratic reading of the Jesus archetype, earlier through the Rosicrucian fusion of the rose and the thorn, and later through his Zen focus on the heart aware of its own suffering, as he explains:

> As I understand it, into the heart of every Christian, Christ comes, and Christ goes. When, by his Grace, the landscape of the heart becomes vast and deep and limitless, then Christ makes His abode in that graceful heart, and His Will prevails. The experience is recognized as Peace. In the absence of this experience much activity arises, division of every sort. Outside of the organizational enterprise, which some applaud and some mistrust, stands the figure of Jesus, nailed to a human predicament, summoning the heart to comprehend its own suffering by dissolving itself in a radical confession of hospitality.[65]

Cohen's songwriting is renowned for being a continuous process of endless revisions. Waves of prophetic fear and priestly love layer the songwriting process. These layers of the prophetic and the priestly, as I have been arguing, are inextricably intertwined as the Montréal bard explains his continuous attraction to the transformative experience of music. Music is both necessary to arouse prophetic inspiration as well as to channel the flow of priestly blessing as discussed in chapter five.[66]

It is fitting to close with a comparison of two different versions of "The Window," that speak to Cohen's provocative image of the soul's ascent to kiss the "New Jerusalem glowing" noted in Wolfson's pioneering study. The eschatological vision of "New Jerusalem" draws at once from the prophets of the Hebrew Bible, like Isaiah 6 (verses 1-3) and 65 (verses 16-18), and the New Testament Book of Revelations 21, seen through the lens of Kabbalah.[67] Through this soul ascent, the self is annihilated, enabling a mystical merging through the luminous symbol of fire, just as in Joan of Arc. What continues to inspire Cohen's songbook is a turning inward, so that "the notion of newness and rebirth of a new cosmos, [*is what*] invites you to unfold that reality in your own heart and in your own life, that dissolving of time."[68] Not only is there a dissolving of time but also of archetypes in time, like the syncretization of the archetypes of Moses and Jesus as the "continuous stutterer."[69]

Redemption is followed by a New Creation in Isaiah which is already eschatological and universal, while also being domestic and historical.[70] "Without the New Jerusalem, then the New Creation is meaningless."[71] This spiritual reality of New Jerusalem is not only the revelatory site of divine sovereignty "more gloriously than any place else,"[72] but for Cohen this becomes the site of restoration, and redemptive reunion of masculine and feminine so that new creativity can emerge in his songbook. This is evinced most strongly in Cohen's reading of Revelation 4-5 and 3 Baruch 11, whereby "the prayers of the saints" worshipping the Lamb "replace the sacrificial offering."[73] "New Jerusalem glowing" envisions the union of the one who is sacrificed and integrated into the spiritual wholeness of Jerusalem. In contrast to John in Revelations 4-5, "who sees the coming of the eschatological New Jerusalem in advance through the Heavenly Temple vision," in other words, as "an ongoing interplay between the temporal transcendence of heavenly worship (in the Heavenly Temple) and the temporal transcendence of eschatological drama (in the New Jerusalem),"[74] Cohen's songbook is embodying the pulsations of the "New

Jerusalem glowing" here and now. This embodiment happens through meditation and song, through humility and incarnation, through self-annihilation and merging.

The question of place and people resounds as this New Jerusalem reveals itself and descends from the heavens to the earth, stretching beyond any imagined dimensions, with gates consisting of but a single pearl, paved with gold as upper and lower realms merge.[75] Returning to Cohen's prophetic "post-Christmas" speech at the Jewish library, he witnesses "an absolute and ruthless longing for the presence of the divine, for the evidence of holiness. Then he [Klein as priest] is alone and I believe him. Then there is no room for the 'we' and if I want to join him, if, even, I want to greet him, I must make my own loneliness."[76] As we conclude with the layering of New Jerusalem *imaginalities* in Cohen, the question remains: is the redemptive power of religion a collective or individual quest? Is there not a certain necessity for every prophet to "make my own loneliness" the very site of this "New Jerusalem glowing"?

To conclude, I juxtapose the recorded lyrics and those printed for "The Window":

> (1)
> The new Jerusalem glowing,
> why tarry all night in the ruin?[77]
>
> (2)
> The code of solitude broken,
> why tarry confused and alone?[78]

From the vantage point of "the New Jerusalem glowing," Cohen demands why his ancestors continue to "tarry all night in the ruin [of the Jerusalem Temple]." This interrogation, through endless revisions of this song, leads to a very different image of New Jerusalem, no longer glowing, but transcended and included, leading to a break through from the grips of solitude, questioning why must the bard "tarry confused and alone?"

The *ethos* of Cohen's post-secular songbook is unabashedly mystical. As I have been arguing, contrary to Doron B. Cohen's mischaracterization, as a popular singer-songwriter, Leonard Cohen remains deeply mystical, whether or not the experiences he conjures in his songbook precisely conform to a merging of human and divine mind and body.[79] This nuanced dialectic is encapsulated in the image of "New Jerusalem glowing" that the singer himself inevitably transcends.[80] What begins as a transposing the *Book of Revelations* really is a rethinking of that previous messianic vision of Jerusalem as "the city [*that*] had no need of the sun or of the moon to shine in it, for the glory of God illuminate[s] it. The Lamb is its light."[81] What emerges in this apocalyptic vision in the *Book of Revelations* is that spiritual reality that there was "no temple in it, for the Lord God Almighty and the Lamb are its temple."[82] Cohen's continual revisions of scriptural archetypes in Isaiah and Revelations, and his continuous cultivating of a *zazen* practice with Roshi at Mount Baldy, all suggest a shift from the archetypal Christian apocalyptic vision, that completely spiritualizes the New Jerusalem as glowing beyond the earth, to return to the ruins of the earthly Jerusalem in the here and now. But this return to the "Jerusalem hidden in Jerusalem,"[83] as Wolfson notes, is an inversion, whereby the incarnational encounter is the elevation being sought rather than an elevation of the flesh into the heavenly realm. Rather than attribute this subtle revision in "The Window" as being prompted by a childhood reaction to Christian proselytizing,[84] I suggest that Cohen once again returns to Jewish archetypal imagery of Jerusalem temple amidst its the ashes, and then sings his way to liberate the sacrificed self through his Zen lens. It is a singular journey towards a more integrated sense of self returning home, until "there was nothing left between/the Nameless and the Name."[85]

10 Standing Where There Used to Be a Street: 9/11 Post-Secularism & Sacred Song

Is it still possible to sing a sacred song, not merely in exile,[1] but moreover in a post-secular age? Disenchantment with religion, a hallmark of the *longue durée*[2] of modernity since the Enlightenment, appears to have reached its nadir. Are there any indices, any movements or pathways of thinking that emerge from modernity that might allow for that impulse toward the sacred to still be sung? The thrust of this question for Judaism in particular, and for religion in general, informs the underlying arc of the entire book before us. There remain no more appropriate exemplars, no more apt prophets of the post-secular age, than a bard and a philosopher—both writing from their Third Solitude in Montréal.[3] I will argue that poet and singer-songwriter, Leonard Cohen, as well as philosopher, Charles Taylor, each contribute to a pathway for thinking through post-secularism as it affects Judaism and religion in their next paradigms. To accomplish this, I will reflect on the religio-cultural matrix of Montréal and then turn to the thought of Taylor, followed by reflections on lyrics by Cohen that I will argue sing an expansive and inclusive sacred song in a post-secular age.

What was the catalyst that launched Cohen into this calling as prophet of the post-secular age? Was it a function of singing in exile and yearning for Zion? Or were his wanderings back and forth to and from Montréal part of his homecoming that was that very road? To answer this question, a momentary reflection on the religio-cultural matrix of Montréal is in order. Montréal—before, during and after the *Shoah*—remains a vibrant site of Jewish culture and religion. During the Nazi storm cloud of the *Shoah* that swept through Europe, Montréal remained a destination for Yiddish-speaking Jewry, even as those very gates of refuge seemed to be forever closing throughout North America.[4] The city remains this messianic promise of welcoming the stranger, encouraging immigration since Confederation.[5] One of those immigrants was Cohen's great-grandfather. Born at the Royal Victoria Hospital in Westmount, Montréal on September 21, 1934, Leonard Norman Cohen straddled the Great Depression and the *Shoah*. Being born into a distinguished Montréal lineage, he was the great grandson of Lazarus Cohen, who had arrived in Canada in 1860 to galvanize and build a small Jewish community.[6] With the rise of pogroms and persecution in Russia, Montréal was quickly becoming the seat of Canadian Jewry. Lazarus witnessed and contributed to this shift in growth of the Jewish community in Montréal, from fewer than five hundred Jews to more than five thousand in the mid-1880s.[7] Lazarus served as president of Congregation Shaar Hashomayim and headed a number of organizations to aid Jewish settlers and immigrants in safe passage to Palestine. His brother (Leonard's great uncle), Tzvi Hirsch Cohen, served as the chief rabbi of Montréal. These pedigrees shed light on the illustrious Jewish strain that Leonard inherited.

Montréal as homecoming for Cohen was always brimming with redemption as evidenced by his claim to have had "a very messianic childhood."[8] Growing up on Belmont Street in Westmount, a classmate recalls how much "Leonard was embedded in religion, … of the synagogue, because of his respect for the elders."[9] Cohen was regularly exposed to traditional synagogue life through his grandfather, Rabbi Solomon Klonitzki-Kline. The Rabbi expressed solidarity with his grandson

Leonard, who was also a writer, and the two of them would sit together many evenings "going through the Book of Isaiah, which the Rabbi knew by heart and which Leonard came to love for its poetry, imagery and prophecy."[10] Early on for Cohen, Montréal—much like Dublin for James Joyce— came to symbolize exile as homecoming.[11]

This yearning for a Promised Land, free from oppression and persecution; the availability of free or inexpensive agricultural land in the Canadian hinterlands and the West at the turn of the twentieth century; and the need for (un)skilled labor in the manufacturing industries in the wake of the *Shoah* compelled so many European Jews to escape to Canada. The modern refugee phenomenon is a function of modernity's greatest challenges—sovereignty and nationalism. Just as European Jewry was welcomed as strangers during the *Shoah*, so too the colonial areas of Africa and Asia capitulated to the modern refugee phenomenon, in the 1950s and 1960s. There may be a distinction between the oppressed refugee and the economic migrant, nonetheless, Canada's immigration policy was meant, at least theoretically, to set Canada apart as a haven for those seeking shelter from the storms of oppression of their respective countries.[12] The echoes of secularization can be heard in the language of the 1951 *Convention Relating to the Status of Refugees*, a document that is salient to our present discussion. Initially signed by twenty-six governments, it is now acceded to by more than sixty as follows:

> As a result of events occurring before 1 January 1951 and owing to a well-founded fear of being persecuted for reasons of race, religion, nationality, membership of a particular social group or political opinion, is outside of his nationality and is unable or owing to such fear, is unwilling to avail himself of the protection of that country, or who, not having a nationality and being outside the country of his former habitual residence as a result of such events, is unable or, owing to such fear is unwilling to return to it.[13]

Secularization, specific to Montréal, figures as part of a larger need to alleviate the "well-founded fear of being persecuted for reasons of race [or] religion" that most European Jewry was feeling before, during, and after the *Shoah*.[14] Montréal remains a unique nexus from which to consider this question of secularization, both for the bard and the philosopher.[15] Whether the reside of ritual life marked by dietary laws, Sabbath observance,[16] or endogamy, Montréal Jews have both the literacy in Hebrew and Yiddish coupled with the audacity to question and critique these remains to the core. One current exemplar is the roving comedy series, *Yidlife Crisis*, shot on location in eateries across Montréal. Each episode is really another example of Jewish appropriation, in this case, of French filmmaker Louis Malle's cult classic, *My Dinner With Andre* (1981). Playing themselves as Pirandello-esque actors in search of the film they happen to be starring in, we encounter actors Wallace Shawn and Andre Gregory. The premise of Malle's film consists of an existential dialogue shared over a meal at a New York restaurant. Gregory is a local theater director who shares with Shawn his tales of dropping out of society, wandering around the world and living an authentic life. That entry into authenticity is what allows Gregory to experience the diversity of ways in which people live. Shawn, his dinner partner, listens intently but also questions those moments where Gregory's quest for authenticity appears to challenge and even at times abandon the pragmatics of lived life in the world.

Fast forward a few decades and *Yidlife Crisis* re-imagines *My Dinner*, but with an anarchic Yiddish-Jewish twist. Yiddish dialogue underscores an authentically Montréal-*esque* meditation on Jewish life and its discontents. Each episode follows a similar formula, featuring Chaimie and Leizer's argument over food and its discontents:[17]

(1) "Breaking the Fast": Assembling at Montréal's Holy Temple of poutine, *La Banquise*, on the Jewish calendar's holiest day of the year, *Yom Kippur*, Chaimie and Leizer argue about

the meaning of the ritual of fasting while inevitably ritually eating.

(2) "The Schmaltz": At *Lester's Deli*, a chance ordering of a lean smoked meat sandwich in lieu of the usual *schmaltzy* one leads to not only the jeopardizing of Chaimie and Leizer's entire relationship but a deep meditation on the joys of fat and being zafdig . . . in all the right places.

(3) "Great Debates": Chaimie and Leizer settle the age old Talmudic argument—*St. Viateur* or *Fairmount Bagel* for the win?

(4) "Bastards": Chaimie tries to get Leizer out of his Maccabean shell by proving the virtues of Hellenistic culture and the power of a pita.

It is important to appreciate that the creators of this post-secular series are proud graduates of the renowned secular Zionist school of Montréal, called Bialik. Eli Batalion and Jamie Elman are two Montréal-born actors who play Chaimie and Leizer, respectively. Each episode follows two thirty-somethings as they grapple with their limits of their secular Jewish identity, reveling in iconic Montréal restaurants, and extolling the virtues of *schmaltz* (an absolute must, when it comes to smoked meat). This would be sufficiently wonderful on its own, but Batalion and Elman deliver something even better: the series is performed almost entirely in the *lingua franca* of so many *émigrés* to Canada—Yiddish! Batalion and Elman studied Yiddish as part of the trilingual curriculum[18] at Bialik High School in Montréal. Years after graduating, these wandering Montréal Jews cross the border and reconnect as aspiring actors in Los Angeles. From Hollywood North to the homeland itself, they began brainstorming ideas for a collaborative project. While not beholden to lofty ideals of ethnicity and identity preservation through the revival of a "dying language," still they decided to create a Yiddish web series. As Canadian comedians, Batalion and Elman were drawn to the vitality and rhythm of Yiddish, so integral in shaping secular identity through comedy in North America, from the Borscht Belt on.[19]

A sophisticated disenchantment is ubiquitous throughout Montréal. So it should come as little surprise, then, that the same university grounds of McGill that nourished the young Leonard Cohen remain the ground of thinking for Montréal philosopher Charles Taylor. The process of disenchantment that indelibly marks modernity while pointing to something beyond it—a re-enchantment of sorts—began with Cohen and continues with Taylor. It is this place of no-place that can be referred to as "post-secular,"[20] insofar as it points beyond the secular but cautious in fully re-embracing the sacred. Taylor's philosophy will provide a context for the turn to post-secularism that marks modernity and how it affects religion in general. From that context, we will then conclude with reflections on Cohen's sacred songs in a post-secular key.

Arguably, there is no more important philosopher who has thought through the implications of modernity on the formation of self and secularism in a pluralistic society than Charles Taylor.[21] Professor emeritus of philosophy at McGill University in Montréal, Taylor is the recipient of the renowned Templeton Prize as well as the Kyoto Prize in Arts and Philosophy. The entire field of modern philosophy has been impacted by Taylor's thinking, especially in his most sustained reflections that abound in, *A Secular Age*[22] and *Sources of the Self.*[23] For purposes of the present investigation, it suffices to consider two of Taylor's seminal essays: "Disenchanment-Reenchantment,"[24] and "What Does Secularism Mean?"[25]

In "Disenchanment-Reenchantment," Taylor draws out the distinctions between existence in the enchanted world that precedes modernity, and the disenchanted world that lies at the core of modernity's project. To truly grasp what is at stake in modernity and how it has indelibly shaped the modern mind, Taylor explains: "The enchanted world, in contrast to our universe of buffered selves and 'minds' shows a perplexing absence of certain boundaries which seem to us so essential."[26] The very compartmentalization of the mind, which privileges the rational over the irrational, is what marks modernity. It is the drawing of such lines as forces of delimitation that marks the modern mind and clarifies further that "in the enchanted world, the line between personal agency and impersonal force was not at all clearly drawn."[27] What the drawing of this line means for modernity, for all intents and purposes, is the elimination of impersonal forces as operative within the modern mind. Rather, that reduction of the transcendent sphere enables the rise of secularism and justifies its rationalization of the modern mind.

Yet amid all of the remarkable discoveries and insights that mark modernity, is it still accurate to claim that this demarcating line "between personal agency and impersonal force" has led to the complete elimination of the unimaginable depths of the cosmos? Perhaps not. What appears to be emerging from the depths of secularization is what Taylor sees as a *rapprochement*, albeit somewhat subconscious at this juncture, between the religious and the materialist:

> The new cosmic imaginary adds a further dimension to [this buffered identity]. Having coming to sense how vast the universe is in time and space, how deep its micro-constitution goes into the infinitesimal, and feeling thus both our insignificance and fragility, we also see what a remarkable thing it is that out of this immense purposeless machine, life and then feeling, and thought emerge. Here is where a religious person will easily confess a sense of mystery. Materialists often want to repudiate this; science in its progress recognizes no mysteries, only temporary puzzles. But nevertheless, the sense that our thinking, feeling life plunges its roots into a system of such unimaginable depths, that our consciousness can emerge out of this, fills [the materialists and physicists] too with awe.[28]

It is precisely at this point where modernity attempts to draw a steadfast demarcating line "between personal agency and impersonal force" that awe begins to emerge—at the precipice of the infinitesimal. At the heart of modernity's project of rationalization lies a sublimated awe with how human consciousness discovers and emerges from a "system of such unimaginable depths." As his insights continue to deepen, Taylor is open to questioning the veracity of another pillar of modernity's project, namely that the human being is the center of the cosmos. That process of meaning-making is unfolding in a plurality of realms, through diverse lenses of knowing. Taylor sees this meaning-making as necessary for providing an alternative to modernity's otherwise reductive approach to knowledge:

> . . . there remains a question whether the purely anthropocentric articulations can do justice to our sense of wonder, and other related evaluations. This will remain a bone of contention between people in different positions—religious, secular, spiritual, indeed of an almost unlimited variety. The discussion between us promises to be fruitful; there is virtual infinity of insights here, of which no single view has the monopoly. But all of these depend on a rejection of a reductive account of human life.[29]

In "What Does Secularism Mean?"[30] Taylor explores how the state attempts to balance the mains goals of secularism by separating "church and state." This is meant to ensure the neutrality of public institutions and spaces that modernity has fought for by all means necessary. Taylor is quick to point out, however, that precisely in this fight for the freedom from the shackles of any particular dogma, there remains a "most pernicious feature of this fetishization [which] is that it tends to hide from view the real dilemmas which we encounter in this realm, and which leap into view once we recognize the plurality of principles at stake."[31] What Taylor goes on to explore and challenge is the Habermasian claim that modern secular states might altogether do without an analogous concept to "political theology," namely, the cosmic-religious terms that once defined political authority. While Taylor advocates for the possibility of civic religion, that is, a "religious view incorporating and justifying the philosophy of civility," he identifies the enigma dwelling at the heart of pluralistic democracy. We quickly come to realize, thanks to Taylor, how "the problem is that a really diverse democracy can't revert to a civil religion, or anti-religion, however comforting this might be, without betraying its own principles."[32] The very real pain that is felt when one heeds the call to live Taylor's ethics of authenticity is that "we are condemned to live an overlapping consensus."[33] This overlap, emerging from the attempt to preserve pristine separation between religion and the public sphere, leaves the latter utterly devoid of meaning. Into this void of meaning, the place of non-place, the enter now the bard in search of restoring some modicum of meaning. The challenge for a poet and lyricist like Leonard Cohen is to confront this "overlapping consensus" as honestly and humbly as possible. As we shall see, it is Cohen's ability to, at once, admit to being bound to the burden of this overlap while being raised by this very burden enabling his songs sacred status in a post-secular reality.

Now that the groundwork of thinking through post-secularism has been outlined, we will conclude with some reflections on the lyrics of Leonard post-secular Cohen, whose sacred songs, I argue, have the uncanny gift of grasping the shift taking place in secularism while pointing to its cracks and providing solace in the post-secular transition. The genius of Cohen and his appeal to the longing of the post-secular age is his gift for continually searching for the transcendent residue within the otherwise mundane neutrality of the public sphere and its claim to utter secularization. Cohen masterfully navigates the materialists' claim to rationality through quantum insights, encapsulated in verses like: "In every atom/broken is the Name."[34] What Taylor refers to as "different positions—religious, secular, spiritual, indeed of an almost unlimited variety," Cohen also envisioned as his "various positions"—at once immanently erotic yet yearning for the transcendent. A closer look at the interplay of these positions embodied in such verses will show how they bridge chasms of fragility and immensity—

what Taylor refers to as the micro-constitution that bleeds into the infinitesimal. We will also see how Cohen uniquely articulates this fleeting feeling of "our insignificance and fragility" within the awe that "out of this immense purposeless machine, life and then feeling, and thought emerge." To bridge this chasm, Cohen takes on the mantle of a new Moses. This Mosaic consciousness is quantum, with an ability to absorb a much more expansive view of the cosmos in which to seek out and to reconstitute the God particle: "In every atom/broken is the Name" and reveal from concealment "a sweet unknowing/Unified the Name." This calling of the quantum prophet is evident in this most recent song, "Born in Chains":[35]

> I was born in chains
> But I was taken out of Egypt
> I was bound to a burden
> But the burden it was raised
> Lord I can no longer
> Keep this secret
> Blessed is the Name
> The Name be praised
> . . .
> Out of Pharaoh's dream
> Word of Words
> And Measure of all Measures
> Blessed is the Name
> The Name be blessed
> Written on my heart
> In burning Letters
> That's all I know
> I cannot read the rest
> I was idle with my soul
> When I heard that you could use me
> I followed very closely
> My life remained the same

> But then you showed me
> Where you had been wounded
> In every atom
> Broken is the Name
> I was alone on the road
> Your Love was so confusing
> And all my teachers told me
> That I had myself to blame
> But in the Grip
> Of Sensual Illusion
> A sweet unknowing
> Unified the Name
>
> Word of Words . . .
>
> I've heard the soul unfolds
> In the chambers of its longing
> And the bitter liquor sweetens
> In the hammered cup
> But all the Ladders
> Of the Night have fallen
> Only darkness now
> To lift the Longing up.[36]

It is through such Mosaic consciousness, that the prophet emerges in Cohen to sing his way to redemption. Notwithstanding Leonard's namesake and patrilineage as a Cohen-Priest, it is the calling of the prophet, rather than the assignment of the priest, to which Cohen responds as early as 1964. Recall that Cohen delivered a speech at the height of his career as a bohemian poet at the Montréal library, days after Christmas, deep in the darkness of the solstice. It is this moment when he heard his calling and articulated the beginning of his lifelong response. According to that recently discovered and reconstructed speech, Cohen laments the loss of his poet mentor, A. M. Klein, who became a recluse and went insane.[37] The community needed something else—a prophet! Realizing that history is just the narrative describing the path of "an idea's journey from generation to generation," Cohen marched on. This prophet continues to chase the idea as it fluctuates, mutates, and changes forms,

> trying never to mistake the cast off shell with the swift changing thing that shed it. Some moment in time very brief, there must have been, among the ancient Hebrews, men who were both prophet and priest in the same office. I tease my imagination when I try to conceive of the energy of that combination. Their lives burned with such an intensity that we here can still feel their warmth. I love the Bible because it honors them.[38]

Another facet of Cohen's prophet calling for a post-secular age is his daring to enter the apparently neutralized space of the public sphere in search of solace and meaning. After 9/11, there was arguably a re-awakening of a need to ritualize the sacred. A critical review of Shoah memorials by James Young for example found that both the idea of the monument and its role in public memory is an integral marker of memory. Moreover, Young argues that every nation remembers the Shoah according to its own traditions, ideals, and experiences, and moreover, these memorials reflect the ever-evolving meanings of the Holocaust in Europe, Israel, and America. What emerges through these embodied memorials is a fascinating reflection on Shoah memory, public art, and their fusion in contemporary life.[39] A further challenge in a post 9/11 world is how this still recent wound is quickly becoming a memory, and how public space and art are now fusing into contemporary American life.[40] This conundrum is at the heart of the post-secular situation—ritualizing memory, hope, and redemption in a space that is no longer sacred yet paradoxically yearning for something like an enchantment of the sacred. Consider how Cohen approaches this very conundrum in his recent song "A Street," which mourns the scars of 9/11 from the place "standing on this corner/where there used to be a street":

You left me with the dishes
And a baby in the bath
You're tight with the militias
You wear their camouflage
You always said we're equal
So let me march with you
Just an extra in the sequel
To the old red white and blue

The party's over
But I've landed on my feet
I'll be standing on this corner
Where there used to be a street.[41]

In reflecting on this challenge of yearning for something like the sacred it strikes me that *Yidlife Crisis* serves as another recent exemplar of post-secularism rather than its earlier counterpart, the bridge into secularism from deep disenchantment, Chaim Grade's short story "My Quarrel with Hersh Rasseyner." It was adapted by David Brandes into *The Quarrel* (1991), as well as into an off-broadway production by Joseph Telushkin. It is set in Montréal in 1948, on the Jewish New Year celebration of *Rosh Hashana*. This is the story of Chaim, a Yiddish writer, who is forced to rethink his Jewish identity and relationship to Judaism when he is asked to be the tenth and completing member of a prayer quorum known as a *minyan*. As Chaim sits and contemplates the decision, suddenly he sees an old friend, Hersh, a rabbi whom he has not seen since their quarrels together as *yeshiva* students. Not only did Rabbi Hersh survive Auschwitz but his convictions about Judaism were strengthened through the ordeal. By contrast, his friend Chaim escaped the Nazis, and in the process lost any and all his convictions about Judaism. As the lost friends reunite and walk together, they reminisce, and argue passionately about themselves, their decisions, their religion, and their long-lost quarrel.

But precisely the conditions of this quarrel are no longer compelling for the Montréal bard. His poetry reflects an outright challenge to remaining an interlocutor engaged in such a quarrel:

> Baby don't ignore me
> We were smokers, we were friends
> Forget that tired story
> Of betrayal and revenge
> I see the Ghost of Culture
> With numbers on his wrist
> Salute some new conclusion
> Which all of us have missed.[42]

The place of religion after Auschwitz for Cohen is caught in an impasse, unable to efface the "numbers on his wrist" while consigned to continue searching for love, despite the horrors of it all. The need to disrupt the post-*Shoah* cloud hovering over the Montréal Judaism of Cohen's early adulthood bristles in this poem from *Flowers for Hitler*, called "The Failure of a Secular Life" with post-secular prescience:

> The pain-monger came home
> from a hard day's torture.
> He came home with his tongs.
> He put down his black bag.
> His wife hit him with an open nerve
> and a cry the trade never heard.
> He watched her real-life Dachau,
> knew his career was ruined.
> Was there anything else to do?
> He sold his bags and tongs,
> went to pieces. A man's got to be able
> to bring his wife something.[43]

In this post-*Shoah* context of the early poetry of Cohen, the Montréal bard is already setting out the case for the failure of a secular life—but what lies beyond such failure? The search for love amid "her real-life Dachau" is a source of continual pain and obstruction. If one can no longer stand in vigil, weeping over the exiled Indwelling Presence, is there not still a vigil to be sung? I suggest this conundrum is at the heart of the post-secular situation captured inimitably throughout Cohen's songbook. In his musical ritualization of memory, hope, and redemption within desacralized space, this yearning for the enchantment of the sacred finds a home amidst his elevation of the ashes, in loving lament.

11 *Never Mind this Neuzeit, Here's Kaddish*: Between the Nameless & the Name

. . . I'm not about to die. But what does it mean to die? To die means to manifest the activity called dying. And to live means to manifest the dynamic activity called life. If life and death activities were separate, some people would just do life activities and some people would just do death. But one has both as one's content. . . . At the time of death you enter a state where the life activity and the death activity both have to act no more. So I'll probably say that I'm going to the world where you don't have to live or die anymore. Bye, bye, Sayonara.

— Rinzai Zen master,
Joshu Sasaki Roshi[1]

. . . and I've been up all night, talking, talking, talking,
reading *Kaddish* aloud, listening to Ray Charles blues shout blind on the phonograph/the rhythm the rhythm—and your memory in my head three years after—And read
Adonai's last triumphant stanzas aloud—wept, realizing how we suffer—
And how Death is that remedy all singers dream of, sing, remember, prophesy as in the
Hebrew Anthem, or the Buddhist Book of Answers—and my own imagination of a
withered leaf—at dawn . . .

—Allen Ginsberg[2]

Amid the suffering of life, to make "the rhythm the rhythm" of each moment count, time must count. A recent outgoing voice mail message heard in Silicon Valley says it all, *"Hello, thanks for calling. You have 30 seconds to add value to my day—start now!"* Part of the tragedy of our accelerated lives in this late capitalist society is that humanity has never fully understood what we were in for with the onset of modernity. When precisely was this moment whereby humanity was inalterably changed? Perhaps modern culture changed with the printing press or the internet. Some may argue the dawn of modernity started earlier, already affecting the human subject after the fall of Constantinople, but in our own lives, the sting of modernity has been most felt since the day that Apple and Facebook went public, because that is the moment when human beings really began to feel how alienated we have become from each other and, since then, how rapidly the "selfie" has become the new "sovereign self."[3]

To be precise about this feeling that life is on hyper-speed, it is helpful consider existence marked by the relationship between *experience* and *expectation*. The distance between the "space of experience" and the "horizon of expectation," according to Reinhart Koselleck, has become so eclipsed within the recent arc of historical time that modernity provides the human subject with a new *experience* of transition. By viewing the arc of historical time frame by frame, Koselleck points to *acceleration* as the means by which one's own time is distinguished from what went before.[4] The acceleration of modern or "new time" (*Neuzeit*) which emerges around the latter half of the eighteenth century, culminates at this "epochal threshold" at which history itself comes to be first perceived as "in motion."[5] Consider the indelible image of Charlie Chaplin in *Modern Times* (1936), in which the Tramp finds himself entangled in the accelerated cogs of the time clock he can no longer control. So in light of these accelerated times we find ourselves in after modernity, what mind can be paid to rituals of an ancient past in our hyper-accelerated world? Is there a prayer for accelerated times? I will argue in this chapter that the prayer of *Kaddish* can reasonably and profitably be read in just that light. This then is a self-conscious journey through popular culture and song, rather than legalistic or exegetical discourse on our situatedness in a post-secular culture.[6] This approach to contextualizing Jewish liturgy within the post-secular will illustrate some specific ways in which *Kaddish* fits the bill.

Prayer demands contemplative time, not accelerated time (even though some *minyanim* today pride themselves on finishing before the arrival of the first commuter train to work!) To dwell on a word, even a letter, for more than a moment strikes us as absurd. The simple answer to the questioning spiritual seeker, caught like the Tramp in the clock of this vexing tension we navigate, is: "Never mind!" A few recent "never mind" moments, bordering on nihilism, seem apt to begin a reflection in this hyper-accelerated world on the timelessness of a prayer, like *Kaddish.*

In his recent novel, later adapted to film, *This is Where I Leave You* (2014), American Jewish novelist, Johnathan Tropper tells the story of a father who passes away, leaving four grown siblings to return to mourn by staying under the same roof together in their childhood home to sit *shiva* and recite *Kaddish.* When two of the four siblings confront this bequest of their late father to mourn according to the tradition, the ensuing discussion is telling:

> **Judd Altman:** I don't understand the *Shiva.* Mom's not even Jewish, and dad was an atheist.
> **Wendy Altman:** A Jewish atheist, and this is what he wanted.[7]

This scene makes for good comedy and in doing so softens the blow of an emergent and accelerated atheism that oftentimes seems to typify the "never mind" generation of post-secular American Judaism. There are some roots and cultural precedent here, whether with in the grunge of Nirvana's *Nevermind* (1991) or with in the punk rock of the Sex Pistols, *Never Mind the Bullocks* (1977).[8] Only decades apart, each of these musical offerings captured that urge not to feel anxiety or stress about the moment, that pervading, nearly nihilistic sense of whateverness, nevermindity—and then comes octogenarian Leonard Cohen with his audacious song, "Never Mind." Like the descendant of the wicked child at the *seder* symposium, Judd is trying to understand what all these mourning rituals, like sitting *shiva* for seven days and reciting *Kaddish,* could possibly mean to someone from a highly assimilated, mixed Jewish background. And yet, this is precisely what the self-proclaimed Jewish atheist father wanted, so that when death would come knocking, he would not remain trapped in a foxhole. The ability to pray beyond one's own circumscribed life story is powerful indeed, as the Altman family finds out.

By contrast, consider the opening scene of the second season of a recent noir television series written by Nic Pizzolatto, called *True Detective* (2015). This show traces the disappearance of a city manager, a man named, Ben Casper. His disappearance disrupts a lucrative land scheme and ignites an investigation involving three police officers and a career criminal, Frank, who yearns to return to legitimate business. As a voracious hustler and somnambulist, Frank is terrified that he has no progeny to leave his fortune to, no land to bequeath, no one to mourn for him. And as the mystery unfolds surrounding the death of Ben Casper, the first and most brutal fact that emerges about this dead man is that he has no living family. Discovered abandoned at the side of a road, comatose, with his eyes burnt out—there is no one left to mourn for him.

The last place on earth one would expect to confront the mourner's prayer known as *Kaddish*, even so much as a trace of it, is in these opening vignettes for the second season of an award-winning noir television series. Aside from the montages that emit sparks of light amid landscapes of deep darkness, it is the music that is so striking—music of the intertwining lives of each character, apparently so vile and depraved, struggling with inner impulses impossible to vanquish or to imagine overcoming—that could only be the sounds of another song by Leonard Cohen, called "Never Mind." Unlike Tropper, Cohen feels no need to soften the blow of atheism; rather, this bard is content with expanding the space of agnosticism—so that any uncertainty within one's relationship to the divine can be accommodated.

What I will argue is for a reconsideration of the *Kaddish* prayer that invokes the Nameless Name in light of Cohen's seemingly alienated lyrics, always crossing that bridge between the nameless and the named. "Never Mind," from his recent release *Popular Problems* (2014), evokes this dance:

> The story's told
> With facts and lies
> I had a name
> But never mind.[9]

The refrain seeks to overcome the paradox of living "with facts and lies" and the consequent loss of a name once one straddles such oscillations of authenticity.

> . . . There's truth that lives
> And truth that dies
> I don't know which
> So never mind.[10]

The space separating the nameless from the named here is infinitesimal, yet it bridges existence, wherein blood is to life as death is to dust. As much as Cohen feigns protesting the need for prayer of any kind in a post-secular world, there remains an abiding appreciation for the power of the Name from which all other names emerge originally in prayer:

> Names so deep
> and Names so true
> They're blood to me
> They're dust to you
>
> There is no need
> That this survive
> There's truth that lives
> And truth that dies.[11]

The divine Name is that name of all names, the source from which all names emerge, holy and broken. This approach, a kind of tending to the broken, holy name through contemplative prayer, predates Cohen's songbook already found in Jewish Mysticism. Let us consider, for example, the musicality of the mysticism in this extended passage from the Zohar:

> Now that [the people of] Israel are in exile, the entire structure, as it were, has collapsed. But in the time that is coming, When the Holy One shall redeem His children, Who [*mi*] and These [*eilleh*]—which were separated in exile—will join as one, the name will be perfectly established, and the world will be fragrantly firm, as is written "Who are these [*mi eilleh*], that fly like a cloud, like doves to their cotes?" (Isaiah 60:8). Since this is one name, it is not written "Who and these" [*mi v'eilleh*], but rather as "Who these" [*mi eilleh*]—one name, indivisible. For in exile, "Who" [*mi*] has withdrawn above—Mother, as it were, away from children, and the children have fallen. And the name that was complete—that supernal, primordial name—has fallen. For this we pray and sanctify in synagogue, that this name may be restored as it was: "May His great Name be enhanced and sanctified!" Who is "His Name"? That "great" one, first of all. For it has no structure without us: "Who" [*mi*] is never built up without "these" [*eilleh*]. So, at that time, "Who are these [*mi eilleh*], that fly like a cloud, like doves to their cotes?" (Isaiah 60:8). The whole worlds will see that the supernal name has been restored to perfection. And if this great Name is perfected and rebuilt, then those who struggle with the divine are responsible for all, and all other names recover their perfection, since they all depend upon "His great name," first structure of all.[12]

Such a depiction of prayer could only appear in this classic text of Jewish theosophic mysticism like the Zohar. (*Theosophic mysticism* means that the mystical shape of the godhead relies heavily on the permutations and reconfigurations of the mystic in prayer and ritual). So strong is this co-dependent relationship between mystic and deity that Charles Mopsik once described theosophy as the rituals that construct God.[13]

As a theosophic moment embedded in standard liturgical ritual life, the *Kaddish* reconfigures the broken divine name. It does so precisely through those who are devoted to the energy within every word, even every letter of liturgy. This is less a fundamentalism and more an approach to prayer, a willingness to enter into a contemplative state with each word, in all its hyperliterality. This hyperliterality obtains in the name *mi eilleh*. While I refrain from entering too deeply into the garden of theosophical delights with this passage, I think it is important to notice why things are broken in prayer. Put another way: a question emerges each time someone's heart is torn in mourning, each time someone encounters and admits the brokenness by reciting "May His great Name be enhanced and sanctified!" The question emerges from those very tears, "Who is 'His Name'?" It is this willingness to make space for questioning, uncertainty, and doubt that allows the *Kaddish* prayer to serve as an elixir to living in accelerated times.

It is no coincidence that brokenness emerges early on in the mystical *imaginaire*, roughly 1296 in Castille, most likely because of a clash between philosophy and mysticism swooping through Spain. The strong influence of ingenious philosopher-rabbi Maimonides, and his search for the rational explanation behind every aspect of ritual life likely led to a dulling of the prayer experience for many seekers. When the contemplative circle of the Zohar, headed by Rabbi Moses ben Shem-Tov de Léon, envisions a way of understanding his own displacement as a Jewish mystic from the Spanish Catholic milieu within Castille. Rabbi de Léon was doubly displaced, first from the Spanish Catholic milieu within Castille where he lived, and secondly as a result of endless disputations with his co-religionists. De Léon envisions a way of understanding his own double displacement through the image of the arc of cosmic exile of the Divine Mother as she withdraws from Her children. In this vision, the rift begins to close.

When a mother is separated from her children, the maternal caress may be interrupted but the bond grows even stronger. At the precise moment when the withdrawn Divine Mother[14] is reunited with Her children, redemption has arrived.[15] The same way that a mother communicates with her children, so too the Divine Mother communicates with Her children, the mystics, who are preoccupied with redeeming the nameless from the named. In this way, the Divine Mother may more effectively serve as the missing modality of intimate communication. Through the reunion of the Divine Mother with Her children, a finer frequency of contemplative communication emerges as the broken names become restored. The finer frequency for Jewish mystics is broadcast in Hebrew in a manner akin to Scrabble, so that *mi eilleh* and *elohim* are really just anagrams of each other. This linguistic intimacy and oddity allows for a more cosmic drama to emerge, namely that *mi eilleh* is the "broken" form of *elohim*. This broken and divided name (*mi eilleh*), which reflects the brokenness of the manifest world, can be restored to its non-dual reality: the "Who are these" of *mi eilleh* equates esoterically with *elohim* as the divine totality. Those mystics in love with every word see how every waking moment in the layers of divisible time manifest the brokenness of eternal light, which continue to illumine limitless lacunae in the fabric of being. This brokenness, as rendered in the *Zohar Hai* commentary, might be repaired only now by the salve of contemplative prayers.[16] And the more restoration the contemplative prayer engages in with this broken, holy Name, the more that prayer must become a contemplative act, engaged in by those who sit and struggle with the divine—Israel. Leonard Cohen remains an intuitive Kabbalist not beholden to any theosophic system. Still, Cohen's rendering of this restoration of the broken, holy name by way of contemplation emerges brilliantly in his magnificent song, "Love Itself":

> In streams of light I clearly saw
> The dust you seldom see,
> Out of which the Nameless makes
> A Name for one like me.
> . . . Then I came back from where I'd been.
> My room, it looked the same

> But there was nothing left between
> The Nameless and the Name.[17]

As one such god-wrestler whose lineage derives from the priestly clan, Cohen, he cannot escape the pull of these prayers that reconstitute the broken, holy name. Cohen is resigned to contemplating and thereby restoring the holy, broken name in a post-secular key. His task comes through in this reprise of this song:

> Never mind
> Never mind
> I live the life
> I left behind
>
> I live it full
> I live it wide
> Through layers of time
> You can't divide[18]

Cohen's post-secular songbook, I would argue, provides seekers with the equivalent of a strong prayer experience that counteracts the erosion of spiritual authenticity caused by living solely in accelerated time. When life is lived in a less accelerated manner, most pronounced as one traverses liminal moments like death, burial, and mourning, this "slowed time" allows for more expansiveness through the indivisible layers of time hovering in a prayer like *Kaddish D'itkhad'ta.* This unique prayer is a liturgical variation based on the regular *Kaddish* and is recited in expanded form during burial at a cemetery. It is also recited at the completion of studying a devotional book and is preceded by the *Hadran* prayer. What is invoked at these liminal moments—an immanent transcendence over space-time—is what allows for de-acceleration of distance between the "space of experience" and the "horizon of expectation." As the devotional book is closed and the coffin is sealed with earth, all of time-space remains open, a crossing-over the threshold into the web of the eternal:

> In the future world which the Holy One will create in unified consciousness, where the Holy One will revive the dead, construct the temple, sustain life, rebuild the city of Jerusalem, uproot idolatrous worship from the Holy Land, and restore the holy devotion of the heavens to its place, along with Her radiance, splendor, and *Shekhinah*, so may the Holy One blossom in redemption to hasten the onset of messianic consciousness.[19]

Contrary to the earlier definition of acceleration as the eliding of distance between the "space of experience" and the "horizon of expectation" as proffered by Reinhart Koselleck, I would argue that strong prayer experiences like the *Kaddish* actually counteract that elision. Accelerated living leads to dysfunctional families like the Altmans in *This is Where I Leave You*, and psychotic hustlers like Frank and Ben in *True Detective*. What normative Jewish liturgy, especially in its mystical undertones, provide is a way to live life in a less accelerated manner, thus allowing for more expansiveness through the indivisible layers of time hovering in a prayer like *Kaddish*. The ritual reciting of *Kaddish* through a Zoharic lens, and its numerous commentaries, sheds light on just how much the Name is in need of restoration. Every one of us is responsible for all names in their process of recovering lost perfection. What Cohen dares to sing of is how to say never mind to the *Neuzeit*, don't worry about those shrinking seconds left to say who was calling. You are free, at least for this eternal moment, to allow yourself an elongation of that distance within; you are beyond those thirty seconds in a post-secular age between the "space of experience" and the "horizon of expectation"; you are free in the contemplative moment of restoring "the rhythm the rhythm" of the Name to its lost wholeness, again and again:

> Worried/of course/defeated/of course/old/of course/יהוה/grateful/of course/ever since/the background/dissolved.[20]

12

Codetta: A Philosophy of Post-Secular Song in Light of *Piyyut* as a Cultural Lens

To close these reflections on the post-secular songbook of Leonard Cohen, I will dance between Canada and Israel—the very exile that the poet finds redemptive. There is a certain type of isolation, aptly termed the "third solitude," is unique to Canada. As we have seen throughout this book, Cohen experienced his most primal *decathexis* from place in the community of Jews caught between the Anglo and Francophone worlds. This is likely an experience that would also describe much of the topography of Cohen's psyche, in a *transcultural traveling homeland,* from Montréal to Hydra, Jerusalem, the Chelsea Hotel in New York, and Mount Baldy Zen Center outside Los Angeles.

The mythic Great White North of the Canadian landscape has something of the "desolation of the wild" that indelibly marks its contours. So much so that this Great White North is no longer strange once one realizes how much "I am bonded to it—and it to me—at the most primordial level."[1] What emerges in exploring this *decathexis* from place is just how much "desolation concerns both the place being left and the new place to which one is going."[2] The psychic topography is no longer limited to the physical. Expressions both barren and unyielding emerge as "no place at all but a site for suffering."[3] Yet amidst such suffering, there is a lucid sense of belonging to this place, the very space in which a home-person called-for-being-welcomed-back is still welcomed, all the while in exile.[4] The pervading melancholia of *placelessness* in Cohen's post-secular songbook, I suggest, is due to the desire to re-inhabit a *home-place,* especially in exile.[5] The irony, of course, is that the journey itself seeks its own displacement, to liberate oneself from being stuck-in-place to begin with.[6] In my own *(dis)placement,* I have been thinking, writing and dwelling outside of Cohen's *(dis)placed* homeland of Canada for almost two decades now. Yet the more I am *(dis)placed* from my homeland of Canada, the more that sense of place returns. But my journey is complicated by almost seven years sojourning in the Holy Land of Israel and then choosing to remain Hebraic in the Diaspora.[7]

And so I cannot avoid the renaissance of *piyyut* in Israel as a cultural phenomenon uniquely linked to the warp of Hebrew culture and the woof of Hebrew language. Still, there is something instructive in how Israeli scholars are navigating through the urgency of post-secular yearning. I return to the opening *circum/fession* now echoing in this Coda, recounting my striking conversation with Jerusalemite Yair Harel, the catalyst of the *piyyut* movement in Israel. I had been trying to explain to him how his holy renaissance work, while close to my heart, is almost irrelevant to seekers in America. "Yair," I pleaded, "Jews in America are less concerned with *piyyut* and more concerned with the following taxonomy of questioning: Is the song of our souls Debbie Friedman or Leonard Cohen?" Without missing beat, Yair retorted: "Well that's obvious—it's Leonard Cohen!" He then went on to teach me how to sing the *piyyut, Yedid Nefesh,* penned by Safed's Rabbi Elazar Moshe Azikri (1533-1600) to the melody of Cohen's *Hallelujah!*

It is true that America and Israel share elements of secular culture. Nonetheless, something markedly different appears to be emerging in each country's unique post-secular cultural landscapes. Haviva Pedaya, an Israeli scholar of *piyyut* and poet in her own right, has dedicated great energy and acumen to *piyyut* renaissance. Pedaya has, first of all, performed the liturgical poetry with her Judeo-Iraqi ensemble, *Yonat Rehokim*. Her scholarship on the subject, also impressive, emerged in great part from the working group she co-founded with Meir Buzaglo at the Van Leer Institute in Jerusalem. What is at stake in Pedaya's sophisticated claim of *Piyyut k'Tzohar Tarbuti* is that this form of liturgical poetry provides a "luminous cultural window" into the culture industry of a given moment within Jewish history.[8] Of course, nothing could be further from the truth as perceived by philosopher and musician Theodor Adorno. Dismissively disparaging the jazz that he experienced while living in America as a German exile, this was a time when Adorno felt a deep sense of loss and yearning for a European classical music that references a lost age in history.[9] Pedaya, by contrast, is more balanced in her critique of memory and forgetfulness of Israeli culture as evidenced in and through its music. Her stated goal is to expand the post-colonialist context of *piyyutim*'s "tool kit," without being limited by any one of the methodologies contained therein.[10] This goal was shared by both the Van Leer working group, "The East Writes Itself," and the colloquiam, "*Piyyut* as a cultural prism."[11]

Several degrees of cultural correlations emerge in Pedaya's investigation surrounding this "tool kit," including modern experiential paradigms of: sight and sound; voice and text; writing and music; music and identity; as well as organizational paradigms of *communitas,* ritual, and mystical *communitas.*[12] Pedaya concludes her magisterial study with the claim that: "*Piyyut* attempts to return and peel away at the place with a liminal language, just after the sealing of the languages of memory as they became final."[13] Most intriguing for our purposes, however, is the comparison Pedaya makes between religious and national cultures, whereby *piyyut* is a key cultural prism for Jewish and Israeli identity. In a similar vein, German-Jewish thinker Franz Rosenzweig claimed the synagogue to be a key cultural prism for Jewish identity in the Diaspora.[14] The problem, of course, in extending the comparison to Rosenzweig, is that Diaspora Judaism in general, and American Judaism in particular, are far removed from the romantic recuperation of Rosenzweig's *Lehrhaus.*[15] Post-colonial discourse seems appropriate to Pedaya when analyzing Israel, but what about analyzing America? Ironically, in this globalized age, organizational paradigms of *communitas,* both ritual and mystical, are emerging as *Kehillot Sharot* or "singing communities." *Kehillot Sharot* are accessed through Yair's website, *An Invitation to Piyut,* in the virtual space between Israel and America.[16] What does the post-colonial song sound like in a globalized age of singing communities?

In an otherwise flat-lined land of globalism where Cohen's post-secular oeuvre strikes a chord—with the decline of affiliation and disaffection from the synagogue, his songbook carries forward a certain modicum of enchantment without the trappings of the institution. It is precisely from those temples his ancestors built—especially his father and grandfather in Montréal—Cohen at once flees and rebuilds as a post-secular prophet. It is from the very stones that builders refused to use that Cohen reconstructs his unique vantage point, elevating the refuse into a song that stirs the soul:

> Now Suzanne takes your hand
> and she leads you to the river
> she is wearing rags and feathers
> from Salvation Army counters
> And the sun pours down like honey
> on our lady of the harbor
> And she shows you where to look
> among the garbage and the flowers
> There are heroes in the seaweed
> there are children in the morning
> they are leaning out for love
> they will lean that way forever
> while Suzanne holds the mirror. . . .[17]

One of Cohen's many muses "leaning out for love" is encountered in this harboring presence of the *Shekhinah*, who is drenched in the golden honey rays of the sun while wearing rags and feathers—yet another glorious tangle of matter and ghost. This is a post-secular poet willing to penetrate all those who appear to be "dressed to kill" and see "the rags of light,"[18] the very rags that precariously hold together embodied human existence.

As a songwriter, Cohen is unflinching in his commitment to redeeming the Jewish liturgy of the very abandoned synagogues his ancestors built. Cohen is unmatched in his audacity for carrying forward the most arcane and theologically problematic liturgical poetry of the holiest day of the year and recasting it in a post-secular context; when he famously sings:

> Who by fire? Who by water? Who in the sunshine? Who in the night time? Who by high ordeal? Who by common trial? Who in your merry, merry month of May? Who by very slow decay? *And who shall I say is calling?*[19]

No one but the high priest of post-secular yearning could succeed in carrying forward the lost lyricism of "*Mi ba'mayim. Mi ba'esh*," rendered as "Who by fire? Who by water?"[20]—which comes from the high holiday's *Netane Tokef piyyut*. Cohen recasts it in this lyric with the most mundane of refrains from which no one can swerve and no deity can answer on time. Everyone has to answer the phone even if no one is home, since a message is always left. That message being left by the *deus absconditus* is that no one can escape the power of this poetry of encounter—even if that encounter is with the presence as absence. Once your ear attunes to it, the sounds imprint upon your heart and mind—and so Canadian media theorist, Herbert Marshall McLuhan (1911-1980) and his apocalyptic prophesy from the television age has come true. But notice here that the *medium* of Cohen's post-secular songs transcends and includes their *message*.[21] As the information age continues to compress its medium microscopically,

Cohen seeks the transcendent, even in that atomization, to ensure the openness to truly see that.[22]

There remains something at once disarming and charming about the ease with which Cohen is able to straddle these worlds. As a ritual artist and rabbi, I have been pleasantly surprised to discover just how canonical Cohen's lyrics have become in liturgical settings. The use of Cohen's lyrical-liturgical words has reached the point where re-inserting them into the very liturgical context that inspired them and allowing them to introduce, or even dialogue with, the original *piyyut* brings solace to American seekers, at the very least in my home of American Jerusalem, San Francisco! A fellow partner in crime, folk singer turned cantor, George Mordecai, has reportedly substituted the canonical cantorial piece, *Hineini* with "If It Be Your Will," with wide acceptance in New York. And what about the original *piyyut*? It would have been imprinted in the apirant's ears through the pale imitations of someone singing, *à la* Yossele Rosenblatt:

> Here I am lowly and downtrodden
> unworthy, trembling with fear from the One Who Sits in Praise of Israel
> I have come to stand and pray before You
> for the sake of this community of Israel that has sent me forth
> even if I am unworthy and mismatched for this task. . . .[23]

Every precintor of high holiday prayers uses the *Hineini* as a way to align his/her intentionality with the solemnity of the day, so that She can then introduce the high holiday additional service repertoire. Undoubtedly, Leonard Cohen suffered through one too many *Hineini* prayers in his Westmount synagogue and was likely repelled by his own experience growing up surrounded by these Ashkenazic sounds during high holidays. What repelled him is what continues to repel most Jews in the pews—the theological dissonance. Having just emerged from the previous liturgical station of "brokenness" through the *Shofar*'s staccato shrills, what words could possibly remain? Instead, the Ashkenzi cantorial tradition turns up the volume and increases the words, to the point of a Purim parody! And so comes the comer: Cohen redeems this near-farcical missed musical moment with a truly poignant, bare-bones rendition of the *piyyut*:

> If it be your will
> that a voice be true,
> from this broken hill
> I will sing to you.
> From this broken hill
> all your praises they shall ring
> if it be your will
> to let me sing.[24]

Only in America—that place for the ex-pat *Canadien érrant*—the only place in all his worldly wanderings—from Hydra and even to Israel—has "that spiritual thirst" and that range for change taken place. How fitting, then, that Cohen's post-secular lyrics (like that "Democracy" he warns about) has taken hold America first. He tells us why:

> It's here they got the range
> and the machinery for change
> and it's here they got that spiritual thirst.
> It's here the family's broken
> and it's here the lonely say
> that the heart has got to open
> in a fundamental way . . .[25]

As halcyon a prism as Pedaya proffers in her claims about *piyyut*, she remains ensconced in a never-ending battling against a hegemonic rabbinic culture of Israel. Cohen, on the other hand, continues to feel at ease with his delicious diasporic dance *to and fro*. Where else could the Montréal bard cloak the climactic moment of the "Closing of the Gates," from the *Yom Kippur piyyut* of *Neilah*, in his own inimitable rendition of "Closing Time"?

> So we struggle and we stagger
> down the snakes and up the ladder
> to the tower where the blessed hours chime
> And I swear it happened just like this:
> a sigh, a cry, a hungry kiss
> the Gates of Love they budged an inch
> I can't say much has happened since
> *but closing time. . . .*[26]

What Cohen captures here again is that nexus between matter and ghost, "when you've fallen on the highway"[27] while continually attempting to make that ascent. What sounds like a juvenile game of Snakes and Ladders really resounds here as a path of no-path,[28] strewn with serpentine *gnosis* intertwined within angelic ladders. That *to and fro* dance, between dualism and undifferentiated oneness, comes through strongest. Take note of the recurring dualistic motifs (mind-body, spirit-limb, reason-heart, altar-Name) and how they are juxtaposed, pointing towards a broken resolution, in a recent lyric by Cohen, called, "Come Healing":

> O gather up the brokenness
> And bring it to me now
> The fragrance of those promises
> You never dared to vow
> The splinters that you carry
> The cross you left behind
> Come healing of the body
> Come healing of the mind
> And let the heavens hear it
> The penitential hymn
> Come healing of the spirit
> Come healing of the limb

Behold the gates of mercy
In arbitrary space
And none of us deserving
The cruelty or the grace
O solitude of longing
Where love has been confined
Come healing of the body
Come healing of the mind
O see the darkness yielding
That tore the light apart
Come healing of the reason
Come healing of the heart
O troubled dust concealing
An undivided love
The Heart beneath is teaching
To the broken Heart above
O let the heavens falter
And let the earth proclaim:
Come healing of the Altar
Come healing of the Name
O longing of the branches
To lift the little bud
O longing of the arteries
To purify the blood
And let the heavens hear it
The penitential hymn
Come healing of the spirit
Come healing of the limb
O let the heavens hear it. . . .[29]

In gathering up the brokenness, of this coda Leonard Cohen's post-secular song invites a remarkably comfortable agnosticism for seekers between America and Israel. If it is nothing more than "the Gates of Love they budged an inch," then there is no need for dogmatic claims about that which eludes it. That agnostic love for life has an expansive enough perspective to embrace the "sigh" within the "hungry kiss."[30] It is within this very interstice that humanity exists and flourishes, if only it can hear the broken song emerging at each and every moment. The poet leaves behind any misgivings of non-dual philosophers by embracing outright "[a]n undivided love." It is the realization of what makes this love unique that allows the poet to make the audacious claim that inverts most mystical expectations, namely, that: "The Heart beneath is teaching/To the broken Heart above." Whereas conventional esoteric language renders the divine-human matrix "As above, so below," Cohen swerves and inverts matters of the heart such that the human-divine matrix is configured otherwise: "As below, so above." In one fell swoop, although a swoop that has gained force over many decades, Cohen masterfully inverts expectations, opening a truly mystical humanism that emerges from the ambivalence of post-secularism. If there is anything left to invent after the human condition,[31] then the invention would not necessarily be as Leonard's son, Adam, also a singer-songwriter, decries: "I'd start a new religion based on your silhouette."[32] Leonard Cohen's songbook masterfully envisions, like no other, that spirit of human fallenness,[33] post-secular religions in their *tangle of matter and ghost.*

13

Coda: Burning Darker Beyond

"You Want it Darker"

"…and it's hell to pay when the fiddler stops: it's CLOSING TIME"[1] — if the *coda* has been sung already in the twelfth chapter of this book, then what happened?[2] How can there be an afterlife of Cohen's post-secular songbook still burning beyond the stated *coda*?!? Perhaps the secret is imbedded in the very *coda* I thought would conclude this book already—*adieu!* After all, is not *adieu* the hope and the promise at the core of philosophic aesthetics? *Adieu* for a pianist-philosopher, like Theodor Adorno might hover in the evanescent, clacking horse hoofs disappearing in Beethoven's sonata *Les Adieux*, [3] while for philosopher, Jacques Derrida *adieu* might emerge in a eulogy to his beloved colleague, Emmanuel Lévinas.[4] Or looking deeper into the ironic "Bye, bye, Sayonara" of Cohen's Rinzai Zen master, Joshu Sasaki Roshi, there hovers the realization that life and death are not separate activities such that "[a]t the time of death you enter a state where the life activity and the death activity both have to act no more. So I'll probably say that I'm going to the world where you don't have to live or die anymore."[5] Each of these hopes points towards an *adieu* that is *à-Dieu —towards the divine* rather than just a *farewell*. Farewell is final; but *à-Dieu* implies eternal return. It is this fearless movement, embodied in that non-dual *à-Dieu* —embodied in Adorno's Beethoven, Derrida's Lévinas, and Cohen's Roshi *towards* the divine embodying the eternal return of the *coda*—where the final notes of return cannot be sung beyond, even by this inimitable Montreal bard. No matter how hard Leonard Cohen's songbook attempts to say farewell, the songs themselves keep singing on through their sympathetic resonance of eternal return.

After all, what is a *coda* but such an invitation to return? Recall the "tail" end of a musical composition lies at the roots of *coda* in Italian, typically at the end of a sonata movement. How surreal then that the Jewish New Year's custom for Sephardim is to pray "not to be the tail [of the ram] but it's head"[6]—so then everyone seated round the table digs into a piece of the head! The only way to enable such a musical extension is if a previous elaboration heard is worth repeating. Yet with every repetition, there is something new—and Leonard's songbook never gets old, even if at times, it sounds like it is repeating. So what if the origins of the *coda* that returns to ornamental sections in medieval music, called *caudae* served were to serve to extend relatively simple polyphonic pieces?!? The typical *coda* section immediately follows the recapitulation section and thus ends the movement. Often it is in the brevity one encounters its brilliance. Just a few measures, or it may be of sizable proportions relative to the rest of the movement. The lingering question repeats: regarding Leonard Cohen's songbook resonates deeper beyond the coda: namely, can darkness get any darker? Or paradoxically, is there a luminosity within the deepest darkness?[7] It is in singing singing such "a paradox to blame" that this calling beyond the *coda* continues hovering.

It is precisely in the recurring sounds of the *coda* that I hear the incipient origin of eternal time returning at the precipice of the New Year, and I find myself once again, struggling with closing time. Whether it is with the perennial encroachment of these Days of Awe in a world bereft of reverence, or in the closing time of this endless book, I am struck by the power of the afterlife of Cohen's *coda* still burning. Little wonder that Jewish mystics reveled in this notion of "the ending being inscribed in the beginning!"[8] That is precisely the feeling that washed over me as the preview of Leonard Cohen's latest single, "You want it darker" was released at the precipice of the New Year, when and two friendly voices concatenated—one, a congregant; the other, a teacher. My congregant, Angie Dalfen, a Montreal ex-pat living here in American Jerusalem, immediately sent me the front-page coverage in the *Montreal Gazette* featuring an interview with Cantor Gideon Zelermyer of Montreal's *Shaar Hashomayim Synagogue.* The story explored the seemingly unlikely collaboration between the Montreal bard and Cantor Zelermyer, as well as an interview with the latter singing and sharing a running commentary on his cantorial riff of the classic liturgical moment from the approaching high holidays, known as, *Hineni,* which means directly, "Here Am I!"[9] Cantor Zelermyer —whose "original face"[10] passed before me in the hallways of Goldsmith residence on W120 and Broadway before taking leave of JTS, now decades ago— regaled how his choir left the Plateau recording studio after midnight, wherein Leonard and son, Adam, asked the cantor to remain. The task? Riff away. What emerged was an ancient-new take on *Hineni.* Cohen was asking himself —through this cantor —to engage in his own deeply personal "death awareness" practice.[11]

Let me explain: there is a kind of poetic justice that this song will be released on 9/21/16, Cohen's 82nd birthday amidst rumors of his battle with cancer, along with the entire album, written by Cohen and produced by his son, Adam, to follow later on after the ebb of the high holidays, 10/21/16. This return to *Shaar* synagogue and its current cantor has a more ancient resonance of eternal recurrence—the site of Cohen's *bar mitzvah,* as well as the tenure of synagogue presidencies held by his grandfather and great-grandfather. Their *original faces* remain resonating in portraits that still hang in the *Shaar* hallway. Last November, Cohen sent Cantor Zelermyer a request, out of the blue: "Would you be interested in collaborating with me on a new record? I'm looking for the sound of the synagogue cantor and choir of my youth. Let me know what you think. Fraternally, Eliezer." Before dawn had broken, this correspondence of eternal recurrence between bard and cantor, concluded with the cantor responding: "*Hallelujah* and *I'm Your Man*!' " Within the course of the following day, Cantor Zelermyer made arrangements with beloved son, Adam, to proceed along with the *Shaar* choir into a Plateau studio together. Could there be any more direct confrontation with Cohen's *original face* than at the *Shaar*?

Then there were the piercing words from my teacher, Elliot Wolfson, written to me immediately in his exile from Santa Barbara, now nestled at Harvard. Wolfson wanted to ensure my high holiday preparations were peaking, just in case I missed this late breaking eternal return of luminal darkness of this darkening *coda* of Cohen:

> …the voice is weakening/and he invokes Abraham's *hineni…*/perhaps portending the end[12]

As always, Wolfson, like no other has that uncanny ability to truly see and channel the imaginal urgency of Cohen's "portending the end" on the precipice of the incipient New Year as another beginning. In gesturing to this (im)possibility of hearing this "portending the end" as beginning, my teacher was pointing me back through allusion to philosopher, Friedrich Nietzsche's notion of "eternal recurrence"—that is, our lives will repeat infinitely. The infinitude of that repetition in each life where every detail has the *appearance of sameness* challenges the philosopher to see *difference* in all that appears to be exactly the same, even in "portending the end". Trapped in such eternal recurrence, there is an unveiling of the horror of existence, which is interwoven throughout Cohen's "You want it darker". The bard continues to struggle within the landscape of all souls, ascending and descending along with his own, amidst a world otherwise filled with meaningless suffering. Yet for the Montreal bard it has never sufficed that eternal recurrence simply be accepted—both philosopher and bard demand that it be loved. I would argue that this call to love approaching death is revealed with great courage than ever in Cohen's "You want it darker". This bold self-assessment of the soul's journey taking place in this song is the work of all real philosophy.[13] There is no *being*, only *becoming* for the philosopher as for the bard—*why?* Because for the philosopher "[e] xistence begins in every instant".[14] The challenge of the philosopher is the "paradox to blame" sung by the bard. Here Nietzsche's challenge is instructive if we want get to the heart of the bard's song, by listening more deeply to the philosopher's following question:

> "What if some day or night a demon were to steal into your loneliest loneliness and say to you: 'This life as you now live and have lived it you will have to live once again and innumerable times again; and there will be nothing new in it, but every pain and every joy and every thought and sigh and everything unspeakably small or great in your life must return to you, all in the same succession and sequence – even this spider and this moonlight between the trees, and even this moment and I myself...' The question in each and every thing, 'Do you want this again and innumerable times again?' would lie on your actions as the heaviest weight! Or how well disposed would you have to become to yourself and to life *to long for nothing more fervently* than for this ultimate eternal confirmation and seal?"[15]

What the philosopher is challenging the bard to sing about is how we all strive to celebrate life *as it is*. So it is "the past", in Kathleen O'Dwyer's reading of Nietzsche, "that is embraced, [where] mistakes, losses and disappointments are acknowledged, as are joys, achievements and fortuitous encounters; and the future is seen as the offshoot of the present."[16] To my ears in this moment, this suggests the delicate interweaving of this inescapable temporality of *Rosh haShannah*—the birthday of creation which strives to celebrate life *as it is* through all temporal spheres. It is a New Year always "portending the end" in its beginning.

Daring to confront these achievements and fortuitous encounters that are part of the fabric of this eternal present is the work of existence as mirrored throughout the Jewish high holidays. In attempting to come to terms with the fabric of this eternal present, the liturgy is replete with moments of introspection. Nevertheless, this opportunity for self-reflection becomes a deeper interrogation for the bard who is not only willing to confront himself, but to also confront the Over-Self which liturgy knows as God. This confrontation is not foreign to dramatic theological images of high holiday liturgy, like in the *Une Tane Tokef*, to which the bard casually riffs on as the divine dealer in his latest song:

> If you are the dealer, I'm out of the game
> If you are the healer, it means I'm broken and lame
> If thine is the glory then mine must be the shame
> You want it darker
> We kill the flame

If, as the philosopher decries, "everything unspeakably small or great in your life must return to you, all in the same succession and sequence" then there is no way out. Existence is clearly a horror, replete with endless suffering. The bard is willing to stare this horror in the face through the "death awareness meditations of *Maranasati* or *hibbut hakever*, but what separates the bard from the philosopher is one thing— *prayer*. What I have been arguing throughout this present book— aptly titled, *Tangle of Matter and Ghost* capturing that hovering non-dual consciousness merging life and death— is that this magnificent post-secular songbook testifies to the power of the Montreal bard who can still offer a prayer, no matter how broken.

There is no brokenness greater than the *Shoah* and the six million souls decimated, and yet, the bard finds a shard of deeper brokenness— those "million candles" for the million souls of children who were also annihilated. Who will remember the loss of all these innocent souls and "the help that never came" to the redeem us from the horrors of the *Shoah* and every other genocide? It is here that the invocation of *Kaddish* emerges in the song that the bard is now recalling as active remembrance, both for these souls and for his own soul:

> Magnified, sanctified, be thy holy name
> Vilified, crucified, in the human frame
> A million candles burning for the help that never came
> You want it darker

The genius of Cohen lies in his daring juxtaposition—here for the first time in his songbook—where he is explicit in his Jewish liturgical moves. Now the aforementioned words of *Kaddish*— discussed already in the eleventh chapter of this book— re-emerge here, but juxtaposed with the prayer leader's prelude of: "*Hineni, hineni*/I'm ready, my lord". While this locution of *Hineni* resonates most strongly within the rubric of liturgy, the bard is blowing on its ancient prophetic resonances—that call which roused prophets like Abraham, Moses and others. However, this new (and perhaps final) song is much more than a mere biblical dirge![17] Rather than rely on the priests of prayer, the bard is calling forth, once again, with his prophetic impulse into a love song:

> There's a lover in the story
> But the story's still the same
> There's a lullaby for suffering
> And a paradox to blame
> But it's written in the scriptures
> And it's not some idle claim
> You want it darker
> We kill the flame

As we come to expect and relish from the bard who uplifts us from the dust and ashes of our lives, this is no simple love song. This octogenarian bard is brimming with righteous indignation, decrying with prophetic impulse that: "There's a lullaby for suffering/And a paradox to blame". Is he yearning to transcend the paradox of religion in favor of the non-dual awareness of the spirit, already discussed in the fourth and fifth chapters of this book? It is the lament of the bard's "lullaby for suffering" that forever condemns every post-Auschwitz listener to remain a witness to all suffering and genocide, even in this age of *postmemory.*[18] Most damning, the bard implicates himself, and every self, in the horrors we confront daily:

> They're lining up the prisoners
> And the guards are taking aim
> I struggled with some demons
> They were middle class and tame
> I didn't know I had permission to murder and to maim
> You want it darker

While this burning beyond the *coda* is both a celebration of rebirthing and portending the end— it is also a prophetic lament. Amidst the fanning of fear-mongering and baseless hatred, America edges into the precipice of the abyss, so the bard offers his lament of this contemporary moment of the broken covenant and complicity within that very brokennes: "You want it darker/We kill the flame." The bard is "portending the end"— at once as *tsaddik* and *bhoddisatva*—for the rest of us as immanent as we are now creating the end before its time in this very moment. In this space of luminal darkness, the tonal counterbalance based on the first and fifth degrees of the scale,[19] respectively, recall "it goes like this: the fourth, the fifth/the minor fall, the major lift/the baffled king composing Hallelujah!"[20] Leonard Cohen sings with an equipoise, for he is clearly disposed to *becoming* himself "and to life *to long for nothing more fervently* than for this ultimate eternal confirmation and seal"—and so, in this openness to *becoming,* all broken prayers here merge. From this fusion of the shards of *Kaddish* to *Hineni,* the bard has crystalized the broken name as One. And so, as I sit mesmerized for twelve hours, listening to these sounds of luminal darkness portending the end of *Elul* with my gypsy girls— Talya and Elyssa— in their rags of light, we come to realize that such a *coda* continues to *sing itself.* Such a burning beyond the *coda* is that lone tonal counterbalance to the horrific tonic—the dominant tragedy of American culture as it is about to unfold again, with eternal recurrence—in this contemporary moment. Only then can darkness burn into such a magnificent afterglow of this redemption song.

Congregation Beth Sholom
San Francisco, California

26th of Elul, 5776

Breaking the Brokenness and the Healing of the Poem: A Brief Meditation

"O gather up the brokenness / And bring it to me now / The fragrance of those promises / You never dared to vow." So begins one of Leonard Cohen's most extraordinary kabbalistic songs, "Come Healing," a poem that is prayer in its purest distillation, a prayer clothed in quintessential nakedness, an anthem that celebrates and laments the wholehearted fragmentariness of the human condition, the brokenness of the promises one never dared to vow. Why is this so? What is a promise that one does not dare to vow, and if the promise is not vowed, how can it broken? The brokenness consists precisely of not having the courage and timidity to make the vow. Even more egregious than the brokenness that results from not keeping a promise one has vowed is the brokenness of the promise that has never been vowed. The promise one does not dare to vow is the deepest lack of belief, a lack of trust in oneself and in the other, a lack of commitment in the possibility of being committed. And yet, the very promises that are never vowed offer a scent, a fragrance, the olfactory trace that calls forth to memory what might have been if one had the audacity to dare to vow. The trace that marks the absence of presence as the presence of absence.

"The splinters that you carry / The cross you left behind / Come healing of the body / Come healing of the mind." Sometimes we carry the reminder of our pain like splinters embedded in the flesh; other times we are condemned to envision the pain as the cross we left behind, the burden of a suffering too burdensome to bear. In either case, the poet offers a prayer for a double healing, the healing of the body and the healing of the mind. Maimonides famously spoke of two perfections, the perfection of the body and the perfection of the soul, *tiqqun ha-guf* and *tiqqun ha-nefesh*, and the kabbalists similarly provided a path that leads to this double healing, a path that forces one to confront the brokenness in all of its stark reality, the brokenness of the world, the human, and the divine. Only prayer in its most destitute form, the prayer divested of prayer, can mend the heart broken by this threefold brokenness, for through the mystery of song, the secret of prayerfulness, we detect that in every moment there is a beginning, and hence each moment is identical because distinctive. Time, as opposed to eternity, must have a point of beginning, but to begin it cannot have begun without compromising its status as the beginning that will begin. The beginning, then, never ends, but only that which ends everlastingly never ends.

"And let the heavens hear it / The penitential hymn / Come healing of the spirit / Come healing of the limb." Long ago the poet admonished that even if the promise be broken, we must keep it nonetheless. No promise can be more devotedly kept than the promise that has been betrayed by never being avowed. Healing of the spirit and healing of the limb are most acutely possible in the place where salvation seems impossible, where hope leaps forth from the depths of hopelessness. In the capriciousness of our expecting the unexpected, of waiting for what cannot arrive, lies our obdurate fidelity to a future that is both present and not present, present as not present, not present as present.

"Behold the gates of mercy / In arbitrary space / And none of us deserving / The cruelty or the grace." Once more, the poet illumines the phenomenological quandary of prayer: only one unworthy is empowered to pray, but one unworthy has no power to pray. There is a Talmudic tradition that from the day the Temple was destroyed the gates of prayer are closed but the gates of weeping remain open. The gates of mercy are these gates of weeping, for tears are the agency that stimulates the compassion necessary in a place of brokenness, the arbitrary space that seems capricious from the standpoint of the strict measure of the law, the place of forgiveness where guilt is transposed into innocence. Mercy, as the kabbalists teach, holds sway between divine wrath and divine love, the response appropriate for the one underserving of cruelty or grace.

"O solitude of longing / Where love has been confined / Come healing of the body / Come healing of the mind." The brokenness is broken in the *solitude of longing where love has been confined*—a curious phrase indeed. *Prima facie*, longing presumes the other, and yet it is engendered most fervently in seclusion. The wasteland of solitude is precisely the womb that bears the possibility of profound relationality. Not only death but desire, too, arises in what Heidegger called the *determinate ring of solitude*. This is reminiscent as well of Soloveitchik's typology of the lonely man of faith, which is not to be construed as loneliness in the sense of being physically isolated from social intercourse, but rather a more intense existential loneliness, the ontic sense of being alone even in, *nay* especially in, the company of others. Being with the other enhances the solitude of longing from which poetic thinking ensues in the aspiration to heal body and mind. The solitude of longing is where love has been confined, where that which by nature extends limitlessly is delimited, the mystery of *tsimtsum* in the kabbalistic tradition, the compression of the boundless light to a point circumscribed in the void emptied of that light. "O see the darkness yielding / That tore the light apart / Come healing of the reason / Come healing of the heart." The inceptual projection is concomitantly a withdrawal, an act expressive of both constrictive judgement and expansive mercy. Attunement to this paradox can bring healing of reason and healing of the heart—only the reason of the heart can ascertain the heart of reason, the truth of love that demands both the contracting that expands and the expansion that contracts.

"O troubled dust concealing / An undivided love / The heart beneath is teaching / To the broken heart above." Here we come to the most esoteric dimension of the poem. The invariable misfortune and turmoil of our all-too-human lot—the troubled dust that gathers in every corner of our lives—conceals an undivided love taught to the broken heart above by the heart that is below. One would expect, first, that the hierarchy would be reversed, that the heart above teaches the heart below, and second, that the heart above would not be described as broken. But, in line with one of the most penetrating insights promulgated by the kabbalists, it is indeed the divine heart that is broken and its mending depends on the action of the human heart below.

"Let the heavens falter / Let the earth proclaim / Come healing of the altar / Come healing of the name." How does the heart below in a world rife with division teach the heart above about undivided love? Even though the heavens falter, the earth will proclaim—through its own brokenness the broken heart will find the path of healing. In the celebrated teaching of Naḥman of Bratzlav, there is no heart as whole as a broken heart. In the chasm of this desolation, all that is left is the possibility of prayer, the possibility to pray for the possibility of prayer. As Cohen put it in another one of his songs, "If it be your will / That a voice be true / From this broken hill / I will sing to you / From this broken hill / All your praises they shall ring / If it be your will / To let me sing."[1] Our finitude is such that even the song of praise can be offered only from the broken hill, the hill ravaged by transgression, indiscretion, and duplicity, the glow of faith ensnared in the shadow of doubt, the face of truth veiled in the mask of untruth. But the possibility of possibility that prayer represents, as impossible as it might seem, has the power to heal the altar and to heal the name.

The melancholic wisdom centers on the discernment that wholeness can be restored only in the fragment, the sacrifice of the aggregate to the suffering of the part. As the final chorus attests: "O longing of the branches / To lift the little bud / O longing of the arteries / To purify the blood." Since the light of the infinite is attired in every detail, each detail can be considered the embodiment of divinity in its entirety; each being displays the craving of the arteries that the life-giving blood that flows through them be purified. The compossible synergy of universality and particularity is expressed in the presumably inestimable refinements and rectifications of the inextensible light. There is no unicity but in the endless divisibility of the indivisible, no integration but in the indefinite disintegration of the indissoluble. And thus the song ends with the repetition of the refrain: "And let the heavens hear it / The penitential hymn / Come healing of the spirit / Come healing of the limb."

Elliot R. Wolfson,
Marsha and Jay Glazer
Endowed Chair in Jewish Studies Area,
UC-Santa Barbara

16th of Av, 5776

Notes

1. *Prelude:* New Skin for a Post-Secular *Circum/fession*

1 Notwithstanding their pre-post-modern context, I am referring to the need for true esoteric meaning of one's political philosophy to remain garbed in the exoteric; see Leo Strauss, *Persecution and the Art of Writing* (Glencoe, IL: Free Press, 1952); see also, Kenneth H. Green, *Jew and Philosopher: The Return to Maimonides in the Jewish Thought of Leo Strauss* (Albany: State University of New York Press, 1993).

2 Leonard Cohen, "Going Home," in *Old Ideas* (New York: Sony Music, 2012).

3 Jacques Derrida and Geoffrey Bennington, "*Circumfession*: Fifty-nine Periods and Periphrases: Written in a Sort of Internal Margin, between Geoffrey Bennington's Book and Work in Preparation" (January 1989-April 1990), (*n.p.*), 37-38.

4 Leonard Cohen, *New Skin for the Old Ceremony* (New York: Columbia, 1974).

5 Leonard Cohen, *Book of Mercy* (New York: Villard Books, 1984).

6 Jeremiah 4:4.

7 Carl Gustav Jung, *Aspects of the Feminine*, vol. 6 (Princeton, NJ: Princeton University Press, 1982); see also, Naomi R. Goldenberg, "A Feminist Critique of Jung," *Signs* 2, no. 2 (1976): 443-449.

8 Adam Maclean, *A Commentary on the Rosearium Philosophorum,* accessed 2/15/16, http://www.levity.com/alchemy/roscom.html.

9 Leonard Cohen, *Death of a Lady's Man* (New York: Columbia, 1977).

10 Zohar I: 224a, tr. D. Matt, Pritzker Edition (Stanford: Stanford University Press, 2006), 346n245, 347n249.

11 I am indebted to the pioneering reflections of Wolfson regarding the phallocentrism of the kabbalistic tradition and the implicit critique that

a rebalancing of gender remains a desideratum. For example, see Elliot R. Wolfson, "The Cut that Binds: Time, Memory, and the Ascetic Impulse," in *God's Voice from the Void: Old and New Studies in Bratslav Hasidism*, ed. Shaul Magid (Albany: State University of New York Press, 2002): 119-120; Idem, "Divine Suffering and the Hermeneutics of Reading: Philosophical Reflections on Lurianic Mythology," *Suffering Religion* (2002): 101-162. It remains an open question whether Leonard Cohen's intuitive Kabbalah manages to rectify this imbalance post-*Death of a Lady's Man* (1974).

12 Leonard Cohen, "Hallelujah," in *Various Positions* (New York: Sony Music, 1995).

13 Leonard Cohen, "Anthem," in *The Future* (New York: Sony Music, 1992).

14 Jacques Derrida, David Shapiro, Michal Govrin, and Kim Shkapich, *Body of Prayer: Written Words, Voices* (New York: Irwin S. Chanin School of Architecture of the Cooper Union, 2001).

15 Leonard Cohen, "Everybody Knows," in *I'm Your Man* (New York: Sony Music, 1988).

16 Michel Foucault, *Archaeology of Knowledge* (London: Routledge, 2002).

17 Aubrey L. Glazer, *Lines of Oblivion*, 1992, accessed 7/15/15, http://www.vtape.org/video?vi=2176.

18 Leonard Cohen, "Who by Fire," in *The Best of Leonard Cohen* (New York: Sony Music,1961).

19 Aubrey L. Glazer, *Fire on the Water*, 1994, accessed 7/15/15, http://www.vtape.org/video?vi=4275.

20 Leonard Cohen, "The Future," in *The Future* (1992).

21 b*Shabbat* 30b.

2. On Exile as Redemption in (Canadian) Jewish Mysticism

1 I am indebted to David Koffman and Stephanie Tara Schwartz for their insights into the nuances at play of "the third solitude" for Canadian Jewish Mysticism. See Sidra D. K. Ezrahi, *Booking Passage: Exile and Homecoming in the Modern Jewish Imagination* (Berkeley: University of California Press, 2000), esp. 3-32, 234-245; Jonathan Boyarin and Daniel Boyarin, *Powers of Diaspora: Two Essays on the Relevance of Jewish Culture* (Minneapolis: University of Minnesota Press, 2002), 1-34; Caryn Aviv and David Shneer, *New Jews: The End of the Jewish Diaspora* (New York: New York University Press, 2005), 1-26.

2 Aviv and Shneer, *New Jews*, 23.

3 See A. M. Klein's unpublished essay "In Praise of the Diaspora," as quoted in Michael Greenstein, *Third Solitude: Tradition and Discontinuity in Jewish Canadian Literature* (Montreal: McGill-Queens Press, 1989), 11.

4 Greenstein, *Third Solitude*, 14.

5 Ibid., 12.

6 For more on how the "two solitudes" of anglophone and francophone linguistic and ethnic clusters give way to Montreal Jews' vibrant and warmly embracing "third solitude," see Harold M. Troper, *The Defining Decade: Identity, Politics, and the Canadian Jewish Community in the 1960s* (Toronto: University of Toronto Press, 2010), 39-80. For the influence of this "third solitude" upon Canadian literature, see Greenstein, *Third Solitude*, 3-17; see also Tom Marshall, "Third Solitude: Canadian as Jew," in *The Canadian Novel: Here and Now*, ed. John Moss (Toronto: NC Press, 1983), 147-155.

7 Ezrahi, *Booking Passage*, 3-4.

8 Ibid., 4: "For Jews who had developed a culture of *substitution* in all the lands of their dispersion, reconnecting Zion, or Jerusalem, meant an intoxicating—and toxic—encounter with the only place that had the status of *the real*. Repudiating mimetic culture in favor of reclamation of 'original space' also activates, at the deepest level, a mechanism for renouncing the workings of the imagination, the invention of alternative worlds, to replace them with the recovery of what is perceived as the bedrock of the collective self."

9 This renowned model for Israel-Diaspora relations in the modern period by Ahad Ha'am (a.k.a. Asher Ginsburg) posited Israel as a center for cultural renewal, radiating outward like spokes on a wheel to the peripheral diaspora. For more on Ahad Ha'am's vision for Zionism, see Steven J. Zipperstein, *Elusive Prophet: Ahad Ha'am and the Origins of Zionism* (Berkeley: University of California Press, 1993).

10 Jonathan Boyarin and Daniel Boyarin, "Diaspora: Generation and the Ground of Jewish Identity," *Critical Inquiry* 19.4 (1993): 711; see also Boyarin and Boyarin, *Powers of Diaspora*, and Aviv and Shneer, *New Jews*.

11 Aviv and Shneer, *New Jews*, 21.

12 Yoram Hazony, *The Philosophy of Hebrew Scripture: An Introduction* (New York: Cambridge University Press, 2012); Daniel Gordis, *Saving Israel: How the Jewish People Can Win a War That May Never End* (Hoboken, NJ: John Wiley & Sons, 2009); Alan M. Dershowitz, *The Case for Israel* (Hoboken, NJ: John Wiley & Sons, 2003).

13 David Hartman, *Israelis and the Jewish Tradition: An Ancient People Debating Its Future* (New Haven: Yale University Press, 2000). See also, Jonathan W. Malino, *Judaism and Modernity: The Religious Philosophy of David Hartman* (Aldershot: Ashgate, 2004). More recently, see David Novak, "Zionism and Jewish Theology" (lecture, The Tikvah Institute for Jewish Thought, New York, March 10, 2011), as well as its fuller length iteration, *Zionism and Judaism: A New Theory* (New York: Cambridge University Press, 2015).

14 Boyarin and Boyarin, *Powers of Diaspora,* 11.

15 Jonathan Garb, "Contemporary Kabbalah and Classical Kabbalah: Breaks and Continuities," in *After Spirituality: Studies in Mystical Traditions*, vol. 1, ed. P. Wexler & J. Garb (New York: Peter Lang, 2012), 19-46.

16 Robert S. Ellwood, *Mysticism and Religion* (New York: Seven Bridges Press, 1999), 39.

17 Ibid., 46.

18 Ibid., 47.

19 Garb, "Contemporary Kabbalah and Classical Kabbalah: Breaks and Continuities," 19-46.

20 Ellwood, *Mysticism and Religion*, 47-48.

21 Greenstein, *Third Solitude,* 4.

22 Ira Robinson, "The Bouchard-Taylor Commission and the Jewish Community of Quebec in Historical Perspective," in *Religion, Culture and the State: Reflections on the Bouchard-Taylor Report*, ed. Howard Adelman and Pierre Anctil (Toronto: University of Toronto Press, 2011), 61.

23 James R. Horne, "Mysticism Demystified," *Dialogue: Canadian Philosophical Review*, 24.2 (1985): 291-296; Donald Evans, "Mysticism and Morality," *Dialogue: Canadian Philosophical Review*, 24.2 (1985): 297-308; James R. Horne, "Reply to Evans" *Dialogue: Canadian Philosophical Review*, 24.2 (1985), 309-312.

24 R. M. Bucke, *Cosmic Consciousness: A Study in the Evolution of the Human Mind* (New York: E. P Dutton, 1901). In 1880, American poet Walt Whitman spent the summer with Bucke at his home in London, Upper Canada. As one of Whitman's most devoted friends and supporters in the poet's later years, Bucke had a messianic view of the poet and drew on his poetic record to inspire his views on Cosmic Consciousness. See "Richard Maurice Bucke," *The Walt Whitman Archive*, accessed 3/1/13, http://whitmanarchive.org/criticism/disciples/bucke/biography/anc.00247.html.

25 Ann Davis, *The Logic of Ecstasy: Canadian Mystical Painting 1920-1940* (Toronto: University of Toronto, 1992), 42-163; Roald Nasgaard, *The Mystic North:*

Symbolist Landscape Painting in Northern Europe and North America 1890-1940 (Toronto: University of Toronto/AGO, 1984).

26 The original formation of painters from 1911-1913 in Toronto included Franklin Carmichael, Lawrence Harris, A. Y. Jackson, Franz Johnston, Arthur Lismer, Jock E. H. MacDonald, and Fred Varley. The group became a national school joined by Montréal's Edwin Holgate in 1930 and Winnipeg's L. L. Fitzgerald in 1932. See Christopher Varley, *The Canadian Encyclopedia*, s.v. "Group of Seven," last modified 3/4/15, accessed 2/10/13, http://www.thecanadianencyclopedia.com/articles/group-of-seven.

27 Davis, *The Logic of Ecstasy*, x.

28 Ibid., 96-97.

29 In the construction of its own history, the Theosophists cite one of its world leaders, Katherine A. Tingley, as having spent formative time leading up to her mystical illumination in a Roman Catholic Convent in Quebec, see *Theosophy*, vol. 12, Issues 1-7 (New York: Theosophical Society, 1896), 46-47. See also M. Lacombe, "Theosophy and the Canadian Idealist Tradition: A Preliminary Exploration," *Journal of Canadian Studies* 17, no. 2 (1982): 100-118; Samuel E. C. Wagar, "Theosophical Socialists in the 1920s Okanagan: Jack Logie's Social Issues Summer Camps" (master's thesis, Burnaby, Simon Fraser University, 2005).

30 For one exception see Boaz Huss, "The Sufi Society From America: Theosophy and Kabbalah in Poona in the Late Nineteenth Century," in *Kabbalah and Modernity: Interpretations, Transformations, Adaptations*, ed. B. Huss, M. Pasi, and K. Von Stuckard (Leiden: Brill, 2012), 167-193. More recently, see Boaz Huss, "Cosmic Kabbalah: Kabbalah and Western Esotericism in the Writings of Max Theon and his Followers" (Chicago: AJS 44th Annual Conference, 2012).

31 Ira Robinson, "Kabbalist and Communal Leader: Rabbi Yudel Rosenberg and the Canadian Jewish Community," *Canadian Jewish Studies* 1 (1993): 41-58.

32 Ibid., 52-53.

33 Jonathan Garb, "After Spirituality: Introducing the Volume and the Series," in *After Spirituality: Studies in Mystical Traditions* (New York: Peter Lang, 2012), 3.

34 Aubrey L. Glazer, *Mystical Vertigo: Contemporary Kabbalistic Hebrew Poetry; Dancing Over the Divide* (Boston: Academic Studies Press, 2013).

35 Greenstein, *Third Solitude*, 14.

36 The Canadian Jewish thinker most preoccupied with the challenges of exile and redemption remains Emil Fackenheim. See Fackenheim's re-articulation of the theosophy of exile through *shevira* and *tikkun* in Lurianic Kabbalah in

Aubrey L. Glazer, "*Tikkun* in Fackenheim's *Leben-Denken* as a trace of Lurianic Kabbalah," in *Emil L. Fackenheim: Philosopher, Theologian, Jew*, ed. J. A. Diamond, S. Portnoff, and Martin D. Yaffe (Leiden: Brill, 2008), 235-249. Another cogent translation of *shevira* and *tikkun* in Lurianic Kabbalah is found in Gershom Scholem, *Major Trends in Jewish Mysticism* (New York: Schocken Books, 1947), 280. Compare with Scholem's 1917 journal entry: "Better to live eternally in exile and carry my sins alone then to lead a hedonistic life in the land of Israel," as quoted in Eric Jacobson, *Metaphysics of the Profane: the Political Theology of Walter Benjamin and Gershom Scholem* (New York: Columbia University Press, 2003), 62.

37 Rodger Kamenetz, *The Jew in the Lotus: A Poet's Rediscovery of Jewish Identity in Buddhist India* (New York: HarperOne, 2007), 11-12.

38 Nicolas James Mount, *When Canadian Literature Moved to New York* (Toronto: University of Toronto Press, 2005).

39 Dany Laferrière, *Comment faire l'amour avec un negre sans se fatiguer* (Ottawa: Archambault, 2007); Idem, *How to Make Love to a Negro without Getting Tired: A Novel*, trans. David Homel (Vancouver: Douglas & McIntyre, 2010). Laferrière's journey from tanning cowhides in a Montréal factory to becoming a wordsmith, from exile to redemption, remains so compelling because he "understands the lesson of the great Jewish-American writers: you can get to the top with words too."(ibid., 3).

40 While I have relied on this synchronic model in the study by Tom Marshall (*Harsh and Lovely Land: The Major Canadian Poets and the Making of a Canadian Tradition* [Vancouver: University of British Columbia Press, 1979]), I have also added musicians as a category for consideration.

41 "Writing about exile, dislocation, memories of an abandoned homeland, loss of mother tongue—some of the themes found in many migrant texts—reflect to a certain extent the nationalistic preoccupations of native Québecois writers": see Frédéric Royall, *Contemporary French Cultures and Societies*, Modern French Identities 26 (Bern: Peter Lang, 2004), 348.

42 Abraham Segal, "The Relation between Lurianic Kabbalah and Hasidism in the Thought of R. Yishaq of Komarno," in *Kabbalah: A Journal for the Study of Jewish Mystical Texts*, vol. 15ed. Daniel Abrams and Avraham Elqayam (Cherub Press: Los Angeles, 2006), 305-334.

43 For more on this Komarno-Zidichov lineage, see Yitzhak Alfasi, *Torat ha'Hasidut*, vol. 2 (Jerusalem: Mossad haRav Kook, 2009), 267-321. The current Tosher Rebbe's great-grandfather was a disciple of R. Yitzhak Ayzik Yehudah Yehiel

of Komarno (1806–1874). R. Yitzhak Ayzik's disciple was R. Meshulam Feish Segal-Loewy, father of Elimelekh Segal-Loewy, father of Mordechai Segal-Loewy of Demescer, father of the current Tosher Rebbe. R. Yitzhak Ayzik was a disciple of R. Tzvi Hirsh of Zidichov (1763-1831), tracing lineage back as a disciple to the Seer of Lublin (1745-1815). The Seer was a disciple of Rebbe Elimelech Lipman of Lizhensk (1717-1787), who was a disciple of Dov Ber, the Maggid of Mezeritch (1704-1772), the primary disciple of the Ba'al Shem Tov (1698-1760).

44 On the prevalence of Komarno-Zidichov customs integrated into contemporary Tosher spiritual practice, see R. Meshulam Feish Segal-Loewy, "*Minhagai ha'Sabah Kadisha*," in *Zemirot 'Avodat haLevi* (Boisbriand: Kiryas Tosh, 2010), 770-774, wherein a sampling of customs allocates prominence to Komarno-Zidichov at a ratio of 8:5.

45 Rather than using terms like "non-normative" or "antinomian," it is more accurate to use the term "hypernomian," which denotes a devotional mode of fulfilling the law by overflowing its traditional form to reformulate its expression, as shown in the extensive work of Elliot R. Wolfson, "Beyond Good and Evil: Hypernomianism, Transmorality, and Kabbalistic ethics," in *Crossing Boundaries: Essays on the Ethical Status of Mysticism*, ed. G. W. Barnard and J. J. Kripal (New York: Seven Bridges Press, 2002), 103–156.

46 Also spelled as *Tash*, adapted from the Hebrew/Yiddish: טאהש

47 Alfasi, *Ha'Hasidut meDor leDor*, 456, 488.

48 Consistently higher levels of anti-Semitism and ethnocentrism have been documented in Québec than elsewhere in Canada. See Paul M. Sniderman, David A. Northrup, Joseph F. Fletcher, Peter H. Russell, et al., "Psychological and Cultural Foundations of Prejudice: The Case of Anti-Semitism in Québec," *Canadian Review of Sociology and Anthropology* 30.2 (1993): 242-270. Compare with anti-Semitism and ethnocentrism as experienced by American Jews with Afro-Americans in Borough Park as opposed to the rest of New York: see Arnold Eisen, "Limits and Virtues of Dialogue," *Society* 31.6 (September-October 1994): 17-22. See also Saul Brenner, "Patterns of Jewish-Catholic Democratic Voting and the 1960 Presidential Vote," *Jewish Social Studies* 26, no. 3 (1964): 169-178, where Brenner analyzes this correlation between anti-Semitism and ethnocentrism in the Borough Park Jewish community as opposed to the Bay Ridge Irish Catholic community.

49 Robinson, "The Bouchard-Taylor Commission and the Jewish Community of Québec in Historical Perspective," 65-66.

50 R. Yitzchak Isaac Yehuda Yechiel Safrin of Komarno, *Zohar Hai* (Premsyln: R. Hayyim Aaron Zupnik & R. Hayyim Knalled, n.d.) part 4, 184b.

51 Hayyim Yaakov Safrin, *Haikhal Berakhah: Deuteronomy* (Premsyln: R. Hayyim Aaron Zupnik & R. Hayyim Knalled, n.d.), 169a.

52 Idem, *Aseereet ha'Aifa* (Premsyln: R. Hayyim Aaron Zupnik & R. Hayyim Knalled, n.d.), 152b, challenges the *Sifra*'s acceptance of never returning to Israel after its curse of desolation and ruin in Leviticus 26:32.

53 R. Yaakov Moshe of Komarno was constantly acquiring and using only *kippot, tzitzit,* and ritual objects from the Land of Israel: see Hayyim Yaakov Safrin, ed., *Shalsheleth haQodesh* (Bnai Brak: n. p., 2003), 519a.

54 R. Yaakov Moshe of Komarno had a deep desire to immigrate to the Land of Israel near the end of his life but was stopped by his disciples. See Safrin, *Shalsheleth haQodesh,* 528b. Consider, for example, R. Barukh of Komarno, who preferred a life removed from the public rabbinate, rather yearning to immigrate to the Land of Israel (ibid., 559a).

55 Ibid., 575a.

56 William Shaffir, "Hassidic Jews and Québec Politics," *Jewish Journal of Sociology* 25 (1983): 105-118.

57 R. Meshulam Feish Segal-Loewy, *Avodat Avodah, Parshat Kedoshim* (Boisbriand, Quebec: Kiryas Tosh, 5771), 96b.

58 Ibid.

59 Ibid, vol. 2, *28th Sivan,* 176b-177a.

60 Ibid, vol. 1, *Parshat Vayetzeh,* 77a; ibid., *Parshat Vayishlakh,* 84b-85b; ibid., vol. 2, *Parshat Tzav-Shabbat haGadol,* 36a-b.

61 Ibid., vol. 2, *Parshat Tzav-Shabbat haGadol,* 36a-b; ibid., *Parshat Acharai Mot,* 90a-b; idem., "*Galut v'Geulat Mitzrayim,*" in *'Avodat haLevi: Haggadah shel Pesach* (Boisbriand, Quebec: Kiryas Tosh, 2005), 279a-296b (emphasis added).

62 Idem, "*Galut v'Geulat Mitzrayim,*" 284b-287b.

63 Idem, *Avodat Avodah,* vol. 1, *Parshat Vayishlakh,* 83a-b; idem, "*Galut v'Geulat Mitzrayim,*" 286b.

64 Idem, *Avodat Avodah,* vol. 1, *Parshat Vayigash,* 144a, 146a-b.

65 Ibid., vol. 2, *Parshat VaYikrah,* 11a-b; compare with similar claims about the exile of the soul and divine portions through improper eating habits: see ibid., vol. 1, *Parshat Hayyai Sarah,* 5oa; ibid., vol. 1, *Parshat Vayetzai,* 77a-b; ibid., vol. 2, *Parshat Shemini,* 52a, 55b; ibid., vol. 2, *Parshat Tzav-Parah,* 23a; ibid., vol. 2, *Parshat Shemini,* 52a, 55b.

66 Ibid., vol. 1, *Parshat Vaera,* 180a-b; ibid., *Parshat Bo,* 185a-b; ibid., *Parshat Ki Tissa,* 279a-b; ibid., vol. 2, *Parshat Shelakh,* 185b-186b.

67 Ibid., vol. 2, *Parshat Nitzavim,* 313b.

68 Ibid., vol. 1, *Parshat Vayakhel,* 282a, 284a-b.

69 Ezrahi, *Booking Passage,* 13.

70 Lewis and Shaffir, "Tosh, Between Earth and Moon: A Hasidic Rebbe's Followersand His Teachings," 147-150.

71 Segal-Loewy, "*Galut v'Geulat Mitzrayim,*" 286b-287b.

72 Ibid., 286b.

73 Segal-Loewy, *Avodat Avodah,* vol. 1, *Parshat Bereshith,* 12b.

74 Ibid., vol. 1, *Parshat Vayishlakh,* 89b; ibid., vol. 1, *Tu B'Shevat,* 209a.

75 Ibid., vol. 1, *Parshat Shemot,* 169a.

76 "Asked directly about the books, the Toshers we spoke with agreed that they accurately represent the Rebbe's approach to spiritual life—except that some of his most demanding teachings were left out because they were seen as being addressed only to an earlier, spiritually stronger generation," see Justin Lewis and William Shaffir, "Tosh, Between Earth and Moon: A Hasidic Rebbe's Followers and His Teachings," in *From Antiquity to the Post-Modern World: Contemporary Jewish Studies in Canada,* ed. Daniel Maoz and Andrea Gondos [Newcastle Upon Tyne: Cambridge Scholars Publishing, 2011], 137-169, esp. 149.

77 Segal-Loewy, "*Galut v'Geulat Mitzrayim,*" 286b.

78 Ibid., 287a-b.

79 Lewis and Shaffir, "Tosh, Between Earth and Moon: A Hasidic Rebbe's Followers and His Teachings," 147-150.

80 Ibid., 149.

81 Segal-Loewy, *Avodat Avodah,* vol. 2, *Parshat Shemini,* 52a.

82 See above.

83 For more on the poet Leonard Cohen as a pop-saint in his own self-imposed sainthood, see Michael Ondaatje, *Leonard Cohen: Canadian Writers Number 5* (Toronto: McClelland and Stewart Limited, 1970), 61; compare to the more recent Alan Light, *The Holy or the Broken: Leonard Cohen, Jeff Buckley, and the Unlikely Ascent of Hallelujah* (New York: Atria Books, 2012). Montréal is recognizing Leonard Cohen as a pop saint of the city with an exhibition dedicated to and featuring his life's work at the Musée d'art contemporain de Montréal for the city's celebration of its 375th anniversary, see http://www.macm.org/en/expositions/leonard-cohen/ accessed 9/11/16.

84 Leonard Cohen, "Un Canadien Errant," in *Recent Songs* (New York: Sony Music, 1988).

85 Sylvie Simmons, *I'm Your Man: The Life of Leonard Cohen* (New York: Harper Collins, 2012), 319-320, accessed 12/25/14, http://www.nytimes.com/2014/08/05/us/joshu-sasaki-a-zen-master-tarnished-by-abuse-claims-dies-at-107.html?_r=0. Joshu Sasaki Roshi's chronology: born in 1907; ordained a monk in 1921; and ordained a priest in 1947; ordained as Roshi and appointed abbot of Yotoku-in, monastery of Zuigan-ji, 1947; Abbot of Shoju-an, 1953; came to America, 1962; founded Cimarron Zen Center, 1968; Mount Baldy Zen Center, 1971; Jemez Bodhi Mandala, 1973; Mount Cobb Sai Sho Zen Ji, 1988, see Yoshin David Radin, ed., *The Great Celebration: A Commemorative Album Published on the Occasion of Joshu Sasaki Roshi's 85th Birthday and 30th Year Teaching Zen in America* (Los Angeles: Rinzai-ji, 1992), 10.

86 Ibid., 325.

87 Michael Harris, "An Interview with Leonard Cohen," *Duel* (1969): 99-100.

88 Hydra small notebook, Leonard Cohen Archive, MS 122: Box 8b, n.d.

89 Sylvie Simmons, *I'm Your Man*, 72.

90 Ibid., 37.

91 Graphic #70, Leonard Cohen Archive, MS 500: Box 74, 2003-2005.

92 Ibid., 37.

93 Ibid., 113-114.

94 Ibid., 122.

95 Ibid.

96 Elliot R. Wolfson, "New Jerusalem Glowing: Songs and Poems of Leonard Cohen in a Kabbalistic Key," *Kabbalah: Journal for the Study of Jewish Mystical Texts* 15 (2006): 103-153.

97 Ibid., 109.

98 Ibid., 124-126.

99 Simmons, *I'm Your Man,* 262-263.

100 Ibid., 105.

101 Ondaatje, *Leonard Cohen,* 61.

102 See Tom Marshall, "A History of Us All: Leonard Cohen," in *Harsh and Lovely Land: The Major Canadian Poets and the Making of a Canadian Tradition*, 142.

103 Graphic #3, Leonard Cohen Archive, MS 500: Box 73, 2003-2005.

104 Leonard Cohen, "Not a Jew,"in *Book of Longing* (Toronto: McClelland & Stuart, 2006), 158.

105 Simmons, *I'm Your Man,* 316.

106 Ibid., 323.

107 Ibid., 186: "Late into the night, says Sanfield, he told me a long version of the tale of Sabbatai Sevi, the false Messiah. I said, 'Why did you tell me that?' He said, 'Well, I just thought you should hear it.' I think it was because I was talking in such superlative praise of my Roshi. Leonard was suspicious of holy men."

108 Wolfson, "New Jerusalem Glowing," 111-122.

109 Radin, *The Great Celebration,* 6.

110 Letter from Neal Donner, Cimarron scholar-in-residence, to Leonard Cohen, Oct. 30, 1978, Leonard Cohen Archive, MS 500: Box 64, 1.

111 Letter from Neal Donner, Cimarron scholar-in-residence, to Leonard Cohen, Oct. 30, 1978, Leonard Cohen Archive, MS 500: Box 64, 2.

112 Radin, *The Great Celebration,* 13.

113 *Lotus Sutra* (1-14), *Heart Sutra* (15-16), *Dharani of Removing Disaster, Dharani of the Great Compassionate One* (17-19), *Dai Segaki* (20-21), *National Teacher Kozen Daito* (22-23), *The Four Great Vows* (24), in *The Rinzai-Ji Daily Sutras* (*n.d., n.p.* included with *Mt. Baldy Zen Center Newsletter,* 1975, Leonard Cohen Archive, Box 64).

114 Radin, *The Great Celebration,* 15-16.

115 "Untitled poem," written on three *Takanawa Prince Hotel Bar* napkins, 03/20/96, Leonard Cohen Archive, MS 500, Box 64. Twenty seven angels appear also in "Tower of Song".

116 Graphic #14, Leonard Cohen Archive, MS 500, Box 64.

117 Leonard Cohen, "Isaiah," in *Stranger Music: Selected Poems and Songs* (New York: Pantheon, 1993), 40.

118 Simmons, *I'm Your Man,* 272.

119 Ibid., 272-273.

120 Leonard Cohen, "Lover Lover Lover," on *New Skin for the Old Ceremony* (released August 11, 1974).

121 Simmons, *I'm Your Man,* 273-274.

122 Ibid., 275: "[I]n traveling to these combat zones [of Israel and Ethiopia], Leonard was avoiding the war that awaited him at home with Suzanne. He was weary, though and ready to make peace. He had seen too much blood and death and hatred in Israel. He felt he should go back and tend this little garden whose seed he had planted and see if somehow he could make a success of family life. But first he went to the monastery to sit in retreat with Roshi. When he finally went home to Suzanne and Adam at the end of the year, peace reigned in the cottage

in Montreal, long enough for Suzanne to become pregnant with their second child [Lorca]."

123 Leonard Cohen, "The Politics of this Book," in *Stranger Music: Selected Poems and Songs* (New York: Pantheon, 1993), 291 (emphasis added).

124 Terry Gross, "Leonard Cohen: Zen And The Art Of Songwriting," NPR, April 03, 2009, accessed 2/7/13, http://www.npr.org/templates/transcript/transcript.php?storyId=102692227 (emphasis added).

125 Ibid.

126 Ibid.: "I wasn't looking for anything exalted or spiritual. I had a great sense of disorder in my life, of chaos, of depression, of distress, and I had no idea where this came from, and the prevailing psychoanalytic explanations at the time didn't seem to address the things I felt. . . So I had to look elsewhere, and I bumped into someone [Zen master Roshi] who seemed to be at ease with himself. It seems a simple thing to say, he seemed to be at ease with himself and at ease with others. And without ever deeply studying at the time what he was speaking about, it was the man himself that attracted me."

127 Leonard Cohen, "I Have Not Lingered in European Monasteries," in *Stranger Music: Selected Poems and Songs* (New York: Pantheon, 1993), 18.

128 Wolfson, "New Jerusalem Glowing," 109.

129 Simmons, *I'm Your Man,* 81-82: "The ritual routine and sparsity of this life [on Hydra] satisfied him immensely. It felt monastic somehow, except this was a monk with benefits; the Hydra arts colony had beaten the hippies to free love by half a decade. Leonard was also a monk who observed the Sabbath. On Friday nights he would light the candles and on Saturday, instead of working, he would put on his white suit and go down to the port to have coffee.

130 Isaiah 56:4.

131 Simmons, *I'm Your Man,* 288.

132 Ibid., 104: "Leonard continued to fast, as he had in Montréal. The discipline of a week of fasting appealed to him, as did the spiritual element of purging and purification and the altered mental state it produced. Fasting focused his mind for writing, but there was vanity in it also; it kept his body thin and his face gaunt and serious (although the amphetamines helped with that too). There seemed to be a deep need in Leonard for self-abnegation, self-control and hunger . . . Leonard abstained from eating meat, but he was less restrained when it came to his appetite 'for the company of women and the sexual expression of friendship.'"

133 Leonard Cohen, *Beautiful Losers* (Toronto: McClelland & Stewart, 1966).

134 Greenstein, *Third Solitude,* 119.

135 Michael Greenstein, *Contemporary Jewish Writing in Canada: An Anthology* (Lincoln: University of Nebraska Press, 2004), xxiv-xxv.

136 Ibid., xxv.

137 Simmons, *I'm Your Man,* 132-133.

138 Gross, "Leonard Cohen: Zen And The Art Of Songwriting."

139 Leonard Cohen, "The Street," *The New Yorker,* March 2, 2009.

140 Graphic #3, Leonard Cohen Archive, MS 500: Box 73, Montreal, 2003.

141 Graphic #39, Leonard Cohen Archive, MS 500, Box 73, January 1, 2004.

142 Elliot R. Wolfson, "Walking as a Sacred Duty: Theological Transformation of Social Reality in Early Hasidism," in *Along the Path: Studies in Kabbalistic Myth* (New York: SUNY Press, 1995), 89-109.

143 Gross, "Leonard Cohen: Zen And The Art Of Songwriting."

144 Leonard Cohen, "Moving into a Period," in *Book of Longing* (Toronto: McClelland & Stuart, 2006), 34.

145 Leonard Cohen, "Fragment from a Journal," in *Stranger Music: Selected Poems and Songs* (New York: Pantheon, 1993), 386.

146 Idem, "Chelsea Hotel," in ibid., 197.

147 Idem, "Dance Me to the End of Love," in ibid., 337.

148 Hydra small notebook, Leonard Cohen Archive, MS 122: Box 8b, n.d.

149 Idem, "By the Rivers Dark," in *Ten New Songs* (New York: Columbia, 2001).

150 Specifically, see Psalm 137:

> By the rivers of Babylon, there we sat, yea, sat and wept, as we remembered Zion. There on the poplars/we hung our lyres,/for our captors asked us for songs, our tormentors, for amusement,/"Sing us one of the songs of Zion."/How can we sing a song of YHVH on alien soil? If I forget you, O Jerusalem,/let my right hand wither;/if I cease to think of you,/if I do not keep Jerusalem in memory/even at my happiest hour . . .

151 Hydra small notebooks, Stratford, CT, Leonard Cohen Archive, MS 122: Box 8b: August 19, 1959.

152 Ezrahi, *Booking Passage,* 9.

153 Ibid., 9.

154 Leonard Cohen, "The Politics of this Book," 291.

155 Nathan Jeffay, "'*Hallelujah*' in Tel Aviv: Leonard Cohen Energizes Diverse Crowd," *Forward,* September 25, 2009, accessed 2/7/13, http://forward.com/articles/115181/hallelujah-in-tel-aviv-leonard-cohen-energizes-di/#ixzz2KLI8BboN: "Even that wasn't the last that concert-goers saw of Leonard Cohen. On the way out of the stadium, there were *Leonard Cohens*

everywhere. Next to the shopping carts purloined from supermarkets by street sellers using them to sell hot bagels was a stall offering black fedora hats, Cohen's trademark. It sold hundreds, and so Leonard Cohen has left behind a different Israel [than] the one that greeted him. Today, you don't have to be *Haredi* to wear a black hat."

156 I am indebted to Wolfson for his usage of "hypernomian" to describe a mystical state whereby a coincidence of opposites allows for a transgression of the boundary of each category. See Elliot R. Wolfson, *Venturing Beyond: Law and Morality in Kabbalistic Mysticism* (New York: Oxford University Press, 2006).

157 See above.

158 H. Bannerji, "On the Dark Side of the Nation: Politics of Multiculturalism and the State of Canada," *Journal of Canadian Studies* 31, no. 3 (1996): 103-128; Danielle Juteau, Marie McAndrew, and Linda Pietrantonio, "Multiculturalism à la Canadian and Intégration à la Québécoise: Transcending Their Limits," *Public Policy and Social Welfare* 23 (1998): 95-110. On the influence of multiculturalism to "reinforce group loyalty and to provide an outlet for the energies of talented Jews to the benefit of those individuals, of the Jewish community, and of the Canadian people at large," see Michael Brown, "Canadian Jews and Multiculturalism: Myths and Realities," *Jewish Political Studies Review* 19, no. 3-4 (2007): 57-75, accessed 04/24/13, http://jcpa.org/article/canadian-jews-and-multiculturalism-myths-and-realities/?print=1.

3. From Darkness, a Love of All This: Seeking the Sacred in Post-Secular Song

1 Osho, *A Bird on the Wind. Zen Anecdotes for Everyday Life*, n.p. 2013, n.p.

2 Vincent Shen Oral teaching (University of Toronto, 2003).

3 On the spiritual quest of jazz in general, see Ingrid Monson, "Oh Freedom: George Russell, John Coltrane, and Modal Jazz," in *The Course of Performance: Studies in the World of Musical Improvisation*, ed. B. Netti and M. Russell (Chicago: University of Chicago Press, 1998), 149-168; Brian Dorsey, *Spirituality, Sensuality, Literality: Blues, Jazz, and Rap as Music and Poetry*, vol. 86, (Lafayette, IN: Purdue University Press, 2000); William Dean, *The American Spiritual Culture and the Invention of Jazz, Football, and the Movies* (New York: Bloomsbury, 2006). On the fusion of jazz and *klezmer* and the search

for illumination through Radical Jewish culture, see David Moscowitz, "Does 'Radical Jewish Culture' Produce Radical Jewish Rhetoric?" *Studies in American Jewish Literature* (2002): 162-171; Mark Slobin, "The Neo-Klezmer Movement and Euro-American Musical Revivalism," *The Journal of American Folklore* 97, no. 383 (1984): 98-104. For the view of critical theory on jazz as fetish, see Theodor W. Adorno, "On Jazz," *Discourse* 12.1, translatd by Jamie Owen Daniel, Center for Twentieth Century Studies (Milwaukee, Bloomington, IN, and Detroit: University of Wisconsin, Indiana University Press, and Wayne State University Press, 1989), 45-69.

4 Specifically, regarding the Beatles and their immersion in Transcendental Meditation through the Maharishi, see Paul Saltzman, *The Beatles in Rishikesh* (New York: Viking Press, 2001); Geoffrey Giuliano and Avalon Giuliano, *Revolver: The Secret History of the Beatles* (London: John Blake, 2005); Phillip Goldberg, *American Veda: From Emerson and the Beatles to Yoga and Meditation, How Indian Spirituality Changed the West* (New York: Doubleday Religious Publishing Group, 2010); more generally, see Camille Paglia, "Cults and Cosmic Consciousness: Religious Visions in the American 1960s," *Arion Austin then Boston* 10 (2003): 57-112, esp. 76.

5 Clinton Heylin, *Bob Dylan: Behind the Shades Revisited* (New York: HarperCollins, 2010), 78.

6 Louis Kaplan, "*Yahweh Rastafari*! Matisyahu and the Aporias of Hasidic Reggae Superstardom," *CR: The New Centennial Review* 7, no. 1 (2007): 15-44.

7 Jerry Adler, "In Search of the Spiritual," *Newsweek* 146 (2005): 46-64. See also, Jody Myers, "The Kabbalah Centre and Contemporary Spirituality," *Religion Compass* 2, no. 3 (2008): 409-420; idem, *Kabbalah and the Spiritual Quest: The Kabbalah Centre in America* (Westport, CT: Praeger Publishers, 2007).

8 See for example, Fredric Jameson, "Postmodernism, or the Cultural Logic of Late Capitalism," *Studies 29* (1984): 54; Slavoj Žižek, *Absolute Recoil: Towards a New Foundation of Dialectical Materialism* (New York: Verso, 2014), esp. 142-154, 245-281; Boaz Huss, "The New Age of Kabbalah: Contemporary Kabbalah, The New Age and Postmodern Spirituality," *Journal of Modern Jewish Studies* 6, no. 2 (2007): 107-125. On the expression "spiritual window shoppers," see Jalāl, al-Dīn Rumi, and E. H. Whinfield, *Masnavi I Ma'navi: Teachings of Rumi; The Spiritual Couplets of Mauláne Jalálu-'d-Dín Muhammad I Rúmí* (London: Octagon Press, 1994), *Mathnawi* VI, 831-845.

9 Jeffrey J. Kripal, *Esalen: America and the Religion of No Religion* (Chicago: University of Chicago Press, 2007).

10 Simmons, *I'm Your Man.*

11 Jurgen Habermas, "A Reply," in *An Awareness of What Is Missing: Faith and Reason in a Post-Secular Age*, ed. N. Brieskorn, Jurgen Habermas, Michael Reder, Joseph Schmidt, and Ciaran Cronin (Cambridge: Polity, 2010), 425-427.

12 S. A. Simpson and E. S. C. Weirer, ed., *The Oxford English Dictionary*, s. v. Enlightenment (Oxford: Clerendon Press, 1989).

13 James Schmidt, "What Enlightenment Was, What it Still Might Be, and Why Karl May Have Been Right After All," *American Behavioral Scientist*, Volume 49, 5: 647-663.

14 Ibid., 652.

15 Ibid.

16 Ba'al Shem Tov, *Ha Shalem* (Kehot Publications, 2004), 3:7-8

17 To trace the history of misreading Adorno's philosophical pronouncement on post-Auschwitz aesthetics, is it necessary to re-examine the following evolving iterations by the thinker himself see:

(1) *Prismen* (Berlin: Suhrkamp Verlag, 1955), vol. 10a, 30: *Kulturkritik findet sich der letzten Stufe der Dialektik von Kultur und Barbarei gegenüber: Nach Auschwitz ein Gedicht zu schreiben, ist barbarisch, und das frißt auch die Erkenntnis an, die ausspricht, warum es unmöglich ward, heute Gedichte zu schreiben.*

(2) *Negative Dialektik* (Frankfurt am Main: Suhrkamp, 1966), 06, 355/356: *Das perennierende Leiden hat soviel Recht auf Ausdruck wie der Gemarterte zu brüllen; Darum mag falsch gewesen sein, nach Auschwitz ließe kein Gedicht mehr sich schreiben. Nicht falsch aber ist die minder kulturelle Frage, ob nach Auschwitz noch sich leben lasse, ob vollends es dürfe, wer zufällig entrann und rechtens hätte umgebracht werden müssen.*

(3) *Ohne Leitbild. Parva aesthetica* (Frankfurt am Main; Suhrkamp, 1967), 10a, 452/453: *Weniger stets verträgt jener Schein sich mit dem Prinzip rationaler Materialbeherrschung, dem er die gesamte Geschichte von Kunst hindurch sich verband. Während die Situation Kunst nicht mehr zuläßt - darauf zielte der Satz über die Unmöglichkeit von Gedichten nach Auschwitz, bedarf sie doch ihrer. Denn die bilderlose Realität das vollendete Widerspiel des bilderlosen Zustands geworden, in dem Kunst verschwände, weil die Utopie sich erfüllt hätte, die in jedem Kunstwerk sich chiffriert.*

(4) *Noten zur Literatur IV* (Frankfurt am Main: Suhrkamp, 1968), vol. 11, 603: *Der Satz, nach Auschwitz lasse kein Gedicht mehr sich schreiben, gilt nicht*

blank, gewiß aber, daß danach, weil es möglich war und bis ins Unabsehbare möglich bleibt, keine heitere Kunst mehr vorgestellt werden kann.

18 Aubrey L. Glazer, *A New Physiognomy of Jewish Thinking: Critical Theory after Adorno as Applied to Jewish Thought* (London: Continuum, 2011).

19 Aaron W. Hughes and Elliot R. Wolfson, "Charting an Alternative Course for the Study of Jewish Philosophy," *New Directions in Jewish Philosophy* (Bloomington: Indiana University Press, 2009), 1. Despite the appearance of recent landmark philosophical studies, like Steven Schwarzschild's *The Pursuit of an Ideal* (New York: SUNY Press, 1990) and Menahēm Kellner's *Must a Jew Believe Anything* (London: Littman Library of Jewish Civilization, 2006), the territory remains remarkably bereft of strong thinking.

20 Hughes and Wolfson, "Charting an Alternative Course for the Study of Jewish Philosophy," 2. One notable exception is the willingness of Fishbane to explore his own Jewish theology as a way of life (despite its apologetic lapses); see Michael Fishbane, *Sacred Attunement: A Jewish Theology* (Chicago: University of Chicago Press, 2008).

21 Hughes and Wolfson, "Charting An Alternative Course for the Study of Jewish Philosophy," 13.

22 Ibid., 14-15.

23 Ibid., 8.

24 Elliot R. Wolfson, *Aleph, Mem, Tau: Kabbalistic Musings on Time, Truth and Death* (Berkeley: University of California Press, 2006).

25 Idem, "Light Does Not Talk but Shines: Apophasis and Vision in Rosenzweig's Theopoetic Temporality," in *New Directions in Jewish Philosophy*, 146n211.

26 Ibid., 123.

27 Hughes and Wolfson, "Charting an Alternative Course for the Study of Jewish Philosophy," 10-11.

28 Ibid., 12.

29 Adorno, "Introduction," in Negative Dialectics, trans. E. B. Ashton (New York: Continuum, 1973), 3-37 [Negative Dialektik (Frankfurt: Suhrkamp, 1966), 3-57]. I have also consulted with the 2001 revised translation of Dennis Redmond; see http://www.efn.org/~dredmond/ndtrans.html (accessed 7/15/15).

30 Axel Honneth, "Pathologies of Reason," in *Pathologies of Reason: On the Legacy of Critical Theory* (New York: Columbia University Press, 2009), 72.

31 Ibid., 75.

32 Ibid.

33 Adorno, *Negative Dialectics*, 35 [57].

34 Slavoj Žižek, *Absolute Recoil*, 4, 148.

35 Ibid., 4.

36 Ibid., 5.

37 Harold Bloom, *Anxiety of Influence* (New York: Oxford University Press, 1997).

38 It is curious that Žižek bases his reading of Lurianic Kabbalah on *Sparknotes* and Bloom bases his reading on Gershom Scholem. Why it is that each thinker is unable to access these cosmogonic myths in the original, and yet recovers it through second- and thirdhand readings is beyond the scope of this investigation but is worthwhile to consider in the post-secular context.

39 Žižek, *Absolute Recoil*, 143.

40 Ibid., 148.

41 Ibid., 245.

42 Friedrich Wilhelm Nietzsche, *The Birth of Tragedy and the Genealogy of Morals* (1872), ed. and trans. Walter Kaufmann (New York: Modern Library, 1967), vol. 81, XX.

43 Žižek, *Absolute Recoil*, 253.

44 Ibid., 260.

45 Ibid., 262.

46 Ibid., 267.

47 Ibid., 275.

48 Arthur Green, "The *Żaddiq* as *Axis Mundi* in Later Judaism," *Journal of the American Academy of Religion* 45, no. 3 (1977): 327-347; Elliot R. Wolfson, "Walking as a Sacred Duty: Theological Transformation of Social Reality in Early Hasidism," *Along the Path: Studies in Kabbalistic Myth, Symbolism, and Hermeneutics* (New York: SUNY Publications, 1995), 89-110.

49 See Shigenori Nagatomo, "Japanese Zen Buddhist Philosophy," in *Stanford Encyclopedia of Philosophy*, accessed 1/6/14, http://plato.stanford.edu/entries/japanese-zen/.

50 Graphic #21, Leonard Cohen Archive, MS 500: Box 73, December 23, 2003.

51 Nagatomo, "Japanese Zen Buddhist Philosophy."

52 Shunryu Suzuki, *Not Always So: Practicing the True Spirit of Zen* (New York: HarperOne, 2003); G. Victor Sogen Hori, "Teaching and Learning in the Rinzai Zen Monastery," *Journal of Japanese Studies* (1994): 5-35.

53 Nyogen Senzaki, Sōen Nakagawa, and Eidō Shimano, *Namu Dai Bosa: A Transmission of Zen Buddhism to America* (New York: Theatre Arts Books, 1976).

54 Hakuyū Taizan Maezumi and Bernard Tetsugen Glassman, eds., *On Zen Practice II*, vol. 2 (Los Angeles: Zen Center of Los Angeles, 1976); Henry C. Finney, "American Zen's 'Japan Connection': A Critical Case Study of Zen Buddhism's Diffusion to the West," *Sociology of Religion* 52, no. 4 (1991): 379-396.

55 Joshu Sasaki, *Buddha Is the Center of Gravity* (Questa, NM: Lama Foundation, 1974).

56 Michael Downing, *Shoes Outside the Door* (Berkeley: Counterpoint, 2001), which describes the sex scandals at the San Francisco Zen Center, once Suzuki handed off leadership to Richard Baker. Regarding these allegations about "Sasaki's routine, widespread, seemingly compulsive, sexual contact with women students," see "Letter from Kim Krull (Spokane, Washington) to Buddhist America," Leonard Cohen Archive, MS 500: Box 64, 1992-1994.

57 Mark Oppenheimer, "Joshu Sasaki, Rinzai Zen Master, Dies at 107: The Influential Teacher Leaves a Mixed Legacy," accessed 1/6/14, http://tricycle.org/trikedaily/joshu-sasaki-roshi-rinzai-zen-master-dies-107/.

58 Leonard Cohen was ordained and became known as Jikan Eliezer Leonard Cohen after the *Dai-sesshin* on August 9, 1996; see *Mount Baldy Zen Center Newsletter*, Issue 7 (Winter 1997), Leonard Cohen Archive, MS 500: Box 64.

59 Nagatomo, "Japanese Zen Buddhist Philosophy."

60 Ibid.

61 Elliot R. Wolfson, "Beyond Good and Evil: Hypernomian Transmorality and Delimiting the Limit," in *Venturing Beyond: Law and Morality in Kabbalistic Mysticism* (Oxford: Oxford University Press, 2006), 186-286; idem, *Luminal Darkness: Imaginal Gleanings From Zoharic Literature* (London: Oneworld Publications Limited, 2007).

62 Leonard Cohen, "Love Calls You by Your Name," in *Songs of Love and Hate* (New York: Sony Music, 1961).

63 Idem, "Ballad of the Absent Mare," *Recent Songs* (September 27, 1979).

64 Idem, "That Don't Make It Junk," *Ten New Songs* (October 9, 2001).

65 Gershom Scholem, "*Shekhinah*: The Feminine Element in Divinity," *On the Mystical Shape of the Godhead: Basic Concepts in the Kabbalah*, foreword by Joseph Dan, trans. Joachim Neugroschel, ed. Jonathan Chipman (New York: Schocken Books, 1991): 140-196; Elliot R. Wolfson, "Occultation of the Feminine and the Body of Secrecy in Medieval Kabbalah," in *Rending the Veil: Concealment and Secrecy in the History of Religions* (New York: Seven Bridges Press, 1999), 113-154; Eric Murphy Selinger, "*Shekhinah* in America," in *Jewish American Poetry: Poems, Commentary, and Reflections*, ed. Jonathan Barron and

Eric Murphy Selinger (Lebanon, NH: University Press of New England, 2000), 250-271.

66 Leonard Cohen, "Lady Midnight," in *Songs from a Room* (New York: Columbia, 1969).

67 Idem, "The Gypsy Wife," in *Recent Songs* (New York: Sony Music, 1988).

68 Idem, "Darkness," in *Old Ideas* (New York: Sony Music, 2012).

69 Ibid.

70 Ibid.

71 Ibid.

72 Isaiah 45:7.

73 Leonard Cohen, "Here It Is," in *Ten New Songs* (New York: Columbia, 2001).

74 Ibid.

75 Ibid.

76 Ibid.

77 Ibid.

78 Ibid.

79 Ibid

80 Donald C. Babcock, "Little Duck," *The New Yorker* 23, no. 33 (October 4, 1947): 38-39. Special thanks to Sheila Peltz-Weinberg for meditating through this poem with me on retreat at Brandeis-Bardein (2014).

81 Leonard Cohen, "Here It Is," in *Ten New Songs* (New York: Columbia, 2001).

82 Idem, "Anthem."

83 I am indebted here to the Piacezener rebbe, whose final homily in the Warsaw Ghetto ended with these words in 1942: "*Es zol zich zingen a shira*"—"So shall the song sing itself." See R. Kalonymous Kalman Shapira, *Esh Kodesh, BeShalakh* 1942 (Jerusalem: Va'ad Hasidai Piacezener, 1990), 154.

4. Tangle of Matter & Ghost: Objective Spirit & Non-Dual Reality in Prayerful Poetry

1 Leonard Cohen, "The Window," in *Recent Songs* (New York: Sony Music, 1988).

2 Friedrich Nietzsche, "Maxims and Barbs," in *Twilight of the Idols,* in *The Portable Nietzsche,* ed. Walter Kaufmann (New York: Viking Press, 1954), 33.

3 Friedrich Nietzsche, *The Birth of Tragedy*, in *Basic Writings of Nietzsche*, ed. and trans. Walter Kaufmann (New York: Modern Library, 1967), 4, 8.

4 Ibid., 1, 5.

5 Ibid., 5. See also Christoph Cox, "Nietzsche, Dionysus, and the Ontology of Music," in *A Companion to Nietzsche*, ed. Keith Ansell Pearson (London: Blackwell Publishing Ltd., 2006), 497.

6 Cox, "Nietzsche, Dionysus, and the Ontology of Music," 497.

7 Charles Taylor, *Hegel* (Cambridge: Cambridge University Press, 1975).

8 Idem, *Sources of the Self: The Making of the Modern Identity* (Cambridge, MA: Harvard University Press, 1989), viii, emphasis added.

9 See above, chapter 2 p.247 n6.

10 See Taylor, *Sources of the Self*, 22. There are over seventy-five references to "spirit" in *Sources of the Self* alone.

11 Rabbi Daniel Wolf, "*Machshevet Yisrael*—Survival or Endurance?" *ATID* (2008): 7 http://www.atid.org/journal/my/docs/wolf5768.pdf.

12 Ibid., 3.

13 Ibid., 24.

14 For one of the earliest iterations of this conceptual triad of God-Torah-Israel, see Zohar III: 73a.

15 Elliot R. Wolfson, *Alef-Mem-Tau: Kabbalistic Musings on Time, Truth, and Death* (Berkeley: University of California Press, 2006).

16 Art Green, *Radical Judaism: Hasidism for a New Era* (New Haven: Yale University Press, 2010).

17 Shaul Magid, "Is 'Radical Theology' Radical?" *Tikkun* 25, no. 2 (March-April 2010): 52; compare with Magid's critique of Green's reticence to enter into a robust *cosmotheism* in idem, *American Post-Judaism: Identity and Renewal in a Postethnic Society* (Bloomington: Indiana University Press, 2013), 88-89, 98-101, 102, 104-105, 109.

18 Taylor, *Sources of the Self*, 107.

19 Ibid., 159.

20 Ibid., 178.

21 Hegel, *Phenomenology of the Spirit*, Part B: no. 207, 208, 216, esp. 218: "The *unhappy consciousness*, however, finds itself merely desiring and toiling; it is not consciously and directly aware that so to find itself rests upon the inner certainty of its self, and that its feeling of real being is this self-feeling. Since it does not in its own view have that certainty, its inner life really remains still a shattered certainty of itself; that confirmation of its own existence, which it would receive through work and enjoyment, is, therefore, just as tottering and insecure; in other words, it must consciously nullify this certification of its own being, so as

to find therein confirmation indeed, but confirmation only of what it is *for itself*, viz. of its disunion."

22 Paul Redding, "Georg Wilhem Friedrich Hegel," in *Stanford Encyclopedia of Philosophy*, accessed 1/18/15, http://plato.stanford.edu/entries/hegel/.

23 Taylor, *Hegel*, esp. 41, 43, 138, 167, 171, 172.

24 Vincent Descombes, "Is There an Objective Spirit?" in *Philosophy in an Age of Pluralism: The Philosophy of Charles Taylor in Question*, ed. Charles Taylor, James Tully, and Daniel M. Weinstock (Cambridge: Cambridge University Press, 1994), 96-118.

25 ibid Barbara C. Scholz, Francis Jeffry Pelletier, and Geoffrey K. Pullum, "Philosophy of Linguistics," in *Stanford Encyclopedia of Philosophy*, accessed 1/18/15, http://plato.stanford.edu/entries/linguistics/.

26 Descombes, "Is There an Objective Spirit?," 116.

27 Ibid., 117.

28 Ibid.

29 Ibid., 118.

30 David E. Cartwright, "Failure in Berlin," in *Schopenhauer: A Biography* (New York: Cambridge University Press, 2010), 378-379.

31 Ibid., 378.

32 Ibid.

33 Arthur Schopenhauer, *The World as Will and Idea*, vol. 1 [114], 131. Project Gutenberg, accessed 1/19/15, http://www.gutenberg.org/files/38427/38427-pdf.pdf.

34 Ibid.

35 Glazer, *A New Physiognomy of Jewish Thinking*, esp. 45-57, 135-146.

36 Schopenhauer, *The World as Will and Idea*, [339], 341.

37 Ibid.

38 Ibid., [339], 342.

39 Ibid., [341], 343.

40 Ibid., [500], 495. Schopenhauer's Christological focus assumes that a universal mysticism emerges from seeing the *New Testament* as primarily an esoteric text, in contradistinction and perhaps in reaction to the exoteric text of the Hebrew Bible. This assumption does not contemplate the esoteric layers within the exoteric text of the *TaNaKh*, which has recently been challenged. See Alex S. Kohav, *The Sod Hypothesis: Phenomenological, Semiotic, Cognitive, and Noetic-Literary Recovery of the Pentateuch's Embedded Inner-Core Mystical Initiation*

Tradition of Ancient Israelite Cultic Religion (PhD thesis, Cincinatti, OH, Union Institute and University, 2011).

41 Schopenhauer, *The World as Will and Idea*, [501], 496.

42 Leonard Cohen, "If It Be Your Will," in *Various Positions* (New York: Sony Music, 1995).

43 Parker J. Palmer, *Let Your Life Speak: Listening for the Voice of Vocation* (San Francisco: Jossey-Bass, 2000), 4.

44 m*Avot* 2:4.

45 On this spiritual process of "truing" religion, see John C. Meagher, *The Truing of Christianity: Visions of Life and Thought for the Future* (New York: Doubleday, 1990).

46 *Hineini*, trans. Rabbi Jeremy Gordon, accessed 1/28,15, http://rabbionanarrowbridge.blogspot.com/2013/08/a-new-translation-of-rosh-hashanah.html.

47 For his riff on another high holiday liturgical poem, called *Netane Tokef*, see Leonard Cohen, "Who by Fire," in *New Skin for the Old Ceremony* (New York: Sony Music, 1974).

48 Leonard Cohen, "If It Be Your Will," in *Various Positions* (New York: Sony Music, 1995).

49 Schopenhauer, *The World as Will and Idea*, [501], 496.

50 Leonard Cohen, "If It Be Your Will."

51 Ibid.

52 Genesis 3:21.

53 *Genesis Rabbah* 20:12.

54 Glazer, *Mystical Vertigo*, esp. 28-35, 52-70.

55 Daisetz Teitaro Suzuki, *An Introduction to Zen Buddhism* (New York: Grove Press, 1964), 38-47; see also Nagatomo, "Japanese Zen Buddhist Philosophy."

56 On Leonard Cohen and Mount Baldy, see most recently, Liel Leibovitz, *A Broken Hallelujah: Rock and Roll, Redemption, and the Life of Leonard Cohen* (New York: W. W. Norton, 2014), esp. 207, 228-231, 243, 244.

57 The founder of the Sōtō school is known as Dōgen (1200–1254).

58 Shunryū Suzuki-Roshi, "Dharma Talk: Soto & Rinzai,"San Francisco Zen Center, July 1969, accessed 1/17/15, http://suzukiroshi.sfzc.org/dharma-talks/tag/soto-rinzai/.

59 Ibid.

60 Kripal, *Esalen: America and the Religion of No Religion.*

61 Suzuki, *An Introduction to Zen Buddhism*, 53.

62 Ibid., 67.

63 Leonard Cohen, "Boogie Street," in *Ten New Songs* (New York: Columbia, 2001).

64 Suzuki, *An Introduction to Zen Buddhism*, 48-57.

65 Nagatomo, "Japanese Zen Buddhist Philosophy."

66 Suzuki, *An Introduction to Zen Buddhism*, 39, 41, 74.

67 This notion of "an embodied divine fragment" is articulated in Jewish thinking as early as 1602, well before its acclaimed Hasidic rendering in the second half of the first chapter of the *Tanya* by R. Shneur Zalman of Lyady. See *Kli Yakar* Genesis 1:31; ad. loc. 9:20.

68 While citations abound, see for example the desire of Shechem precipitating his rape of Dinah in Genesis 34:3, 8, or the desire for consuming flesh in Deuteronomy 12:15.

69 The origin of this dichotomy in Jewish Mysticism between the bestial soul, or *nefesh ha'behemit*, and the divine soul, or *nefesh 'elohi*, is found in discussions surrounding the bestial soul in the second half of the first chapter in R. Shneur Zalman of Lyady, the *Tanya*.

70 A more sophisticated psychic mapping emerges by the sixteenth century in Safed in Lurianic Kabbalah that posits a five-fold soul system: ". . . inter-inclusive nature of the soul, all five levels of the collective soul are represented in it. In particular, the *yechidah* corresponds to pleasure, *chayah* corresponds to will, *neshamah* corresponds to the intellect, *ru'ach* corresponds to the character attributes, and *nefesh* corresponds to the garments, while the root of the *nefesh* is found already in the lowest of the character attributes, *malchut*." See R. Yitzhak Ginsburgh, *Anatomy of the Soul*, accessed 1/28/15, http://www.inner.org/torah_and_science/psychology/anatomy-of-the-soul/root-of-the-soul.php#_ednref30.

71 See above note 21.

72 Nietzsche, *The Birth of Tragedy*, 4, 8.

73 Ibid., 1, 5.

74 Ibid., 5. See also, Cox, "Nietzsche, Dionysus, and the Ontology of Music," 497.

5. A Question of Pure Consciousness in the Priestly Blessing of Love

1 While his studies are prolific on the *imaginal*, one of the most important book length treatments can be found in Elliot R. Wolfson, *Through a Speculum that*

Shines: Vision and Imagination in Medieval Jewish Mysticism (Princeton, NJ: Princeton University Press, 1994) as well as 58-73, 380-392..

2 Kalman P. Bland, *The Artless Jew: Medieval and Modern Affirmations and Denials of the Visual* (Princeton, NJ: Princeton University Press, 2000); Zachary Braiterman, *The Shape of Revelation: Aesthetics and Modern Jewish Thought* (Stanford: Stanford University Press, 2007); Martina Urban, *Aesthetics of Renewal: Martin Buber's Early Representation of Hasidism as Kulturkritik* (Chicago: University of Chicago Press, 2008).

3 Steven Fine, ed., *Images: A Journal of Jewish Art and Visual Culture* (Leiden: Brill, 2007); Bracha Yaniv, Sara Offenberg, Mirjam Rajner, Ilia Rodov, eds., *Ars Judaica: The Bar-Ilan Journal of Jewish Art* (Ramat-Gan, Israel: Dept. of Jewish Art, Bar-Ilan University, 2005).

4 For example, most recently, see Moshe Idel, "Color in Kabbalah," in *Ars Judaica: The Bar-Ilan Journal of Jewish Art*. Ramat-Gan, Israel: Dept. of Jewish Art, Bar-Ilan University, *forthcoming*.

5 For a more sustained reflection on the challenges intrinsic to the dualism of beauty/ugliness, see Harry Fox, "Poet*h*ics: How Every Jew is a Poet," in Aubrey L. Glazer, *Contemporary Hebrew Mystical Poetry* (New York: Mellen Press, 2009), i–xxxiv.

6 See James Shelley, "The Concept of the Aesthetic," accessed 7/22/15, http://plato.stanford.edu/entries/aesthetic-concept/.

7 I have in mind the Existentialist Aesthetics of Gabriel Marcel and Maurice Merleau-Ponty. On Marcel and Jewish theological philosophy, see Aubrey L. Glazer, "Living the Death of God in the Hope of Words: On Gillman, Jabès, Marcel & Badiou," in *Personal Theology: Essays in Honor of Neil Gillman*, ed. William Plevan and Neil Gillman (Boston: Academic Studies Press, 2013), 220-335. On Merleau-Ponty and Jewish theological philosophy, see Aubrey L. Glazer, "Touching God: Vertigo, Exactitude, and Degrees of Devekut in the Contemporary Nondual Jewish Mysticism of R. Yitzhaq Maier Morgenstern," *The Journal of Jewish Thought and Philosophy* 19.2 (2011): 147-192.

8 Edward S. Casey, "Keep Art to Its Edge," in *Rethinking Facticity*, ed. F. Raffoul and E. S. Nelson (New York: SUNY Press, 2008), 273-287.

9 Ibid., 281.

10 Ibid.

11 Ibid., 285.

12 Ibid., 286.

13 Ibid.
14 Ibid., 273.
15 Ibid., 274.
16 Ibid., 275.
17 Kripal, *Esalen: America and the Religion of No Religion*, 262, 485.
18 Thomas F. Cleary, *Classics of Buddhism and Zen: The Collected Translations of Thomas Cleary* (Boston: Shambhala, 2001).
19 Leonard Cohen, "Not a Jew," in *Book of Longing*, 158.
20 Simmons, *I'm Your Man*, 316.
21 Leonard Cohen, "Lover Lover Lover," in *New Skin for the Old Ceremony* (New York: Sony Music, 1974).
22 Idem, "The Politics of this Book," 291.
23 Yehuda Amichai, *Pa'amonim Ṿe-Rakavot: Maḥazot Ṿe-Taskitim* (Yerushalayim [Jerusalem]: Shocḳen, 1992).
24 Nili Scharf Gold, *Yehuda Amichai: The Making of Israel's National Poet* (Waltham, MA: Brandeis University Press, 2008) 5-7, 20, 22, 38-9, 44-5, 50, 64-5, 69, 70, 72, 74-84, 86-90.
25 Yehuda Amichai, "I Wasn't One of the Six Million: And What Is My Life Span? Open Closed Open," in *Open Closed Open*, trans. Chana Bloch and Chana Kronfeld (New York: Harcourt, Inc., 2000) 7-8.
26 Idem, "A Man in his Life," in The Poetry of Yehuda Amichai, tr. R. Atter Farrar, Straus and Giroux; New York, 2015, 323.
27 Ibid, 324.
28 A few exceptions to this rule ca be found in the following collections, see: Morris M. Faiers teint, tr. Jewish Mystical Autobiographies: book of visions and of secrets, Paulist Press: New York, 1999; Louis Jacobs, tr. Jewish Mystical Testimonies, Schocken Books, New York, 1976. Kripal suggests that mystical texts do two things very skillfully: (1) "rhetorically both reveal and conceal the religious experiences of their authors, and (2) such texts have the power to semantically re-enact analogous 'experiences' in the hermeneutical events of their readings." See Jeffrey J. Kripal, *Roads of Excess, Palaces of Wisdom: Eroticism & Reflexivity in the Study of Mysticism* (Chicago: University of Chicago Press, 2001), 9.
29 Jacob Milgrom, *JPS Commentary to Numbers* 6:27 (Philadelphia: JPS, 1990), 52.
30 Shaul Magid, *Hasidism on the Margin: Reconciliation, Antinomianism, and Messianism in Ishbitzer Rebbe/Radzin Hasidism* (Madison: University of Wisconsin Press, 2003), xviii-xix.

31 Ibid., xvii.

32 Steven S. Schwarzschild and Menaḥēm Kellner, "On Jewish Eschatology," in *The Pursuit of the Ideal: Jewish Writings of Steven Schwarzschild* (Albany: State University of New York Press, 1990), 209-228.

33 b*Niddah* 61b, *s.v. mitzvoth betailot l'atid l'vo.*

34 This recurring motif of the unified will appears over fifty times in the *Mai haShiloah* commentary to the Pentateuch of the Ishbitzer Rebbe, to be discussed below; see Magid, *Hasidism on the Margin*, 205-207.

35 Ibid., 216.

36 *Mai haShiloah*, vol. 1, 51d-52a, quoted in Magid, *Hasidism on the Margin*, 223.

37 Ibid., 217.

38 Ibid., 227.

39 Ibid., 224.

40 Ibid., 233.

41 Ibid., 237-238.

42 This eightfold division of the priestly garbing described in Exodus 28:1-43 consists of the following: (1) the *Ephod* (6-12); (2) the Breastplate of Judgment and the *Urim* and *Thummim* (13-30); (3) the Robe (31-35); (4) the Frontlet (36-38); (5) the Tunic (39); (6) the Headdress (39); (7) the Sash (39); and (8) the Turban (40).

43 This eightfold division of spiritual qualities is divided in the liturgy of the *Shema* as follows: "Endow us with: (1) understanding (2) and discernment, (3) that we may study (4) and teach your Torah with devotion, (5) heed its words, (6) transmit its precepts, (7) follow its instruction and (8) fulfill its teachings in love."

44 R. Mordecai Yosef Leiner of Izbica, *Mai haShiloah, Parshat Tezaveh* (Bnai Brak: Meishor Publications, 5755), vol. 1, 89a.

45 Ibid., *Parshat Nasso,* vol. 1, 146a.

46 The Ishbitzer Rebbe tends to refer to a reconciliation between the exilic messianic consciousness of Joseph and the redeeming messianic consciousness symbolized by Judah. See Magid, *Hasidism on the Margin*, 205.

47 Sri Aurobindo Ghose, *On Himself* (Pondicherry: Sri Aurobindo Ashram, 1972), 102.

48 Idem, *The Divine Life* (Pondicherry: Sri Aurobindo Ashram, 1973), 345. See also Ernest L. Simmons Jr., "Mystical Consciousness in a Process Perspective," accessed 12/24/13, http://www.religion-online.org/showarticle.asp?title=2585.

49 Magid, *Hasidism on the Margin*, 240.

50 This nuanced point of straddling the struggle for pure consciousness in contemplative and mystical Judaism is something that still needs to be redressed in recent popular works; for example, see Jay Michaelson, *Everything Is God: The Radical Path of Nondual Judaism* (Boston: Trumpeter, 2009); Idem, *Evolving Dharma: Meditation, Buddhism, and the Next Generation of Enlightenment* (Berkeley: Evolver Editions, 2013).

6. *Amen* to American Agnosticism

1 Leonard Cohen, "Hallelujah," in *Stranger Music: Selected Poems and Songs* (New York: Pantheon Books, 1993), 347.

2 "Growth of the Nonreligious: Many Say Trend is Bad for American Society," *PEW Forum on Religion & Public Life*, July 2, 2013.

3 Hauke Brunkhorst, *Adorno and Critical Theory* (Cardiff: University of Wales Press, 1999), 59.

4 Ibid., 34.

5 Castoriadis, "The Discovery of the Imagination," in *World in Fragments: Writings on Politics, Society, Psychoanalysis, and the Imagination*, trans. David A. Curtis (Stanford: Stanford University Press, 1997), 213-245, esp. 245.

6 Brunkhorst, *Adorno and Critical Theory*, 36.

7 *Zohar Hadash, Bereishith,* 5d.

8 Abraham Kook, *'Orot haQodesh* (Jerusalem: Mossad haRav Kook, 1963) vol. 3, 106-107. The ecstatic moment of song, *Shir 'El*, is what makes creative thinking possible for Isra'El. For a study of mystical sources on music in the Zohar, see Shiloah, *Nossei Musiqa baZohar: Textim uMaftaihot*, Jerusalem 1977. Compare with Moshe Idel, "Music and Prophetic Kabbalah," *Yuval* 4 (1982): 150-169; idem, "Music in Sixteenth-Century Kabbalah in Northern Africa," *Yuval* 7 (2002): 154-170.

9 Theodor Adorno, *Beethoven: The Philosophy of Music*, ed. R. Tiedmann, trans. E. Jephcott (Stanford: Stanford University Press, 1998), 176-177:

> Relate the end of my study to the teaching of Jewish mysticism about the grass angels, who are created for an instant only to perish in the sacred fire. Music—modeled on the glorification of God, even and especially, when it opposes the world—resembles these angels. Their very transience, their ephemerality, is glorification. That is, the incessant destruction of nature.

> Beethoven raised this figure to musical self-consciousness. His truth is the destruction of the particular. He composed to its end the absolute transcience of music. The fire, which according to his stricture against weeping, is to be struck from a man's soul, is the fire which consumes [nature] . . .

The metaphysics of musical time reveals the transience of these angels created on the second day of Creation as a flaming fire, as well as grass, according to the Zoharic passage Adorno received from Scholem. That original passage does not speak of grass angels *per se,* but rather vacillates between the (im)possibility of such a tenuous symbolic register. That register is what connects the transience of angels to the growing grass being eaten in the Psalm itself as expressed in Zohar III: 217a:

> R. Hiyya opened [the discourse thus]: (Psalm 104: 16) "The trees of the Lord are satiated, the cedars of Lebanon which he has planted," why is it written in the verse prior (Psalm 104: 15) . . . Yet the verse "Who causes the grass to sprout for the beast" (Psalm 104: 14)—these are two thousand ten thousands angels sent as emissaries from the day of creation (Gen. R. 81). These are grass, but why "grass"? [The angels] grow like grass in a world where each day the grass is cut every day, and then grow again as in the beginning. And so it is written, "Who causes the grass to grow for the cattle" (Psalm 104: 14).

10 See for example, Heidi M. Ravven, "Some Thoughts on What Spinoza Learned from Maimonides about the Prophetic Imagination: Part 1. Maimonides on Prophecy and the Imagination," *Journal of the History of Philosophy* 39, no. 2 (2001): 193-214. For a critical re-reading of Maimonides on dreams and prophecy as correlated with the imagination, see Elliot R. Wolfson, *A Dream Interpreted within a Dream: Oneiropoiesis and the Prism of Imagination* (New York: Zone Books, 2011), 109-142; compare with techniques of visualization proffered and practiced by Maimonides's son, see R. Avraham ben Maiumun, *Ham-maspiq Le-ʿovde Haš-Sem (The Guide to Serving God)* (Jerusalem: Feldheim, 2008), 474-479.

11 Paul Ricoeur refers to a "second naïveté" wherein scripture and religious concepts are read as symbols (i.e. metaphorical constructs) to be interpreted "in the full responsibility of autonomous thought." See Paul Ricoeur, *The Symbolism of Evil* (Boston: Beacon Press, 1967), 349-350.

12 Brunkhorst, *Adorno and Critical Theory,* 15.

13 Ibid., 18.

14 For a preliminary attempt at addressing the interworld of colors in Jewish Thinking, see Aubrey L. Glazer, *Contemporary Hebrew Mystical Poetry: How It Redeems Jewish Thinking* (New York: Edwin Mellen Press, 2009), 243-290.

15 Adorno, "Criteria for New Music," in *Sound Figures*, trans. R. Livingstone (Stanford: Stanford University Press, 1999), 179.

16 Ibid., 196.

17 See *Guitar School Magazine*: *For The Practicing Musician* 3.4 (July 1991).

18 Cohen, "Hallelujah," 347.

19 Tanya Luhrman, "Belief Is the Least Part of Faith," *New York Times* (May 29, 2013).

20 J Kameron Carter, "Christian Atheism: The Only Response Worth its Salt to the Zimmerman Verdict," *Religion Dispatches* (July 23, 2013).

21 Fyodor Dostoevsky, *Crime and Punishment,* trans. David Magarshack (Harmondsworth, Middlesex: Penguin Books, 1951), VI: VII:52.

22 See PeterRollins.net/friendly-fire-online/

23 Peter Rollins, *How (Not) to Speak About God* (New York: Paraclete Press, 2006), 166.

24 Aubrey Glazer, *New Physiognomy of Jewish Thinking* (Resling Press: Tel Aviv, *forthcoming*) [Hebrewy].

25 A wonderful introduction to the Kotzker rebbe for the contemporary seeker is found in Abraham J. Heschel, *A Passion for Truth* (New York: Farrar, Straus and Giroux, 1973).

26 Oral communication from Rabbi Morris Shapiro, (JTS: New York, 1994). Compare with Sefer Emeth v'Emunah (Yeshivat Amshinav: Jerusalelm, 2005), n. 645, p. 457; see also Martin Buber, "What Does it Matter to you?" in Tales of the Hasidim: The Late Masters (Schocken Books: New York, 1991), p. 280.

27 Paul's Letter to the Galatians, 2:1-14. For more on Paul's theology within its Jewish context, see Daniel Boyarin, A radical Jew: Paul and the politics of identity (Berkeley: University of California Press, 1994).

28 R. Yitzhaq Maier Morgenstern, *Y"AM HaHokhmah* (Jerusalem: Mechon Y"AM HaHokhmah, 5770), 520b.

29 A. J. Heschel, *Between God and Man* (New York: Free Press, 1997), 81.

30 "*Credo quia absurdum*"—"I believe because it is absurd." See Tertullian, *De carne Christi,* 5:4: The usual implication is that Tertullian believed in Christianity because it was absurd. Some still argue that Tertullian thought nothing of the kind, as evinced in *De Paenitentia* 1:2, but the argument remains weak. See http://www.tertullian.org/works/de_carne_christi.htm (accessed 12/171/14).

31 Bob Dylan, "Highway 61 Revisited" (1965), accessed 12/17/14, http://www.bobdylan.com/us/songs/highway-61-revisited.

32 See R. Baruch Epstein, *Torah Temimah* (Jerusalem: Feldheim Publishers, 1989) Genesis 15: 6.

33 The literature on this incident in Kotzk has been largely shrouded in mystery and/or self-censored. See Joseph Fox, *Rabbi Menachem Mendel of Kotzk: A Biographical Study of the Chasidic Master* (New York: Bash Publications, 1988) 119, 120. Abraham J. Heschel, *Ḳotzḳ: In Gerangl Far Emeśdiḳeyṭ,* 2 vols (Tel-Aviv: *HaMenorah*, 1973); idem, *A Passion for Truth*. For a more satirical rendering of this and other events in Kotzk, see most recently, Menasheh Unger, Jonathan Boyarin, and Glenn Dynner, trans., *A Fire Burns in Kotsk: A Tale of Hasidism in the Kingdom of Poland* (Detroit: Wayne State University Press, 2015).

34 Martin Buber, *Tales of the Hasidim: The Later Masters* (New York: Schocken, 1991), 288-289.

35 *Zohar* III:73a.

36 Thanks to Art Green for reminding me of this story.

37 b Yebamoth 65b, b Ketubot 16b-17a, b Bobo Metzia 13b-24a, b Nedarim 27b.

38 I am grateful to Shaul Magid for being my *havruta* in this shared *derasha*-conversation and for sharing this story and prayer space with me at WLSS (JTSA).

39 Shaul Magid, "Why the Jewish Now (and Future) Can't Be Confined to the Paradigms of the Past," *Zeek* (11/20/14), accessed 12/8/14, http://zeek.forward.com/articles/118426/.

40 Leonard Cohen, "Amen," in *Old Ideas* (New York: Sony Music, 2012).

41 I am referring here to dogmatic misunderstandings that abound from the Skverer transmissions of these teachings. For one example of many: "Faith," said the master Reb Mendel of Vitebsk, "is to believe without reason whatsoever. Anything else leads to an erosion of our pure faith and, ultimately, to heresy." See Shulem Deen, *All Who Go Do Not Return* (New York: MacMillan, 2015).

42 R. Menachem Mendel of Vitebsk, *Peri haAretz,* vol. 1, *Parshat VaYera* (Jerusalem: *Mechon Peri haAretz*, 5774 [2014]).

43 Compare with Ba'al Shem Tov, *Keter Shem Tov Hashalem*, ed. E. Shohat (New York: Kehot Publications, 2004), 3:7–8.

44 R. Menachem Mendel of Vitebsk, *Parshat VaYera.*

7. Nothing as Whole as a Broken Middle *Matzah*

1 Graphic #50, Leonard Cohen Archive, MS 500, Box 64.

2 Pew recently found that 70 percent of Jews say they participated in a Passover *seder* in the past year: see "A Portrait of American Jews," Pew Study (10/1/15), accessed 4/9/15, http://www.pewforum.org/2013/10/01/jewish-american-beliefs-attitudes-culture-survey/.

3 Yiẕhak Yudolov, *Otzar ha-Haggadot* (Jerusalem: Magnus Press, 1997); Yosef Goldman, Ari Kinsberg, and Ephraim Deinard, *Hebrew Printing in America* (Brooklyn, NY: YG Books, 2006), 170; Abraham Yaari, *Bibliography of the Passover Haggadah* (Jerusalem: Bamberer & Wahrman, 1960).

4 Emma Morris, "Haggadot on View at the University of Chicago," *Jewcy*, 4/5/12, accessed 4/12/15, http://jewcy.com/jewish-arts-and-culture/haggadot-on-view-at-the-university-of-chicago.

5 Lambert Zuidervaart, "Theodor W. Adorno," *Stanford Encyclopedia of Philosophy*, accessed 4/12/15, http://plato.stanford.edu/entries/adorno/.

6 Edward S. Casey, *Getting Back into Place: Toward a Renewed Understanding of the Place-World* (Bloomington: Indiana University Press, 1993), xiv.

7 Ibid., xvi.

8 Ibid., xvi-xvii.

9 Idem, *The Fate of Place: A Philosophic History* (Los Angeles: University of California Press, 1996), 255. Compare the paradoxical nearness of *no where* and *absence* with Elliot R. Wolfson, *Giving Beyond the Gift: Apophasis and Overcoming Theomania* (New York: Fordham University Press, 2014), 128-129, 244, esp. 300n2.

10 Ibid., 255.

11 Ibid., 261.

12 Aubrey L. Glazer, "What Does Heidegger's Anti-Semitism Mean for Jewish Philosophy? An Interview with Elliot R. Wolfson on the publication of *Giving Beyond the Gift: Apophasis and Overcoming Theomania* (2014)," *Religion Dispatches,* April 3, 2014, accessed 7/17/15, www.religiondispatches.org/what-does-heideggers-anti-semitism-mean-for-jewish-philosophy. Wolfson's forthcoming sustained study of the correlation of Kabbalah and Heideggerean hermeneutics will require a complete re-orientation of the nature of Jewish studies, in general, as well as Jewish Mysticism in particular.

13 Casey, *Getting Back Into Place*, xiv.

14 Ibid.

15 Ibid., 36.
16 Ibid., 37.
17 Ibid., 198.
18 Ibid., 197.
19 Ibid., 198.
20 Ibid.
21 Ibid., 199.
22 Honneth, *Pathologies of Reason,* 78.
23 Theodor W Adorno, *Minima Moralia: Reflections from Damaged Life*, trans. E. F. N. Jephcott (London: Verso, 1978) [*Minima Moralia: Reflexionen aus dem beschädigten Leben* (Frankfurt am Main: Suhrkamp, 1951)].
24 Brunkhorst, *Adorno and Critical Theory,* 51.
25 Honneth, *Pathologies of Reason,* 81.
26 Ibid.
27 Ibid., 82.
28 Rabbi Adam Scheier and Richard Marceau, *Canadian Haggadah Canadienne* (Montreal: Congregation Sha'ar Hashomayim, 2015).
29 Walter Benjamin, "The Task of the Translator," in *Walter Benjamin: Selected Writings, Volume 1* (1913-1926), ed. M. W. Jennings (Cambridge: Belknap Press, 2002), 261.
30 Sasha Weiss, "A *Haggadah* for the Internet Age," *The New Yorker*, 4/6/12, accessed 4/9/15, http://www.newyorker.com/books/page-turner/a-haggadah-for-the-internet-age.
31 Ibid.
32 Leon Wieseltier, "Comes the Comer," *Jewish Review of Books*, Spring 2012, accessed 4/9/15, http://jewishreviewofbooks.com/articles/92/comes-the-comer/?login=1428599493.
33 Ibid.
34 Ibid.
35 Regarding the inspiration for this haggadah by these "bridge figures" we learn the following about their process: "The two talked and concluded, 'Maybe we're the ones who should be on that bridge, making sure that Canadian Jews can celebrate together,' Marceau said." See Ron Csillag, "First Canada Haggadah Takes Passover North of the Border," *The Forward*, 3/6/15, accessed 4/9/15, http://forward.com/articles/216137/first-canada-haggadah-takes-passover-north-of-bord/#ixzz3Wk7nYaSc.
36 See above, chapter 2.

37 Ron Csillag, "First Ever Canadian Haggadah Has Distinctly North-of-the-Border Vibe," *JTA* (3/5/15), accessed 4/9/15, http://www.jta.org/2015/03/05/news-opinion/the-telegraph/first-ever-canadian-haggadah-has-a-distinctly-north-of-the-border-vibe.

38 Csillag, "First Canada Haggadah Takes Passover North of the Border."

39 Benjamin, "The Task of the Translator," 253-263.

40 Scheier and Marceau, *Canadian Haggadah Canadienne*, 20.

41 Ibid., 31.

42 Ibid., 79.

43 Ibid., 93.

44 Ibid., 33.

45 Ibid., 105.

46 Benjamin, "The Task of the Translator," 262-263.

47 Rabbi Ron Aigen, *Wellsprings of Freedom: The Renew Our Days Haggadah* (Montreal: Congregation Dorshai Emet, 2012), 18.

48 Leonard Cohen, "Democracy," in *The Future* (New York: Sony Music, 1992).

49 Ibid.

50 Ibid

51 Cohen, "Anthem."

52 Ibid.

53 See above, chapter 2.

54 Rabbi Meshulam Feish Segal-Loewy, *'Avodat haLevi: Haggadah shel Pesah* (Boisbriand, Quebec: Kiryas Tosh, 2005), 61a-62b.

8. Falling with Our Angels, So Human

1 Harold Bloom, *Fallen Angels* (New Haven: Yale University Press, 2007), 27.

2 Leonard Cohen, "Angel Eyes," in *Night Magic* (New York: Sony Music, 1985).

3 Bloom, *Fallen Angels*, 29.

4 Leonard Cohen, "Tower of Song" in *I'm Your Man* (New York: Sony Music, 1988).

5 *Tiqqunai Zohar, Tiqqun* 11, 26b, trans. A. Glazer.

6 Zohar III: 165a, Matt, 84n87; I am grateful to Danny Matt for sharing these Zohar passages on the Tower of Song with me.

7 Zohar III: 165a, Matt, 85.

8 b*Hagigah* 14a.

9 Matt, 133n197.

10 Matt, 142n267. Zohar III: 165a, Matt, 523n66.

11 *Lamentations Rabbah* 8, 201.

12 R. Shaul Yedidya Elazar Taub of Modzitz, *Sefer Imrei Shaul*, 309. I am grateful to Shir Yaakov Feit for sharing this source with me.

13 R. Arele Roth, *Sefer Shomer 'Emunim*, vol. 2, *Ma'amar Tzahali v'Rani* (Jerusalem: Yeshivat Toldot Aharon, 5758) 2: 381.

14 Joshua Trachtenberg, *Jewish Magic and Superstition: A Study in Folk Religion* (Philadelphia: University of Pennsylvania Press, 2012), esp. 69-77, 97-103.

15 Moshe Idel, "Enoch is Metatron," *Immanuel* 24-25 (1990): 23-38.

16 Ibid., 233.

17 Ibid., 234.

18 Ibid., 236.

19 Ibid., 53.

20 Moshe Idel, *The Angelic World-Apotheosis and Theophany*, (Tel Aviv: Miskal-Yedioth Ahronoth Books and Chemed Books, 2008), esp. 19-73 [Hebrew].

21 Graphic #54, Leonard Cohen Archive, MS 500, Box 73, January 11, 2004.

22 Cohen, "The Window."

23 For example, see Zohar I: 1a; III: 38a; III: 278b etc.

24 Song of Songs 2:2.

25 Rather than searching for incarnational theology in Catholicism as influence, it seems more fruitful to consider things in a post-secular key. Consider, for example, the rise of Jewish Masons in the process of secularization that comes with the Enlightenment and their eagerness to possess the *Rose-Croix* as well as the complexity of Counter-Enlightenment strains in Masonry; see Christopher McIntosh, *The Rose Cross and the Age of Reason: Eighteenth-Century Rosicrucianism in Central Europe and Its Relationship to the Enlightenment* (New York: SUNY Press, 2012), 176-177; on the motif of the rose and the cross portrayed in Rosicrucianism, see Hereward Tilton, *The Quest for the Phoenix: Spiritual Alchemy and Rosicrucianism in the Work of Count Michael Maier* (1569-1622), vol. 88 (Boston: Walter de Gruyter, 2003), 90, 91, 120, 123.

26 Cohen, "The Window."

27 Regarding my swerving from reading strains of Catholic theology as a meaningful influence on Leonard Cohen, specifically from his nursemaid of youth, see the previous note on the complexity of Jewish Masonry and Counter-Enlightenment strains therein. See Bernard Avishai, "Leonard Cohen's Montreal," *The New Yorker* (February 28, 2015), accessed 2/28/15, http://www.newyorker.com/

culture/culture-desk/leonard-cohens-montreal. Also compare with Alexandra Pleshoyano, "La poésie lyrique de Leonard Cohen: Lieu d'un deployment de la mystique juive," *Theologiques* 18/2 (2010): 163-164. In contradistinction to Pleshoyano's unresolved theological claims about Catholic theology, I follow the work of Wolfson and Magid, whose pioneering scholarship on incarnation in Jewish Mysticism is mirrored within Cohen's lyrical exploration of incarnation in his songs, see for example, Elliot R. Wolfson, "Judaism and Incarnation: The Imaginal Body of God," *Christianity in Jewish Terms* (2000): 239-254; see also more recently, Shaul Magid, *Hasidism Incarnate: Hasidism, Christianity, and the Construction of Modern Judaism* (Stanford: Stanford University Press, 2014). It is no coincidence then that the cover of Magid's recent book features a painting by Chagall, see for example, Marc Chagall, "White Crucifixion" (1938), accessed 2/17/15, http://www.artic.edu/aic/collections/artwork/59426. For the counterpoint to the usage of any kind of incarnational language whatsoever in Jewish Mysticism rather preferring "sonship," see Moshe Idel, *Ben: Sonship and Jewish Mysticism*, vol. 5 (New York: Continuum, 2007), esp. 603, 604.

28 Leonard Cohen, "So Long, Marianne," in *The Best of Leonard Cohen* (New York: Sony Music, 1961).

29 Idem., "Paper Thin Hotel," on *Death of a Ladies' Man* (New York: Columbia, 1977).

30 Idem, "The Law," on *Various Positions* (New York: Sony Music, 1995).

31 Bloom, *Fallen Angels*, 71.

32 Leonard Cohen, "Closing Time," in *The Future* (New York: Sony Music, 1992).

33 Idem, "Ain't No Cure for Love," in *I'm Your Man* (New York: Sony Music, 1988).

34 Idem, "Tonight Will Be Fine," in *Live Songs* (New York: Sony Music, 1973); *Live at the Isle of Wight* 1970 (October 20, 2009)

35 Bloom, *Fallen Angels*, 61.

36 Leonard Cohen, "Amen," in *Old Ideas* (New York: Sony Music, 2012).

37 Bloom, *Fallen Angels*, 63.

38 Ibid., 63-64.

39 Zohar III: 170a-170b, trans. Matt, vol. IX, 123-125n215: "An orphaned song: that is, whose author is anonymous. The newness of this psalm refers to the fact that the angels have not yet sung it, and also to the identity of one particular angel, namely the chief angel, Metatron, who is designated as 'the one who renews his youth.' . . . according the Rabbi Shimon, the heavenly creatures-

hayyot, chant this same psalm while carrying the divine throne. Here, though, the spiritual messenger informs Rabbi Shimon that 'until now, holy angels did not offer[it] in praise.'"

9. "An Appetite for Something Like Religion": *Un*binding the Binding of Isaac, Jesus Christ & Joan of Arc through Zen

1 Leonard Cohen, preamble to *"Show Me the Place,"* Montreal Jazz Festival 2012, accessed 6/15/16, https://www.youtube.com/watch?v=zkOk_r7wTdI (emphasis added).

2 Kripal, *Esalen: America and the Religion of No Religion.*

3 Leonard Cohen, "Got a Little Secret-Live in Auckland Soundcheck," in *Can't Forget* (New York: Sony Music, 2015).

4 Ibid.

5 Jurgen Habermas, "A Reply," 78.

6 *Ladies and Gentlemen . . . Mr. Leonard Cohen*, directed by: Donald Brittain and Don Owen (Toronto: National Film Board, 1965), DVD.

7 Armelle Brusq, "Leonard Cohen: Portrait Spring" (Interview with Leondard Cohen), Mount Baldy: 1996, accessed 4/24/13, https://www.youtube.com/watch?v=HJuJQI0RMiw.

8 Elliot R. Wolfson, "New Jerusalem Glowing," 147-153. Compare with idem, "Afterword: To Pray after Praying/To Dance with No Feet," in *Mystical Vertigo*, by Aubrey Glazer (Boston: Academic Studies Press, 2014), 267-273.

9 Wolfson, "New Jerusalem Glowing," 147.

10 Cohen, *Live in Montreal* (emphasis added).

11 Franz Kafka, Max Brod, and Joseph Kresh, *The Diaries of Franz Kafka* (New York: Schocken Books, 1948), 398.

12 Wolfson, "New Jerusalem Glowing," 119.

13 Idem, "Afterword: To Pray after Praying/To Dance with No Feet," 273.

14 Carl A. Raschke, "Derrida and the Return of Religion: Religious Theory After Postmodernism," 1, accessed 9/9/15, http://www.jcrt.org/archives/06.2/raschke.pdf.

15 Ibid., 2.

16 Jacques Derrida, "Faith and Knowledge: The Two Sources of 'Religion' at the Limits of Reason Alone," trans. S. Webb, in *Acts of Religion* (Stanford: Stanford

University Press, 1998), 1-78; idem, *The Gift of Death*, trans. David Wills (Chicago: University of Chicago Press, 1995), 49; idem, *Acts of Religion*, 92.

17 Moshe Halbertal, *On Sacrifice* (Princeton, NJ: Princeton University Press, 2012).

18 Derrida, *The Gift of Death.*

19 Wolfson, "New Jerusalem Glowing," 119.

20 See note 6.

21 Ibid.

22 Cass Fisher, *Contemplative Nation: A Philosophical Account of Jewish Theological Language* (Stanford: Stanford University Press, 2012), esp. 1-100.

23 Leonard Cohen, "Story of Isaac," in *Songs from a Room* (New York: Columbia, 1969).

24 Lyle Liebowitz, *A Broken Hallelujah: Rock and Roll, Redemption and the Life of Leonard Cohen* (New York: Knopf Press, 2014), 83, 254n13.

25 Ibid., 83.

26 Ibid.

27 Ibid (emphasis added).

28 Leonard Cohen, "Story of Isaac."

29 Ibid.

30 Ibid.

31 Ibid.

32 Ibid.

33 Leonard Cohen, "Show me the Place," *Old Ideas* (New York: Song Music, 2012).

34 Heschel, *Between God and Man*, 81.

35 Cohen, "Show me the Place."

36 Cohen, "Going Home."

37 James Hillman, "Betrayal," *A Blue Fire: Selected Writings by James Hillman* (New York: Harper & Ran, 1989), 281.

38 Zohar I: 119b, trans. Matt, 193-194.

39 Zohar I: 119b, trans. Matt, 193n600.

40 Zohar I: 119b, trans. Matt, 193n601.

41 Martha Hanna, "Iconology and Ideology: Images of Joan of Arc in the Idiom of the Action Française, 1908-1931," *French Historical Studies* 14 (1985): 215-239.

42 Leonard Cohen, "Joan of Arc," in Songs of Love and Hate (New York: Sony Music, 1961).

43 Wolfson, "New Jerusalem Glowing," 103-106.

44 For one of his earliest iterations, see for example Elliot R. Wolfson, "Circle in the Square," in *Studies in the Use of Gender in Kabbalistic Symbolism* (New York: SUNY Press, 1995), 1-48.

45 Wolfson, "New Jerusalem Glowing," 131-135.

46 Leonard Cohen, "Joan of Arc."

47 Ibid.

48 Cohen, "The Window."

49 Cohen, "Suzanne."

50 "Suzanne: You Probably Think This Song is About You: Suzanne Verdal McCallister interviewed by Kate Saunders," BBC Radio 4 FM, June 1998, accessed 9/9/15, www.leonardcohenfiles.com.

51 Leonard Cohen, "Suzanne," in *Songs from a Room* (New York: Sony Music, 1961).

52 "Suzanne: You Probably Think This Song is About You."

53 Wolfson, "New Jerusalem Glowing," 106-122.

54 Leonard Cohen, "Jazz Police," in *Recent Songs* (New York: Sony Music, 1988).

55 See Géza Vermés, *The Religion of Jesus the Jew* (Fortress Press: Minneapolis, 1993).

56 Jason Murray, "Fragmented Absurdity: An Analysis of Leonard Cohen's Jazz Police," accessed 9/9/15, www.leonardcohenfiles.com. See also Levi, *The Aquarian Gospel of Jesus the Christ: The Philosophic and Practical Basis of the Religion of the Aquarian Age of the World* (DeVorss: Los Angeles, 1964).

57 N. Halliwell, trans., "*Synergie* Interview with Leonard Cohen: France-Inter with Jean-Luc Esse," October 6, 1997, accessed 9/9/15, www.leonardcohenfiles.com.

58 Ibid.

59 James Hillman, *A Terrible Love of War* (Penguin Press: New York, 2004).

60 Cohen, "The Future."

61 Heidi Hochenedel, "A Reading of the Future" (1996), accessed 9/9/15, www.leonardcohenfiles.com.

62 Cohen, "The Future."

63 Ibid.

64 "Interview" last modified 1996, accessed 9/9/15, www.leonardcohenfiles.com.

65 "Internet Chat with Leonard Cohen" (October 1991), accessed 9/9/15, www.leonardcohenfiles.com. Compare with Jacques Derrida and Anne Dufourmantelle, Of Hospitality. (Stanford University Press: Stanford, 2000).

66 Moshe Idel, "Music and Prophetic Kabbalah," *Yuval Studies of the Jewish Music Research Centre* 4 (1982), 150-169; Moshe Idel and Shahar Arzy, *Kabbalah:*

A Neurocognitive Approach to Mystical Experiences (New Haven: Yale University Press, 2015).

67 Wolfson, "New Jerusalem Glowing," 143n149.

68 Ibid.

69 Ibid., 144.

70 Pilchan Lee, *The New Jerusalem in the Book of Revelation: A Study of Revelation 21-22 in the Light of Its Background in Jewish Tradition*, vol. 129 (Tübingen: Mohr Siebeck, 2001), 20.

71 Ibid.

72 Ibid., 21.

73 Ibid., 252.

74 Ibid., 253.

75 Celia Deutsch, "Transformation of Symbols: The New Jerusalem in Rv 21:1–22:5," *Zeitschrift für die Neutestamentliche Wissenschaft und die Kunde der Älteren Kirche* 78.1-2 (1987): 106-126; see also, Robert H. Gundry, "The New Jerusalem: People as Place, Not Place for People," *Novum Testamentum* 29, no. 3 (1987): 254-264.

76 Liebowitz, *A Broken Hallelujah,* 83.

77 Cohen, "The Window."

78 Leonard Cohen, "The Window," in *Stranger Music* (New York: Pantheon, 1993), 299-300. Compare with the interpretation of Doron B. Cohen, "Speaking Sweetly from 'The Window': Reading Leonard Cohen's Song," 16-17, accessed 9/9/15, www.leonardcohenfiles.com.

79 Mystical experience is more nuanced than a reductive definition that measures whether the aspirant merges with the divine or not, thus qualifying as a (Christian) mystic or not. This very misguided presumption plagues an otherwise noble appreciation of Cohen's poetics; see Doron B. Cohen's commentary to his recent translation, epilogue, and annotations to Leonard Cohen's *Book of Mercy* a second time into Hebrew: *Sefer Rahamim (Book of Mercy),* Hebrew trans., epilogue and notes (Jerusalem: Carmel, 2015), esp. 72. For more nuanced perspectives on the nature of mystical experience, see Idel and Arzy, *Kabbalah: A Neurocognitive Approach to Mystical Experiences.*

80 Transcending and including alludes to the "Integrative Principle," see Jean Aebser, *The Ever-Present Origin*, 385; 431.

81 *Book of Revelations* 21:23.

82 *Book of Revelations* 21:22.

83 Wolfson, "New Jerusalem Glowing," 146-147.

84 Cohen, "Speaking Sweetly from 'The Window': Reading Leonard Cohen's Song," 16-17; compare with Doron B. Cohen's recent translation, epilogue and [annotations to Leonard Cohen's *Book of Mercy* a second time into Hebrew, see *Ibid, Sefer Rahamim (Book of Mercy)*, 67-135.

85 Cohen, *Book of Longing*, 54. On the Name, YHVH as the locus of the intuitive introvert returning to the collective unconscious, see C.G. Jung and Erich Neumann, Analytical Psychology in Exile: The Correspondence of C.G. Jung and Erich Neumann, ed. M. Liebscher (Princeton University Press: Princeton, 2015), 24-25, 28-30, 32-33, 37, 39-47, 49-50, 65, 68-70, 73, 93, 102, 115, 148, 152, 272-274.

10. Standing Where There Used to Be a Street: 9/11 Post-Secularism & Sacred Song

1 "How shall we sing a song so divine in exile?/Should I forget You, O Jerusalem, may my right hand wither" (Psalm 137:4-5).

2 On this expression first used by *Annaliste* historian, Fernand Braudel, see David Armitage, "What's the Big Idea?" *TLS*, 9/20/12, accessed 12/24/14, http://www.the-tls.co.uk/tls/public/article1129685.ece.

3 For more on the role of the "Third Solitude" in the mystical *imaginaire* of Leonard Cohen, see above, chapter 2.

4 Irving Abella and Harold Troper, *None Is Too Many: Canada and the Jews of Europe, 1933-1948* (Toronto: University of Toronto Press, 2012); Harold Martin Troper, *The Defining Decade: Identity, Politics, and the Canadian Jewish Community in the 1960s* (Toronto: University of Toronto Press, 2010); Lita-Rose Betcherman, *The Swastika and the Maple Leaf: Fascist Movements in Canada in the Thirties* (Toronto: Fitzhenry & Whiteside, 1975); Valerie Knowles, *Strangers at Our Gates: Canadian Immigration and Immigration Policy, 1504-1990* (Tonawanda, NY: Dundurn, 1997).

5 Simmons, *I'm Your Man*, 4 (New York: Ecco, 2012).

6 Ibid., 6.

7 Ibid.

8 Ibid., 72.

9 Ibid., 37.

10 Ibid.

11 Ibid., 113-114.

12 Freda Hawkins, *Canada and Immigration: Public Policy and Public Concern* (Montreal: McGill-Queen's University Press, 1988).

13 Gerald E. Dirks, *Canada's Refugee Policy: Indifference or Opportunism?* (Montreal: McGill-Queen's University Press, 1977).

14 Ibid.

15 B. Shatenstein, P. Ghadirian, and J. Lambert, "Patterns of Observance of the Jewish Dietary Laws (*kashruth*) among Secular Jews in Montreal," *Journal of the Canadian Dietetic Association* (1992).

16 Myer Siemiatycki, "Contesting Sacred Urban Space: The Case of the *Eruv*," *Journal of International Migration and Integration/Revue de l'integration et de la migration international* 6, no. 2 (2005): 255-270.

17 *Yidlife Crisis*, accessed 12/24/2014, http://www.yidlifecrisis.com/video/. I am grateful to Angie Dalfen for sharing these sources with me.

18 Yiddish, Hebrew, and French.

19 Brigit Katz, "Spotlight On: Eli Batalion and Jamie Elman of 'YidLife Crisis'" (October 27, 2014), accessed 12/14/14, http://jewcy.com/jewish-arts-and-culture/spotlight-on-eli-batalion-jamie-elman-yidlife-crisis-montreal#sthash.Xu2SlEQF.dpuf. See also Lawrence J Epstein, *The Haunted Smile: The Story of Jewish Comedians in America* (New York: PublicAffairs, 2002); Phil Brown, "Catskill Culture: The Rise and Fall of a Jewish Resort Area Seen through Personal Narrative and Ethnography," *Journal of Contemporary Ethnography* 25, no. 1 (1996): 83-119; Margaret Malamud, "Brooklyn-on-the-Tiber," *Imperial Projections: Ancient Rome in Modern Popular Culture* (Baltimore: Johns Hopkins University Press, 2001), 191; Rob Drew, "Going Home for All Tomorrow's Parties: Indie Culture, the Borscht Belt, and the Romance of Ruins," *Cultural Studies in Critical Methodologies* 11, no. 5 (2011): 446-452.

20 James A. Beckford, "Public Religions and the Post-Secular: Critical Reflections; SSSR Presidential Address," *Journal for the Scientific Study of Religion* 51, no. 1 (2012):1–19.

21 James Tully and Daniel M. Weinstock, *Philosophy in an Age of Pluralism: The Philosophy of Charles Taylor in Question* (Cambridge: Cambridge University Press, 1994).

22 Charles Taylor, *A Secular Age* (Cambridge, MA: Belknap Press of Harvard University Press, 2007).

23 Taylor, *Sources of the Self.*

24 Idem, "Disenchanment-Reenchantment," *Dilemmas and Connections: Selected Essays* (Cambridge, MA: Belknap Press of Harvard University, 2011), 287-302.

25 Idem, "What Does Secularism Mean?" *Dilemmas and Connections: Selected Essays* (Cambridge, MA: Belknap Press of Harvard University, 2011), 303-325.

26 Idem, "Disenchanment-Reenchantment," 290.

27 Ibid.

28 Ibid., 296.

29 Ibid., 302.

30 Idem, "What Does Secularism Mean?," 303-325.

31 Ibid., 315.

32 Ibid.

33 Ibid.

34 Leonard Cohen, "Born in Chains," in *Popular Problems* (New York: Sony Music, 2014).

35 Ibid.

36 Ibid.

37 For more on A. M. Klein, see Caplan Usher, *Like One that Dreamed: A Portrait of A. M. Klein.* (New York: McGraw-Hill, 1982); Zailig Pollock and A. M. Klein, *The Story of the Poet* (Toronto: University of Toronto Press, 1994).

38 Liel Leibovitz, "The Previously Undiscovered Speech that Launched Leonard Cohen's Career," *The New Republic,* March 29, 2014, accessed 12/24/14, http://www.newrepublic.com/article/117177/leonard-cohens-previously-undiscovered-montreal-library-speech.

39 James E. Young, *The Texture of Memory: Holocaust Memorials and Meaning* (New Haven: Yale University Press, 1993). Compare more recently with Brett A. Kaplan, *Landscapes of Holocaust Postmemory*, (New York: Routledge, 2011).

40 David Simpson, *9/11: The Culture of Commemoration* (Chicago: University of Chicago Press, 2006).

41 Leonard Cohen and Anjani Thomas, "A Street," in *Popular Problems* (New York: Sony Music, 2014).

42 Ibid.

43 Leonard Cohen, "The Failure of a Secular Life," *Flowers for Hitler*, in *Stranger Music: Selected Poems and Songs* (New York: Pantheon Books, 1993), 56.

11. *Never Mind this Neuzeit, Here's Kaddish*: Between the Nameless & the Name

1 Radin, *The Great Celebration,* 20.

2 Allen Ginsberg, "*Kaddish,*" accessed 7/15/15, http://www.poetryfoundation.org/poem/179391.

3 See S. M. Cohen and A. Giser, *The Jew Within: Self, Family, and Community in America* (Bloomington: Indiana University Press, 2000).

4 Reinhart Koselleck, "Is There an Acceleration of History?" in *High-Speed Society: Social Acceleration, Power, and Modernity*, ed. Hartmut Rosa and William E. Scheuerman (University Park: Pennsylvania State University Press, 2009), 113-134.

5 David Cunningham, "A Marxist Heresy? Accelerationism and Its Discontents," *Radical Philosophy* 191 (May/June 2015): 29-38.

6 Undoubtedly, the magisterial study on *Kaddish* in English has already been written; see Leon Wieseltier, *Kaddish* (Knopf: New York, 1998). Wieseltier's reflections on the prayer emerge from his own *Kaddish*, journal which he kept fastidiously during the eleven-month period of mourning marking his father's passing. Wieseltier based his reflection primarily upon dense legalistic and exegetical commentaries only available in Hebrew or Aramaic to the *Kaddish* prayer itself, and so the author is at times resistant and thus hyper-critical of the age and what he sees as Jewish illiteracy in America.

7 Jonathan Tropper, *This is Where I Leave You* (New York: Dutton, 2009); adapted into a film of the same name (New York: Warner Brothers, 2014).

8 For more on influence of the punk ideology on cultural memes, see the prescient analysis in Dick Hebdige, *Subculture: The Meaning of Style* (London: Methuen, 1979).

9 Leonard Cohen, "Never Mind," in *Popular Problems* (New York: Sony Music, 2014).

10 Ibid.

11 Ibid.

12 Zohar II: 105a, *Pritzker Edition*, vol. 5, trans. D. Matt (Standford: Stanford University Press, 2009), 76, slightly altered by myself.

13 Charles Mopsik, *Les Grandes Textes de la Cabale: Les Rites qui Font Dieu: Pratiques religieuses et efficacite theurgique dans la Cabale, des origins au milieu du XVIIIe siecle* (Paris: Lagrasse Verdier, 1993).

14 Known as sphere of divine consciousness called, *Binah.*

15 Zohar II: 105a, *Pritzker Edition*, 76-77n219.

16 See R. Yitzhak Izik Yehudah Yehiel ben Alexander Sander of Kamorna, *Zohar Hai*, Zohar II: 105a (Premsyln: R. Hayyim Aaron Zupnik & R. Hayyim Knalled, n.d.), 139a-b.

17 Leonard Cohen, "Love Itself," in *Ten New Songs* (New York: Columbia, 2001).

18 Cohen, "Never Mind."

19 Anonymous, *Kaddish De'itkhad'ta, Siddur* (my translation).

20 Graphic #28, Leonard Cohen Archive, MS 500, Box 73, ca. December 2003.

12. *Codetta*: A Philosophy of Post-Secular Song in Light of *Piyyut* as a Cultural Lens

1 Casey, *Getting Back into Place*, 246.

2 Ibid., 261.

3 Ibid.

4 Ibid., 300.

5 Ibid., 302.

6 Ibid., 308.

7 On the Hebraic Diaspora See Alan L. Mintz, *Sanctuary in the Wilderness: A Critical Introduction to American Hebrew Poetry* (Stanford: Stanford Univerisity, 2012); See also, Mati Shemoelof, "Creating a Radical Hebrew Culture in the Diaspora", 972 blog (August 19, 2016), 972mag.com/creating-a-radical-hebrew-culture-in-the-diaspora/121470, accessed 9/14/16).

8 Haviva Pedaya, *ha-Piyuṭ ke-tsohar tarbuti: Kiṿunim ḥadashim la-havanat ha-piyuṭ ule-havnayuto ha-tarbutit*; *The Piyyut as a Cultural Prism: New Approaches* (Jerusalem: Van Leer Institute, 2012), 14-26.

9 Theodor W. Adorno, "Perennial Fashion—Jazz" (1953), in *Prisms,* trans. Samuel and Shierry Weber (London: Neville Spearman, 1967), 119-132. Compare more recently with Max Paddison, "The Critique Criticised: Adorno and Popular Music," *Popular Music* 2 (1982): 201-218.

10 Pedaya, *The Piyyut as a Cultural Prism*, 24.

11 Ibid.

12 Ibid.

13 Ibid.

14 Ibid.

15 Some in San Francisco might disagree, as the Jewish learning community refers to its truly blossoming nexus as *Lehrhaus*.

16 *An Invitation to Piyut*, accessed 4/13/15, http://www.piyut.org.il/communities/.

17 Cohen, "Suzanne," 96.

18 Idem, "If It Be Your Will," in *Stranger Music*, 343.
19 Idem, "Who by Fire," in *Stranger Music*, 207.
20 "*Hineni*," in *Mussaf Rosh haShanna, Mahzor Lev Shalem* (New York: Rabbinical Assembly, 2010).
21 Herbert Marshall McLuhan, *Understanding Media* (New York: McGraw-Hill, 1964), 8-9.
22 "In every atom/ broken is the Name." Cohen, "Born in Chains".
23 "*Hineni*."
24 Cohen, "If It Be Your Will."
25 Idem, "Democracy," in *Stranger Music*, 368.
26 Idem, "Closing Time," in *Stranger Music*, 378 (emphasis added).
27 Idem, "Waiting for the Miracle," in *Stranger Music*, 382.
28 I am indebted to Elliot R. Wolfson's locution of "the path beyond the path" delivered for his investiture of the Glazer Chair in Religion (Santa Barbara, University of California-Santa Barbara, 2015).
29 Leonard Cohen, "Come Healing," in *Old Ideas* (New York: Sony Music, 2012).
30 Cohen, "Closing Time."
31 Harold Bloom, *Shakespeare: The Invention of the Human* (New York: Riverhead Books, 1998).
32 Adam Cohen, "Out Of Bed," on *Like a Man* (New York: Rezolute-EMI, 2011).
33 Mark H. Podwal, *Fallen Angels* (New Haven: Yale University Press, 2007).

13. *Coda*: Burning Darker Beyond "You Want it Darker"

1 Leonard Cohen, "Closing Time," on *The Future* (1992).
2 Leonard Cohen, "Closing Time," on *The Future* (1992).
3 Theodor W. Adorno, *Aesthetic Theory*, Tr. Rolf Tiedemann, Stanford, Calif: Stanford University Press, 1984, 490. For further reflections on musical thinking of Adorno, see also Aubrey L. Glazer. *A New Physiognomy of Jewish Thinking: Critical Theory After Adorno As Applied to Jewish Thought*. London: Continuum, 2011.
4 Jacques Derrida, *Adieu to Emmanuel Levinas*. Stanford, Calif: Stanford University Press, 1999.
5 Radin, *The Great Celebration*, 20.

6 *Mahzor Rosh haShannah, minhagai Rosh haShannah*: *"Sh'nehi l'rosh v'lo l'zanav"*

7 I am indebted once again to Wolfson in my thinking through the issue of luminal darkness in Cohen, which he has already explored in Zohar, see Elliot R. Wolfson, *Luminal Darkness: Imaginal Gleanings from Zoharic Literature*. Oxford: Oneworld, 2007.

8 While the most familiar liturgical reference to "the ending being inscribed in the beginning!" is found in Shlomo Alkabetz's renowned *piyyut, Lecha Dodi*, recited weekly for welcoming the Sabbath, there are over two hundred references to this expression in kabbalah and Hasidism.

9 Angie Dalfen (e-mail communication 9/21/16) http://montrealgazette.com/news/local-news/montreal-cantor-collaborates-on-leonard-cohens-new-album

10 I am referring here to a foundational Zen *koan* which asks one to contemplate this question: *What was your original face?* Or sometimes rendered as: *What did your face look like before your parents were born?* See *The Platform Sutra: The Zen Teaching of Hui-neng*, Counterpoint Press, Red Pine (2008), 120.

11 *Maranasati* is a meditative practice of "death awareness" that originates with the Buddha's own teaching. See Larry Rosenberg, "Shining the Light of Death on Life: *Maranasati* Meditation (Part I), Barre Center for Buddhist Studies, Spring 1994. (accessed 10/5/16) https://www.bcbsdharma.org/article/shining-the-light-of-death-on-life-maranasati-meditation-part-i/ It is worthwhile noting that there is a parallel practice in Judaism known as *Hibbut haKever*, literally: "beating the grave". This meditation beckons one to consider after their own death that the Angel of Death beats him in a terrible fashion for his sins. For its earliest iteration in the ninth century, see Rav Amram Gaon, *Seder Rav Amram Gaon*, in *Hilkhot Seudah*, ed. Goldschmidt, Jerusalem, 1971, p. 41, parag. 78). The practice was once so commonplace that it was even included at the conclusion of every meal with the recitation of one of the *Harahaman* verses at the end of Grace After Meals where one prays: "*Harahaman yatzilenu mei-hibbut hakever*", "May the Merciful save us from *Hibbut Hakever*".

12 Elliot R. Wolfson (e-mail communication 9/21/16) http://www.rollingstone.com/music/news/hear-leonard-cohens-hypnotic-new-song-you-want-it-darker-w441274

13 https://philosophynow.org/issues/93/The_Challenge_of_Eternal_Recurrence (accessed 9/21/16)

14 Friedrich Nietzsche, *Thus Spoke Zarathustra*, tr. R. J. Hollingdale, p.234

15 Friedrich Nietzsche, *The Gay Science*, tr. Walter Kaufmann, p.341

16 Kathleen O'Dwyer, "The Challenge of Eternal Recurrence," https://philosophynow.org/issues/93/The_Challenge_of_Eternal_Recurrence (accessed 9/21/16)

17 For timely and thoughtful reflections on this perfect offering, see Jay Michaelson, "Leonard Cohen's New Biblical Dirge Is Among His Best Songs Ever" http://www.thedailybeast.com/articles/2016/09/21/leonard-cohen-s-new-biblical-dirge-is-among-his-best-songs-ever.html (accessed 9/21/16)

18 Murray Baumgarten, "Not Knowing What I Should Think: the Landscape of Postmemory in W. G. Sebald's the Emigrants." *Partial Answers: Journal of Literature and the History of Ideas*. 5.2 (2007): 267-28

19 https://www.britannica.com/art/coda-music (accessed 9/21/16)

20 Leonard Cohen, "Hallelujah", *Stranger Music: Selected Poems and Songs*, 347.

Breaking the Brokenness and the Healing of the Poem: A Brief Meditation

1 Cohen, "If it be your will."

Bibliography

PRIMARY SOURCES:

Scriptures

m Mishna

b Babylonian Talmud

j Jerusalem Talmud

Hebrew Bible (1916 JPS translation)

Exegesis and TORAH commentary

Midrash Rabbah. Translated by M. Simon. London: Soncino, 1939.

Ephraim, Solomon A. *Sefer Keli Yaḳar: Ha-shalem; Perush Raḥav 'al Ha-Torah Be-Ve'ur Ha-Miḳra'ot U-Midreshe Ḥazal.* Bnai Braḳ: Agudat Shelomoh, 1984.

Epstein, R. Baruch. *Torah Temimah Commentary.* Jerusalem: Feldheim Publishers, 1989.

Kabbalah

Zohar Hadash. Translated by A. Glazer.

Zohar, Tiqqunai. Translated by A. Glazer.

Zohar. Translated by D. Matt, 10 vols. Pritzker Edition. Stanford: Stanford University Press, 2006-2016.

Hasidism

Ba'al Shem Tov, R. Israel Eliezer. *Keter Shem Tov Hashalem.* Edited by E. Shohat. New York: Kehot Publications, 2004.

Kook, Abraham I., and David Cohen. *Orot Ha-Ḳodesh.* Jerusalem: Mossad haRav Kook, 1963.

Leiner, R. Mordecai Yosef of Izbica. *Mai haShiloah, Parshat Tezaveh.* 2 vols. Bnai Brak: Meishor Publications, 1995.

Lyady, R. Shneur Zalman of. *Likuṭe Amarim Tanya: ʻim Perush Ḥasidut Mevoʼeret.* Brooklyn, NY: Hekhal Menaḥem, 2006.

Maiumun, R. Avraham ben. *Ham-maspiq Le-ʻovde Haš-Sem (The Guide to Serving God).* Jerusalem: Feldheim, 2008.

Morgenstern, R. Yitzhaq Maier. *Y"AM HaHokhmah.* Jerusalem: Mechon Y"AM HaHokhmah, 2010.

Roth, R. Arele. "Ma'amar Tzahali v'Rani." In *Sefer Shomer 'Emunim.* 2 vols. Jerusalem: Yeshivat Toldot Aharon, 1998.

Safrin, R. Yitzhak Izik Yehudah Yehiel ben Alexander Sander of Kamorna. *Zohar Hai.* Premsyln: R. Hayyim Aaron Zupnik & R. Hayyim Knalled, n.d.

Safrin, R. Hayyim Yaakov, ed. *Shalsheleth haQodesh.* Bnai Brak: n. p., 2003.

------. *Aseereet ha'Aifa.* Premsyln: R. Hayyim Aaron Zupnik & R. Hayyim Knalled, n.d.

------. *Haikhal Berakhah.* Premsyln: R. Hayyim Aaron Zupnik & R. Hayyim Knalled, n.d.

Segal-Loewy, R. Meshulam Feish. *Zemirot 'Avodat haLevi.* Boisbriand, Quebec: Kiryas Tosh, 2010.

------. *Avodat Avodah.* 2 vols. Boisbriand, Quebec: Kiryas Tosh, 2005.

------. *'Avodat haLevi: Haggadah shel Pesah.* Boisbriand, Quebec: Kiryas Tosh, 2005.

Shapira, R. Kalonymous Kalman. *Esh Kodesh.* Jerusalem: Va'ad Hasidai Piacezener, 1990.

Taub, Saul J. E. I, and Shemu'el E. S. Y. Taub. *Sefer Imre Sha'ul: Ha-kolel Me-Imrotaṿ ʻal Yeme Ha-Noraʼim, Moʻadim, Ḥagim Ṿe-Shabatot U-Sheʼar ʻinyanim.* Tel-Aviv: Yiśraʼel Dan Ṭaub, 1959.

Vitebsk, R. Menachem Mendel. *Peri haAretz.* 2 vols. Jerusalem: Mechon Peri haAretz, 5774 (2014).

Leonard Cohen sources

Cohen, Leonard. "Got a Little Secret-Live in Auckland Soundcheck." In *Can't Forget.* New York: Sony Music, 2015.

------. "Born in Chains." In *Popular Problems.* New York: Sony Music, 2014.

------. "Never Mind." In *Popular Problems*. New York: Sony Music, 2014.

------. "Going Home." In *Old Ideas*. New York: Sony Music, 2012.

------. "Darkness." In *Old Ideas*. New York: Sony Music, 2012.

------. "Amen," *Old Ideas*. New York: Sony Music, 2012.

------. "Come Healing." In *Old Ideas*. New York: Sony, 2012.

------. "Show Me the Place." Montreal Jazz Festival. Montreal, 2012. https://www.youtube.com/watch?v=zkOk_r7wTdI.

------. *Live at the Isle of Wight 1970*. New York: Columbia, 2009.

------. "The Street." *The New Yorker.* March 2, 2009.

------. *Book of Longing*. Toronto: McClelland & Stuart, 2006.

------. "By the Rivers Dark." In *Ten New Songs*. New York: Columbia, 2001.

------. "Boogie Street." In *Ten New Songs*. New York: Columbia, 2001.

------. "Here It Is." In *Ten New Songs*. New York: Columbia, 2001.

------. "Love Itself." In *Ten New Songs*. New York: Columbia, 2001.

------. "That Don't Make It Junk." In *Ten New Songs*. New York: Columbia, 2001.

------. "Hallelujah." In *Various Positions*. New York: Sony Music, 1995.

------. "If It Be Your Will." In *Various Positions*. New York: Sony Music, 1995.

------. "The Law." In *Various Positions*. New York: Sony Music, 1995.

------. "Closing Time." In *Stranger Music: Selected Poems and Songs*. New York: Pantheon, 1993.

------. "The Window." In *Stranger Music: Selected Poems and Songs*. New York: Pantheon, 1993.

------. "Democracy." In *Stranger Music: Selected Poems and Songs*. New York: Pantheon, 1993.

------. "Anthem." In *The Future*. New York: Sony Music, 1992.

------. "Democracy." In *The Future*. New York: Sony Music, 1992.

------. "Waiting for the Miracle." In *The Future*. New York: Sony Music, 1992.

------. "Closing Time." In *The Future*. New York: Sony Music, 1992.

------. "The Future." In *The Future*. New York: Sony Music, 1992.

------. "Jazz Police." In *Recent Songs*. New York: Sony Music, 1988.

------. "Un Canadien Errant." In *Recent Songs*. New York: Sony Music, 1988.

------. "Ballad of the Absent Mare." In *Recent Songs*. New York: Sony Music, 1988.

------. "The Gypsy Wife." In *Recent Songs*. New York: Sony Music, 1988.

------. "The Window." In *Recent Songs*. New York: Sony Music, 1988.

------. "Everybody Knows." In *I'm Your Man*. New York: Sony Music, 1988.

------. "Tower of Song." In *I'm Your Man*. New York: Sony Music, 1988.
------. "Ain't No Cure for Love." In *I'm Your Man*. New York: Sony Music, 1988.
------. "Angel Eyes." In *Night Magic*. New York: Sony Music, 1985.
------. *Book of Mercy*. New York: Villard Books, 1984.
------. *Sefer Rahamim (Book of Mercy,* 1984*)*. Hebrew translation and epilogue and notes by Doron B. Cohen. Jerusalem: Carmel, 2015.
------. "Paper Thin Hotel." In *Death of a Ladies' Man*. New York: Columbia, 1977.
------. "Lover Lover Lover." In *New Skin for the Old Ceremony*. New York: Sony Music, 1974.
------. "Who by Fire." In *New Skin for the Old Ceremony*. New York: Sony Music, 1974.
------. "Tonight Will Be Fine." In *Live Songs*. New York: Sony Music, 1973.
------. "Lady Midnight." In *Songs from a Room*. New York: Columbia, 1969.
------. "Story of Isaac." In *Songs from a Room*. New York: Columbia, 1969.
------. "Suzanne." In *Songs from a Room*. New York: Columbia, 1969.
------. *Beautiful Losers*. Toronto: McClelland & Stewart, 1966.
------. *Flowers for Hitler*. Toronto: McClelland and Stewart, 1964.
------. "Joan of Arc." In *Songs of Love and Hate*. New York: Sony Music, 1961.
------. "Love Calls You by Your Name." In *Songs of Love and Hate*. New York: Sony Music, 1961.
------. "So Long, Marianne." In *The Best of Leonard Cohen*. New York: Sony Music, 1961.
------. "Who by Fire." In *The Best of Leonard Cohen*. New York: Sony Music, 1961.
Cohen, Leonard, and Anjani Thomas. "A Street." In *Popular Problems*. New York: Sony, 2014.
"Internet Chat with Leonard Cohen." October 1991. www.leonardcohenfiles.com.
"Interview (with Leonard Cohen)." Last modified 1996. www.leonardcohenfiles.com.

Leonard Cohen Archive:

Cohen, Leonard. Graphic #14. Leonard Cohen Archive, MS 500, Box 64, n.d.
------. "Untitled poem," written on three Takanawa Prince Hotel Bar napkins, 03/20/96. Leonard Cohen Archive, MS 500, Box 64.

------. Graphic #3. Leonard Cohen Archive, MS 500: Box 73, Montreal, 2003.

------. Graphic #39. Leonard Cohen Archive, MS 500, Box 73, January 1, 2004.

------. Graphic #70. Leonard Cohen Archive, MS 500: Box 74, 2003-2005.

------. Hydra small notebook. Leonard Cohen Archive, MS 122: Box 8b, n.d.

------. Hydra small notebook. Leonard Cohen Archive, MS 122: Box 8b, n.d.

------. Hydra small notebooks, Stratford, CT. Leonard Cohen Archive, MS 122: Box 8b: August 19, 1959.

------. Letter from Neal Donner, Cimarron scholar-in-residence, to Leonard Cohen, Oct. 30, 1978. Leonard Cohen Archive, MS 500: Box 64, 1.

------. Letter from Neal Donner, Cimarron scholar-in-residence, to Leonard Cohen, Oct. 30, 1978. Leonard Cohen Archive, MS 500: Box 64, 2.

------. *Lotus Sutra* (1-14), *Heart Sutra* (15-16), *Dharani of Removing Disaster, Dharani of the Great Compassionate One* (17-19), *Dai Segaki* (20-21), *National Teacher Kozen Daito* (22-23), *The Four Great Vows* (24), in *The Rinzai-Ji Daily Sutras.* N.d., n.p. Included with *Mt. Baldy Zen Center Newsletter,* 1975. Leonard Cohen Archive, Box 64.

------. Graphic #21. Leonard Cohen Archive, MS 500: Box 73, December 23, 2003.

------. Graphic #28. Leonard Cohen Archive, MS 500, Box 73, ca. December 2003.

------. Graphic #50. Leonard Cohen Archive, MS 500, Box 64.

------. Graphic #54. Leonard Cohen Archive, MS 500, Box 73, January 11, 2004.

Krull, Kim. "Letter from Kim Krull (Spokane, Washington) to Buddhist America." Leonard Cohen Archive, MS 500: Box 64, 1992-1994.

Mount Baldy Zen Center Newsletter, Issue 7 (Winter 1997). Leonard Cohen Archive, MS 500: Box 64.

Secondary sources

Abella, Irving, and Harold Troper. *None Is Too Many: Canada and the Jews of Europe, 1933-1948.* Toronto: University of Toronto Press, 2012.

Adler, Jerry. "In Search of the Spiritual." *Newsweek* 146 (2005): 46-64.

Adorno, Theodor W. *Negative Dialectics.* Translated by E. B. Ashton. New York: Continuum, 1973.

------. *Negative Dialektik.* Frankfurt am Main: Suhrkamp, 1966.

------. *Negative Dialektik*. Revised translation of Dennis Redmond. 2001. http://www.efn.org/~dredmond/ndtrans.html.

------. *Noten zur Literatur IV.* Frankfurt am Main: Suhrkamp Verlag, 1968.

------. *Ohne Leitbild. Parva aesthetica.* Frankfurt am Main: Suhrkamp Verlag, 1967.

------. "Criteria for New Music." In *Sound Figures,* translated by R. Livingstone, 145-196. Stanford: Stanford University Press, 1999.

------. "Perennial Fashion –Jazz." In *Prisms,* trans. Samuel and Shierry Weber, 119-132. London: Neville Spearman, 1967.

------. *Beethoven: The Philosophy of Music*. Edited by R. Tiedmann. Translated by E. Jephcott. Stanford: Stanford University Press, 1998.

------. *Minima Moralia: Reflections from Damaged Life*. Translated by E. F. N. Jephcott. London: Verso, 1978.

------. *Minima Moralia: Reflexionen aus dem beschädigten Leben.* Frankfurt: Suhrkamp, 1951.

------. *Prismen,* vol. 10a. Berlin: Suhrkamp Verlag, 1955.

------. "On Jazz." In *Discourse* 12.1, translated by Jamie Owen Daniel, 45-69. Center for Twentieth Century Studies. Milwaukee, Bloomington, and Detroit: University of Wisconsin, Indiana University Press, and Wayne State University Press, 1989.

Aigen, Rabbi Ron. *Wellsprings of Freedom: The Renew Our Days Haggadah.* Montreal: Congregation Dorshai Emet, 2012.

Alfasi, Yitzhak. *Torat ha'Hasidut.* 2 vols. Jerusalem: Mossad haRav Kook, 2009.

Amichai, Yehuda. *Open Closed Open.* Translated by Chana Bloch and Chana Kronfeld. New York: Harcourt, Inc., 2000.

------. *Pa'amonim Ṿe-Rakavot: Maḥazot Ṿe-Taskitim.* Jerusalem: Shocḳen, 1992.

Armitage, David. "What's the Big Idea?" *TLS.* Last modified September 20, 2012. http://www.the-tls.co.uk/tls/public/article1129685.ece.

Avishai, Bernard. "Leonard Cohen's Montreal." *The New Yorker.* Last modified February 28, 2015. http://www.newyorker.com/culture/culture-desk/leonard-cohens-montreal.

Aviv, Caryn, and David Shneer. *New Jews: The End of the Jewish Diaspora*. New York: New York University Press, 2005.

Babcock, Donald C. "Little Duck." *The New Yorker*, October 4, 1947.

Bannerji, H. "On the Dark Side of the Nation: Politics of Multiculturalism and the State of Canada." *Journal of Canadian Studies* 31, no. 3 (1996): 103-128.

Beckford, James A. "Public Religions and the Post-Secular: Critical Reflections; SSSR Presidential Address." *Journal for the Scientific Study of Religion* 51, no. 1 (2012): 1–19.

Benjamin, Walter. "The Task of the Translator." In *Walter Benjamin: Selected Writings, Volume 1* (1913-1926), edited by M. W. Jennings, 253-263. Cambridge: Belknap Press, 2002.

Betcherman, Lita-Rose. *The Swastika and the Maple Leaf: Fascist Movements in Canada in the Thirties.* Toronto: Fitzhenry & Whiteside, 1975.

Bland, Kalman P. *The Artless Jew: Medieval and Modern Affirmations and Denials of the Visual.* Princeton, NJ: Princeton University Press, 2000.

Bloom, Harold. *Anxiety of Influence.* New York: Oxford University Press, 1997.

------. *Fallen Angels.* New Haven: Yale University Press, 2007.

------. *Shakespeare: The Invention of the Human.* New York: Riverhead Books, 1998.

Boyarin, Jonathan, and Daniel Boyarin. "Diaspora: Generation and the Ground of Jewish Identity." *Critical Inquiry* 19, no. 4 (1993): 693-725.

------. *Powers of Diaspora: Two Essays on the Relevance of Jewish Culture.* Minneapolis: University of Minnesota Press, 2002.

Braiterman, Zachary. *The Shape of Revelation: Aesthetics and Modern Jewish Thought.* Stanford: Stanford University Press, 2007.

Brenner, Saul. "Patterns of Jewish-Catholic Democratic Voting and the 1960 Presidential Vote." *Jewish Social Studies* 26, no. 3 (1964): 169-178.

Brown, Michael. "Canadian Jews and Multiculturalism: Myths and Realities." *Jewish Political Studies Review* 19, no. 3-4 (2007): 57-75.

Brown, Phil. "Catskill Culture: The Rise and Fall of a Jewish Resort Area Seen through Personal Narrative and Ethnography." *Journal of Contemporary Ethnography* 25, no. 1 (1996): 83-119.

Brunkhorst, Hauke. *Adorno and Critical Theory.* Cardiff: University of Wales Press, 1999.

Brusq, Armelle. "Leonard Cohen: Portrait Spring" (Interview with Leondard Cohen). Mount Baldy: 1996. Accessed April 24, 2013. https://www.youtube.com/watch?v=HJuJQI0RMiw.

Buber, Martin. *Tales of the Hasidim: The Later Masters.* New York: Schocken, 1991.

Bucke, R. M. *Cosmic Consciousness: A Study in the Evolution of the Human Mind.* New York: E. P Dutton, 1901.

Carter, J. Kameron. "Christian Atheism: The Only Response Worth Its Salt to the Zimmerman Verdict." *Religion Dispatches,* July 23, 2013.

Cartwright, David E. "Failure in Berlin." In *Schopenhauer: A Biography*, 336-401. New York: Cambridge University Press, 2010.

Casey, Edward S. "Keep Art to Its Edge." In *Rethinking Facticity*, edited by F. Raffoul and E. S. Nelson, 273-287. New York: SUNY Press, 2008.

------. *Getting Back into Place: Toward a Renewed Understanding of the Place-World.* Bloomington: Indiana University Press, 1993.

------. *The Fate of Place: A Philosophic History.* Los Angeles: University of California Press, 1996.

Castoriadis, Cornelius. "The Discovery of the Imagination." In *World in Fragments: Writings on Politics, Society, Psychoanalysis, and the Imagination*, translated by David A. Curtis, 213-245. Stanford: Stanford University Press, 1997.

Chagall, Marc. "White Crucifixion" (1938). Accessed April 24, 2013. http://www.artic.edu/aic/collections/artwork/59426.

Cleary, Thomas F. *Classics of Buddhism and Zen: The Collected Translations of Thomas Cleary.* Boston: Shambhala, 2001.

Cohen, Adam. "Out Of Bed." In *Like a Man.* New York: Rezolute-EMI, 2011.

Cohen, Doron B. "Speaking sweetly from" The Window": reading Leonard Cohen's Song (Feature: The Philosophy of Martin Buber and His Biblical Hermeneutics: Between Germanness and Jewishness)." *Journal of the Interdisciplinary Study of Monotheistic Religions: JISMOR* 6 (2010): 106-129.

Cox, Christoph. "Nietzsche, Dionysus, and the Ontology of Music." In *A Companion to Nietzsche*, edited by Keith Ansell Pearson, 495-514. London: Blackwell Publishing Ltd., 2006.

Csillag, Ron. "First Canada Haggadah Takes Passover North of the Border." *The Forward.* Last modified March 6, 2015. http://forward.com/articles/216137/first-canada-haggadah-takes-passover-north-of-bord/#ixzz3Wk7nYaSc.

------. "First Ever Canadian Haggadah Has Distinctly North-of-the-Border Vibe." *JTA.* Last modified March 5, 2015. http://www.jta.org/2015/03/05/news-opinion/the-telegraph/first-ever-canadian-haggadah-has-a-distinctly-north-of-the-border-vibe.

Cunningham, David I. "A Marxist Heresy? Accelerationism and Its Discontents." *Radical Philosophy* 191 (2015): 29-38.

Davis, Ann. *The Logic of Ecstasy: Canadian Mystical Painting 1920-1940.* Toronto: University of Toronto, 1992.

Dean, William. *The American Spiritual Culture and the Invention of Jazz, Football, and the Movies.* New York: Bloomsbury, 2006.

Deen, Shulem. *All Who Go Do Not Return.* New York: MacMillan, 2015.

Derrida, Jacques. "Faith and Knowledge: The Two Sources of 'Religion' at the Limits of Reason Alone." In *Acts of Religion*, translated by S. Webb, 1-78. Stanford: Stanford University Press, 1998.

------. *The Gift of Death.* Translated by David Wills. Chicago: University of Chicago Press, 1995.

Derrida, Jacques, and Geoffrey Bennington. "*Circumfession*: Fifty-nine Periods and Periphrases: Written in a Sort of Internal Margin, between Geoffrey Bennington's Book and Work in Preparation" (January 1989-April 1990). N.p., 1993.

Derrida, Jacques, David Shapiro, Michal Govrin, and Kim Shkapich. *Body of Prayer: Written Words, Voices.* New York: Irwin S. Chanin School of Architecture of the Cooper Union, 2001.

Dershowitz, Alan M. *The Case for Israel.* Hoboken, NJ: John Wiley & Sons, 2003.

Descombes, Vincent. "Is There an Objective Spirit?" In *Philosophy in an Age of Pluralism: The Philosophy of Charles Taylor in Question*, edited by Charles Taylor, James Tully, and Daniel M. Weinstock, 96-118. Cambridge: Cambridge University Press, 1994.

Deutsch, Celia. "Transformation of Symbols: The New Jerusalem in Rv 21:1–22:5." *Zeitschrift für die Neutestamentliche Wissenschaft und die Kunde der Älteren Kirche* 78, no. 1-2 (1987): 106-126.

Dirks, Gerald E. *Canada's Refugee Policy: Indifference or Opportunism?* Montreal: McGill-Queen's University Press, 1977.

Dorsey, Brian. *Spirituality, Sensuality, Literality: Blues, Jazz, and Rap as Music and Poetry*, vol. 86. Lafayette, IN: Purdue University Press, 2000.

Dostoevsky, Fyodor. *Crime and Punishment.* Translated by David Magarshack. Harmondsworth, Middlesex: Penguin Books, 1951.

Downing, Michael. *Shoes Outside the Door.* Berkeley: Counterpoint, 2001.

Drew, Rob. "Going Home for All Tomorrow's Parties: Indie Culture, the Borscht Belt, and the Romance of Ruins." *Cultural Studies↔Critical Methodologies* 11, no. 5 (2011): 446-452.

Dylan, Bob. *Highway 61 Revisited.* New York: Sony Music, 1965. http://www.bobdylan.com/us/songs/highway-61-revisited.

Eisen, Arnold. "Limits and Virtues of Dialogue." *Society* 31, no. 6 (September-October 1994): 17-22.

Elman, Jamie, and Eli Batalion. *Yidlife Crisis.* October 27, 2014. Accessed December 14, 2014. http://www.yidlifecrisis.com/video/.

Ellwood, Robert S. *Mysticism and Religion.* New York: Seven Bridges Press, 1999.

Epstein, Lawrence J. *The Haunted Smile: The Story of Jewish Comedians in America.* New York: Public Affairs, 2002.

Evans, Donald. "Mysticism and Morality." *Dialogue: Canadian Philosophical Review* 24, no. 2 (1985): 297-308.

Ezrahi, Sidra D. K. *Booking Passage: Exile and Homecoming in the Modern Jewish Imagination.* Berkeley: University of California Press, 2000.

Fine, Steven, ed. *Images: A Journal of Jewish Art and Visual Culture.* Leiden: Brill, 2007.

Finney, Henry C. "American Zen's 'Japan Connection': A Critical Case Study of Zen Buddhism's Diffusion to the West." *Sociology of Religion* 52, no. 4 (1991): 379-396.

Fishbane, Michael. *Sacred Attunement: A Jewish Theology.* Chicago: University of Chicago Press, 2008.

Fisher, Cass. *Contemplative Nation: A Philosophical Account of Jewish Theological Language.* Stanford: Stanford University Press, 2012.

Foucault, Michel. *Archaeology of Knowledge.* Translated by Alan Sheridan. New York: Pantheon Books, 1972.

Fox, Harry. "Poet*h*ics: How Every Jew Is a Poet." In *Contemporary Hebrew Mystical Poetry*, edited by Aubrey L. Glazer, i-xxxiv. New York: Edwin Mellen Press, 2009.

Fox, Joseph. *Rabbi Menachem Mendel of Kotzk: A Biographical Study of the Chasidic Master.* New York: Bash Publications, 1988.

Garb, Jonathan. "After Spirituality: Introducing the Volume and the Series." In *After Spirituality: Studies in Mystical Traditions*, edited by P. Wexler and J. Garb, 1-18. New York: Peter Lang, 2012.

------. "Contemporary Kabbalah and Classical Kabbalah: Breaks and Continuities." In *After Spirituality: Studies in Mystical Traditions*, vol. 1, edited by P. Wexler and J. Garb, 19-46. New York: Peter Lang, 2012.

Ghose, Sri Aurobindo. *On Himself*. Pondicherry: Sri Aurobindo Ashram, 1972.

------. *The Divine Life*. Pondicherry: Sri Aurobindo Ashram, 1973.

Ginsberg, Allen. "*Kaddish*." Accessed July 15, 2015. http://www.poetryfoundation.org/poem/179391.

Ginsburgh, R. Yitzhak. *Anatomy of the Soul*. Accessed January 28, 2015. http://www.inner.org/torah_and_science/psychology/anatomy-of-the-soul/root-of-the-soul.php#_ednref30.

Giuliano, Geoffrey, and Avalon Giuliano. *Revolver: The Secret History of the Beatles*. London: John Blake, 2005.

Glazer, Aubrey L. *A New Physiognomy of Jewish Thinking: Critical Theory after Adorno as Applied to Jewish Thought*. London: Continuum, 2011.

------. *Contemporary Hebrew Mystical Poetry: How It Redeems Jewish Thinking*. New York: Edwin Mellen Press, 2009.

------. *Fire on the Water*. Toronto, 1994. http://www.vtape.org/video?vi=4275.

------. *Lines of Oblivion*. Toronto, 1992. http://www.vtape.org/video?vi=2176.

------. "Living the Death of God in the Hope of Words: On Gillman, Jabès, Marcel & Badiou." In *Personal Theology: Essays in Honor of Neil Gillman*, edited by William Plevan and Neil Gillman. Boston: Academic Studies Press, 2013, 220-235.

------. *Mystical Vertigo: Contemporary Kabbalistic Hebrew Poetry; Dancing Over the Divide*. Boston: Academic Studies Press, 2013.

------. "Preface to Hebrew Edition." In *New Physiognomy of Jewish Thinking* [Hebrew]. Tel Aviv: Resling Press, 2015.

------. "*Tikkun* in Fackenheim's *Leben-Denken* as a trace of Lurianic Kabbalah." In *Emil L. Fackenheim: Philosopher, Theologian, Jew,* edited by J. A. Diamond, S. Portnoff, and Martin D. Yaffe (Leiden: Brill, 2008), 235-249.

------. "Touching God: Vertigo, Exactitude, and Degrees of Devekut in the Contemporary Nondual Jewish Mysticism of R. Yitzhaq Maier Morgenstern." *The Journal of Jewish Thought and Philosophy* 19, no. 2 (2011): 147-192.

------. "What Does Heidegger's Anti-Semitism Mean for Jewish Philosophy? An Interview with Elliot R. Wolfson on the publication of *Giving Beyond the*

Gift: Apophasis and Overcoming Theomania (2014)." *Religious Dispatches.* Last modified April 3, 2014. www.religiondispatches.org/what-does-heideggers-anti-semitism-mean-for-jewish-philosophy.

Goldberg, Phillip. *American Veda: From Emerson and the Beatles to Yoga and Meditation; How Indian Spirituality Changed the West.* New York: Doubleday Religious Publishing Group, 2010.

Goldenberg, Naomi R. "A Feminist Critique of Jung." *Signs* 2, no. 2 (1976): 443-449.

Goldman, Yosef, Ari Kinsberg, and Ephraim Deinard. *Hebrew Printing in America 1735-1926: A History and Annotated Bibliography.* Brooklyn, NY: YG Books, 2006.

Gordis, Daniel. *Saving Israel: How the Jewish People Can Win a War That May Never End.* Hoboken, NJ: John Wiley & Sons, 2009.

Gordon, Jeremy, trans. *Hineini.* Accessed January 28, 2015. http://rabbionanarrowbridge.blogspot.com/2013/08/a-new-translation-of-rosh-hashanah.html.

Green, Art. *Radical Judaism: Hasidism for a New Era.* New Haven: Yale University Press, 2010.

------. "The *Żaddiq* as *Axis Mundi* in Later Judaism." *Journal of the American Academy of Religion* 45, no. 3 (1977): 327-347.

Green, Kenneth H. *Jew and Philosopher: The Return to Maimonides in the Jewish Thought of Leo Strauss.* Albany: State University of New York Press, 1993.

Greenstein, Michael. *Contemporary Jewish Writing in Canada: An Anthology.* Lincoln: University of Nebraska Press, 2004.

Gross, Terry. "Leonard Cohen: Zen and the Art Of Songwriting." *NPR.* Last modified April 3, 2009. http://www.npr.org/templates/transcript/transcript.php?storyId=102692227.

"Growth of the Nonreligious: Many Say Trend Is Bad for American Society." *PEW Forum on Religion & Public Life*, July 2, 2013.

Guitar School Magazine: *For The Practicing Musician* 3, no. 4 (July 1991).

Gundry, Robert H. "The New Jerusalem: People as Place, Not Place for People." *Novum Testamentum* 29, no. 3 (1987): 254-264.

Habermas, Jurgen. "A Reply." In *An Awareness of What Is Missing: Faith and Reason in a Post-Secular Age*, edited by N. Brieskorn, Jurgen Habermas, Michael

Reder, Josef Schmidt, Ciaran Cronin, et al., 425-427. Cambridge: Polity, 2010.

Halbertal, Moshe. *On Sacrifice*. Princeton, NJ: Princeton University Press, 2012.

Halliwell, N., trans. "*Synergie* Interview with Leonard Cohen: France-Inter with Jean-Luc Esse." Last modified October 6, 1997. www.leonardcohenfiles.com.

Hanna, Martha. "Iconology and Ideology: Images of Joan of Arc in the Idiom of the Action Française, 1908-1931." *French Historical Studies* 14 (1985): 2.

Harris, Michael. "An Interview with Leonard Cohen." *Duel* (1969): 99-100.

Hartman, David. *Israelis and the Jewish Tradition: An Ancient People Debating Its Future*. New Haven: Yale University Press, 2000.

Hawkins, Freda. *Canada and Immigration: Public Policy and Public Concern*. Montreal: McGill-Queen's University Press, 1988.

Hazony, Yoram. *The Philosophy of Hebrew Scripture: An Introduction*. New York: Cambridge University Press, 2012.

Hebdige, Dick. *Subculture: The Meaning of Style*. London: Methuen, 1979.

Hegel, Georg Wilhelm Friedrich. *Georg Wilhelm Friedrich Hegel: Lectures on the Philosophy of Spirit 1827-8*. Translated by Robert R. Williams. Oxford: Oxford University Press, 2007.

Heschel, Abraham J. *A Passion for Truth*. New York: Farrar, Straus and Giroux, 1973.

------. *Ḳotzḳ: In Gerangl Far Emes̀diḳeyṭ*. 2 vols. Tel-Aviv: HaMenorah, 1973.

Heylin, Clinton. *Bob Dylan: Behind the Shades Revisited*. New York: HarperCollins, 2010.

"*Hineni*." In *Mussaf Rosh haShanna, Mahzor Lev Shalem*. New York: Rabbinical Assembly, 2010.

Hochenedel, Heidi. "A Reading of the Future." Last modified 1996. www.leonardcohenfiles.com.

Honneth, Axel. *Pathologies of Reason: On the Legacy of Critical Theory*. New York: Columbia University Press, 2009.

Hori, G. Victor Sogen. "Teaching and Learning in the Rinzai Zen Monastery." *Journal of Japanese Studies* (1994): 5-35.

Horne, James R. "Mysticism Demystified." *Dialogue: Canadian Philosophical Review* 24, no. 2 (1985): 291-296.

------. "Reply to Evans." *Dialogue: Canadian Philosophical Review* 24, no. 2 (1985): 309-312.

Huss, Boaz. *Cosmic Kabbalah: Kabbalah and Western Esotericism in the Writings of Max Theon and His Followers.* Chicago: AJS 44th Annual Conference, 2012.

------. "The New Age of Kabbalah: Contemporary Kabbalah, The New Age and Postmodern Spirituality." *Journal of Modern Jewish Studies* 6, no. 2 (2007): 107-125.

------. "The Sufi Society From America: Theosophy and Kabbalah in Poona in the Late Nineteenth Century." In *Kabbalah and Modernity: Interpretations, Transformations, Adaptations*, edited by B. Huss, M. Pasi, and K. Von Stuckard, 167-193. Leiden: Brill, 2012.

Idel, Moshe. "Color in Kabbalah." In *Ars Judaica: The Bar-Ilan Journal of Jewish Art*. Ramat-Gan: Department of Jewish Art, Bar-Ilan University, *forthcoming.*

------. "Enoch is Metatron." *Immanuel* 24-25 (1990): 23-38.

------. "Music and Prophetic Kabbalah." *Yuval Studies of the Jewish Music Research Centre* 4 (1982): 150-169.

------. "Music in Sixteenth-Century Kabbalah in Northern Africa." *Yuval* 7 (2002): 154-170.

Idel, Moshe, and Shahar Arzy, *Kabbalah: A Neurocognitive Approach to Mystical Experiences.* New Haven: Yale University Press, 2015.

------. *The Angelic World-Apotheosis and Theophany* [Hebrew]. Tel Aviv: Miskal-Yedioth Ahronoth Books and Chemed Books, 2008.

------. *Ben: Sonship and Jewish Mysticism*, vol. 5. New York: Continuum, 2007.

Jacobson, Eric. *Metaphysics of the Profane: The Political Theology of Walter Benjamin and Gershom Scholem.* New York: Columbia University Press, 2003.

Jameson, Fredric. "Postmodernism, or the Cultural Logic of Late Capitalism." *Studies* 29 (1984).

Jeffay, Nathan. "'*Hallelujah*' in Tel Aviv: Leonard Cohen Energizes Diverse Crowd." *Forward.* Last modified September 25, 2009. http://forward.com/articles/115181/hallelujah-in-tel-aviv-leonard-cohen-energizes-di/#ixzz2KLI8BboN.

Jung, Carl Gustav. *Aspects of the Feminine*, vol. 6. Princeton, NJ: Princeton University Press, 1982.

Juteau, Danielle, Marie McAndrew, and Linda Pietrantonio. "Multiculturalism à la Canadian and Intégration à la Québécoise: Transcending Their Limits." *Public Policy and Social Welfare* 23 (1998).

Kafka, Franz, Max Brod, and Joseph Kresh, eds. *The Diaries of Franz Kafka*. New York: Schocken Books, 1948.

Kamenetz, Rodger. *The Jew in the Lotus: A Poet's Rediscovery of Jewish Identity in Buddhist India*. New York: HarperOne, 2007.

Kaplan, Louis. "*Yahweh Rastafari*! Matisyahu and the Aporias of Hasidic Reggae Superstardom." *CR: The New Centennial Review* 7, no. 1 (2007): 15-44.

Katz, Brigit. "Spotlight On: Eli Batalion and Jamie Elman of 'YidLife Crisis.'" *Jewcy*. Last modified October 27, 2014. http://jewcy.com/jewish-arts-and-culture/spotlight-on-eli-batalion-jamie-elman-yidlife-crisis-montreal#sthash.Xu2SlEQF.dpuf.

Kellner, Menaḥēm. *Must a Jew Believe Anything*. London: Littman Library of Jewish Civilization, 2006.

Klein, A. M. "In Praise of the Diaspora." As quoted in Michael Greenstein, *Third Solitude: Tradition and Discontinuity in Jewish Canadian Literature*. Montreal: McGill-Queen's University Press, 1989.

Knowles, Valerie. *Strangers at Our Gates: Canadian Immigration and Immigration Policy, 1504-1990*. Tonawanda, NY: Dundurn, 1997.

Kohav, Alex S. *The Sod Hypothesis: Phenomenological, Semiotic, Cognitive, and Noetic-Literary Recovery of the Pentateuch's Embedded Inner-Core Mystical Initiation Tradition of Ancient Israelite Cultic Religion*. PhD thesis, Cincinatti, OH, Union Institute and University, 2011.

Koselleck, Reinhart. "Is There an Acceleration of History?" In *High-Speed Society: Social Acceleration, Power, and Modernity*, edited by Hartmut Rosa and William E. Scheuerman, 113-134. University Park: Pennsylvania State University Press, 2009.

Kripal, Jeffrey J. *Esalen: America and the Religion of No Religion*. Chicago: University of Chicago Press, 2007.

------. *Roads of Excess, Palaces of Wisdom: Eroticism & Reflexivity in the Study of Mysticism*. Chicago: University of Chicago Press, 2001.

Lacombe, M. "Theosophy and the Canadian Idealist Tradition: A Preliminary Exploration." *Journal of Canadian Studies* 17, no. 2 (1982): 100-118.

Ladies and Gentlemen . . . Mr. Leonard Cohen. Directed by Donald Brittain and Don Owen. Toronto: National Film Board, 1965. DVD.

Laferrière, Dany. *Comment faire l'amour avec un negre sans se fatiguer*. Ottawa: Archambault, 2007.

------. *How to Make Love to a Negro without Getting Tired: A Novel.* Translated by David Homel. Vancouver: Douglas & McIntyre, 2010.

Lee, Pilchan. *The New Jerusalem in the Book of Revelation: A Study of Revelation 21-22 in the Light of Its Background in Jewish Tradition*, vol. 129. Tübingen: Mohr Siebeck, 2001.

Leibovitz, Liel. "The Previously Undiscovered Speech that Launched Leonard Cohen's Career." *The New Republic.* Last modified March 29, 2014. http://www.newrepublic.com/article/117177/leonard-cohens-previously-undiscovered-montreal-library-speech.

------. *A Broken Hallelujah: Rock and Roll, Redemption, and the Life of Leonard Cohen.* New York: W. W. Norton, 2014.

Liebowitz, Lyle. *A Broken Hallelujah: Rock and Roll, Redemption and the Life of Leonard Cohen.* New York: Knopf Press, 2014.

Light, Alan. *The Holy or the Broken: Leonard Cohen, Jeff Buckley, and the Unlikely Ascent of Hallelujah*. New York: Atria Books, 2012.

Luhrman, Tanya. "Belief Is the Least Part of Faith." *New York Times.* May 29, 2013.

Maclean, Adam. *A Commentary on the Rosearium Philosophorum.* Accessed February 15, 2016. http://www.levity.com/alchemy/roscom.html.

Maezumi, Hakuyū Taizan, and Bernard Tetsugen Glassman, eds. *On Zen Practice II*, vol. 2. Los Angeles: Zen Center of Los Angeles, 1976.

Magid, Shaul. *American Post-Judaism: Identity and Renewal in a Postethnic Society.* Bloomington: Indiana University Press, 2013.

------. *Hasidism on the Margin: Reconciliation, Antinomianism, and Messianism in Ishbitzer Rebbe/Radzin Hasidism.* Madison: University of Wisconsin Press, 2003.

------. "Is 'Radical Theology' Radical?" *Tikkun* 25, 2 (March-April 2010): 52.

------. "Why the Jewish Now (and Future) Can't Be Confined to the Paradigms of the Past." *Zeek.* Last modified November 20, 2014. http://zeek.forward.com/articles/118426/.

------. *Hasidism Incarnate: Hasidism, Christianity, and the Construction of Modern Judaism*. Stanford: Stanford University Press, 2014.

Malamud, Margaret. "Brooklyn-on-the-Tiber." In *Imperial Projections: Ancient Rome in Modern Popular Culture.* Baltimore: Johns Hopkins University Press, 2001.

Malino, Jonathan W. *Judaism and Modernity: The Religious Philosophy of David Hartman.* Aldershot: Ashgate, 2004.

Marshall, Tom. "A History of Us All: Leonard Cohen." In *Harsh and Lovely Land: The Major Canadian Poets and the Making of a Canadian Tradition*, 142. Vancouver: University of British Columbia Press, 1979.

------. *Harsh and Lovely Land: The Major Canadian Poets and the Making of a Canadian Tradition.* Vancouver: University of British Columbia Press, 1979.

------. "Third Solitude: Canadian as Jew." in *The Canadian Novel: Here and Now*, edited by John Moss, 147-155. Toronto: NC Press, 1983.

McIntosh, Christopher. *The Rose Cross and the Age of Reason: Eighteenth-Century Rosicrucianism in Central Europe and Its Relationship to the Enlightenment.* New York: SUNY Press, 2012.

McLuhan, Herbert Marshall. *Understanding Media.* New York: McGraw-Hill, 1964.

Meagher, John C. *The Truing of Christianity: Visions of Life and Thought for the Future.* New York: Doubleday, 1990.

Michaelson, Jay. *Everything Is God: The Radical Path of Nondual Judaism.* Boston: Trumpeter, 2009.

------. *Evolving Dharma: Meditation, Buddhism, and the Next Generation of Enlightenment.* Berkeley: Evolver Editions, 2013.

Milgrom, Jacob. *JPS Commentary to Numbers* 6:27. Philadelphia: JPS, 1990.

Monson, Ingrid. "Oh Freedom: George Russell, John Coltrane, and Modal Jazz." In *The Course of Performance: Studies in the World of Musical Improvisation,* edited by B. Netti and M. Russell, 149-168. Chicago: University of Chicago Press, 1998.

Mopsik, Charles. *Les Grandes Textes de la Cabale: Les Rites qui Font Dieu; Pratiques religieuses et efficacite theurgique dans la Cabale, des origins au milieu du XVIIIe siecle.* Paris: Lagrasse Verdier, 1993.

Morris, Emma. "Haggadot on View at the University of Chicago." *Jewcy.* Last modified April 5, 2012. http://jewcy.com/jewish-arts-and-culture/haggadot-on-view-at-the-university-of-chicago.

Moscowitz, David. "Does 'Radical Jewish Culture' Produce Radical Jewish Rhetoric?" *Studies in American Jewish Literature* (2002): 162-171.

Mount, Nicolas James. *When Canadian Literature Moved to New York*. Toronto: University of Toronto Press, 2005.

Murray, Jason. "Fragmented Absurdity: An Analysis of Leonard Cohen's Jazz Police." Accessed September 9, 2015. www.leonardcohenfiles.com.

Myers, Jody Elizabeth. "The Kabbalah Centre and Contemporary Spirituality." *Religion Compass* 2, no. 3 (2008): 409-420.

------. *Kabbalah and the Spiritual Quest: The Kabbalah Centre in America*. Westport, CT: Praeger Publishers, 2007.

Nagatomo, Shigenori. "Japanese Zen Buddhist Philosophy." In *Stanford Encyclopedia of Philosophy.* http://plato.stanford.edu/entries/japanese-zen/.

Nasgaard, Roald. *The Mystic North: Symbolist Landscape Painting in Northern Europe and North America 1890-1940*. Toronto: University of Toronto/AGO, 1984.

Nelson, Howard. "Richard Maurice Bucke." *The Walt Whitman Archive*. Accessed March 1, 2013. http://whitmanarchive.org/criticism/disciples/bucke/biography/anc.00247.html.

Nietzsche, Friedrich Wilhelm. *The Birth of Tragedy and the Genealogy of Morals* (1872), vol. 81. Edited and translated by Walter Kaufmann. New York: Modern Library, 1967.

------. *Twilight of the Idols.* In *The Portable Nietzsche,* edited by Walter Kaufmann, 33. New York: Viking Press, 1954.

Novak, David. *Zionism and Judaism: A New Theory*. New York: Cambridge University Press, 2015.

------. "Zionism and Jewish Theology." Lecture, The Tikvah Institute for Jewish Thought, New York, March 10, 2011.

Ondaatje, Michael. *Leonard Cohen: Canadian Writers Number 5*. Toronto: McClelland and Stewart Limited, 1970.

Oppenheimer, Mark. "Joshu Sasaki, Rinzai Zen Master, Dies at 107: The Influential Teacher Leaves a Mixed Legacy." Accessed January 6, 2014. http://tricycle.org/trikedaily/joshu-sasaki-roshi-rinzai-zen-master-dies-107/.

Paddison, Max. "The Critique Criticised: Adorno and Popular Music." *Popular Music* 2 (1982): 201-218.

Paglia, Camille. "Cults and Cosmic Consciousness: Religious Visions in the American 1960s." *Arion Austin Then Boston* 10 (2003): 57-112.

Palmer, Parker J. *Let Your Life Speak: Listening for the Voice of Vocation*. San Francisco: Jossey-Bass, 2000.

Pedaya, Haviva. *Ha-Piyuṭ ke-tsohar tarbuti: Kiṿunim ḥadashim la-havanat ha-piyuṭ ule-havnayuto ha-tarbutit*; *The Piyyut as a Cultural Prism: New Approaches*. Jerusalem: Van Leer Institute, 2012.

Pleshoyano, Alexandra. "La poésie lyrique de Leonard Cohen: Lieu d'un déploiement de la mystique juive." *Théologiques* 18, no. 2 (2010): 163-186.

Podwal, Mark H. *Fallen Angels*. New Haven: Yale University Press, 2007.

Pollock, Zailig. *A. M. Klein: The Story of the Poet*. Toronto: University of Toronto Press, 1994.

"Portrait of American Jews, A." Pew Study. October 1, 2013. http://www.pewforum.org/2013/10/01/jewish-american-beliefs-attitudes-culture-survey/.

Radin, Yoshin David, ed. *The Great Celebration: A Commemorative Album Published on the Occasion of Joshu Sasaki Roshi's 85th Birthday and 30th Year Teaching Zen in America*. Los Angeles: Rinzai-ji, 1992.

Raschke, Carl A. "Derrida and the Return of Religion: Religious Theory After Postmodernism." Accessed September 9, 2015. http://www.jcrt.org/archives/06.2/raschke.pdf.

Ravven, Heidi M. "Some Thoughts on What Spinoza Learned from Maimonides about the Prophetic Imagination: Part 1. Maimonides on Prophecy and the Imagination." *Journal of the History of Philosophy* 39, no. 2 (2001): 193-214.

Redding, Paul. "Georg Wilhem Friedrich Hegel." *Stanford Encyclopedia of Philosophy.* Accessed January 18, 2015. http://plato.stanford.edu/entries/hegel/.

Ricoeur, Paul. *The Symbolism of Evil*. Boston: Beacon Press, 1967.

Robinson, Ira. "The Bouchard-Taylor Commission and the Jewish Community of Quebec in Historical Perspective." In *Religion, Culture and the State: Reflections on the Bouchard-Taylor Report*, edited by Howard Adelman and Pierre Anctil, 58-68. Toronto: University of Toronto Press, 2011.

------. "Kabbalist and Communal Leader: Rabbi Yudel Rosenberg and the Canadian Jewish Community." *Canadian Jewish Studies* 1 (1993): 41-58.

Rollins, Peter. *How (Not) to Speak About God*. New York: Paraclete Press, 2006.

Royall, Frédéric. *Contemporary French Cultures and Societies*. Modern French Identities 26. Bern: Peter Lang, 2004.

Rumi, Jalāl, al-Dīn, and E. H. Whinfield. *Masnavi I Ma'navi: Teachings of Rumi; The Spiritual Couplets of Mauláná Jalálu-'d-Dín Muhammad I Rúmí.* London: Octagon Press, 1994.

Saltzman, Paul. *The Beatles in Rishikesh.* New York: Viking Press, 2001.

Sasaki Roshi, Joshu. *Buddha Is the Center of Gravity.* Questa, NM: Lama Foundation, 1974.

Saunders, Kate. "Suzanne: You Probably Think This Song is About You: Suzanne Verdal McCallister." *BBC Radio 4 FM.* Last modified June 1998. leonardcohenfiles.com.

Scharf Gold, Nili. *Yehuda Amichai: The Making of Israel's National Poet.* Waltham, MA: Brandeis University Press, 2008.

Scheier, Rabbi Adam, and Richard Marceau. *Canadian Haggadah Canadienne.* Montreal: Congregation Sha'ar Hashomayim, 2015.

Scholem, Gershom. "*Shekhinah*: The Feminine Element in Divinity." In *On the Mystical Shape of the Godhead: Basic Concepts in the Kabbalah,* foreword by Joseph Dan, translated by Joachim Neugroschel, edited by Jonathan Chipman, 140-196. New York: Schocken Books, 1991.

------. *Major Trends in Jewish Mysticism.* New York: Schocken Books, 1947.

Scholz, Barbara C. Francis, Jeffry Pelletier, and Geoffrey K. Pullum. "Philosophy of Linguistics." *Stanford Encyclopedia of Philosophy.* Accessed January 18, 2015. http://plato.stanford.edu/entries/linguistics/.

Schopenhauer, Arthur. *The World as Will and Idea,* vol. 1. Project Gutenberg. Accessed January 19, 2015.
http://www.gutenberg.org/files/38427/38427-pdf.pdf.

Shwartz, Dov. "Editorship Vs Authorship/
עריכה מול יצירה (עוד על עריכת "אורות הקודש" לרב קוק)."
Daat: A Journal of Jewish Philosophy & Kabbalah/
דעת: כתב-עת לפילוסופיה יהודית וקבלה. (1990): 87-92.

Schwarzschild, Steven S. *The Pursuit of the Ideal: Jewish Writings of Steven Schwarzschild.* Edited by Menaḥēm Kellner. Albany: State University of New York Press, 1990.

Segal, Abraham. "The Relation between Lurianic Kabbalah and Hasidism in the Thought of R. Yishaq of Komarno." In *Kabbalah: A Journal for the Study of Jewish Mystical Texts,* edited by Daniel Abrams and Avraham Elqayam, vol. 15, 305-334. Los Angeles: Cherub Press, 2006.

Selinger, Eric Murphy. "*Shekhinah* in America." In *Jewish American Poetry: Poems, Commentary, and Reflections,* edited by Jonathan Barron and Eric Murphy Selinger, 250-271. Lebanon, NH: University Press of New England, 2000.

Senzaki, Nyogen, Sōen Nakagawa, Eidō Shimano, and Louis D. Nordstrom. *Namu Dai Bosa: A Transmission of Zen Buddhism to America.* New York: Theatre Arts Books, 1976.

Shaffir, William. "Hassidic Jews and Quebec Politics." *Jewish Journal of Sociology* 25 (1983): 105-118.

Shaffir, William, and Justin Lewis. "Tosh, Between Earth and Moon: A Hasidic Rebbe's Followers and His Teachings." In *From Antiquity to the Post-Modern World: Contemporary Jewish Studies in Canada,* edited by Daniel Maoz and Andrea Gondos, 137-169. Newcastle upon Tyne: Cambridge Scholars Publishing, 2011.

Shatenstein, B., P. Ghadirian, and J. Lambert. "Patterns of Observance of the Jewish Dietary Laws (*kashruth*) among Secular Jews in Montreal." *Journal of the Canadian Dietetic Association* 53, no. 3 (1992): 198.

Shelley, James. "The Concept of the Aesthetic." Accessed July 22, 2015. http://plato.stanford.edu/entries/aesthetic-concept/.

Shiloah, Amnon, Ruth Tene, and Lea Shalem. *Nośe Musiḳah Ba-Zohar: Ṭeksṭim U-Mafteḥot.* Yerushalayim: Hotsa'at sefarim 'a. sh. Y.L Magnes, ha-Universiṭah ha-'Ivrit, 1977.

Shunryū Suzuki-Roshi. "Dharma Talk: Soto & Rinzai." San Francisco Zen Center. July 1969. Accessed January 17, 2015. http://suzukiroshi.sfzc.org/dharma-talks/tag/soto-rinzai/.

Siemiatycki, Myer. "Contesting Sacred Urban Space: The Case of the *Eruv.*" *Journal of International Migration and Integration/Revue de l'integration et de la migration international* 6, no. 2 (2005): 255-270.

Simmons, Ernest L. Jr. "Mystical Consciousness in a Process Perspective." Accessed December 24, 2013. http://www.religion-online.org/showarticle.asp?title=2585.

Simmons, Sylvie. *I'm Your Man: The Life of Leonard Cohen.* New York: HarperCollins, 2012.

Simpson, David. *9/11: The Culture of Commemoration.* Chicago: University of Chicago Press, 2006.

Slobin, Mark. "The Neo-Klezmer Movement and Euro-American Musical Revivalism." *The Journal of American Folklore* 97, no. 383 (1984): 98-104.

Sniderman, Paul M. David, A. Northrup, Joseph F. Fletcher, Peter H. Russell, et al. "Psychological and Cultural Foundations of Prejudice: The Case of Anti-Semitism in Quebec." *Canadian Review of Sociology/Revue Canadienne De Sociologie* 30, no. 2 (1993): 242-270.

Strauss, Leo. *Persecution and the Art of Writing*. Glencoe, IL: Free Press, 1952.

Suzuki, Daisetz Teitaro. *An Introduction to Zen Buddhism*. New York: Grove Press, 1964.

Suzuki, Shunryu. *Not Always So: Practicing the True Spirit of Zen*. New York: HarperOne, 2003.

Taylor, Charles. *Dilemmas and Connections: Selected Essays*. Cambridge, MA: Belknap Press of Harvard University, 2011.

------. *A Secular Age*. Cambridge, MA: Belknap Press of Harvard University Press, 2007.

------. *Hegel*. Cambridge: Cambridge University Press, 1975.

------. *Sources of the Self: The Making of the Modern Identity*. Cambridge, MA: Harvard University Press, 1989.

Tertullian. *De carne Christi*. 11th century Payerne MS, Codex Paterniacensis 439 (P). Accessed December 17, 2014. http://www.tertullian.org/works/de_carne_christi.htm.

------. *Tertullien: De Paenitentia. De Pudicitia. Texte Latin, Traduction Française*. Translated by Pierre Labriolle. Paris: A. Picard, 1906. Accessed December 17, 2014. http://www.tertullian.org/works/de_carne_christi.htm.

Theosophy, vol. 12, Issues 1-7. New York: Theosophical Society, 1896.

This Is Where I Leave You. Directed by Sean Levy, written by Jonathan Tropper. New York: Warner Brothers, 2014. DVD.

Tilton, Hereward. *The Quest for the Phoenix: Spiritual Alchemy and Rosicrucianism in the Work of Count Michael Maier (1569-1622)*, vol. 88. Boston: Walter de Gruyter, 2003.

Trachtenberg, Joshua. *Jewish Magic and Superstition: A Study in Folk Religion*. Philadelphia: University of Pennsylvania Press, 2012.

Troper, Harold Martin. *The Defining Decade: Identity, Politics, and the Canadian Jewish Community in the 1960s*. Toronto: University of Toronto Press, 2010.

Tropper, Jonathan. *This Is Where I Leave You*. New York: Dutton, 2009

Tully, James, and Daniel M. Weinstock. *Philosophy in an Age of Pluralism: The Philosophy of Charles Taylor in Question*. Cambridge: Cambridge University Press, 1994.

Unger, Menasheh. *A Fire Burns in Kotsk: A Tale of Hasidism in the Kingdom of Poland.* Translated by Jonathan Boyarin, and Glenn Dynner. Detroit: Wayne State University Press, 2015.

Urban, Martina. *Aesthetics of Renewal: Martin Buber's Early Representation of Hasidism as Kulturkritik*. Chicago: University of Chicago Press, 2008.

Usher, Caplan. *Like One that Dreamed: A Portrait of A. M. Klein*. New York: McGraw-Hill, 1982.

Varley, Christopher. *The Canadian Encyclopedia, s.v.* "Group of Seven." Last modified March 4, 2015. http://www.thecanadianencyclopedia.com/articles/group-of-seven.

Vitello, Paul. "Joshu Sasaki, 107, Tainted Zen Master." *New York Times*. Last modified August 4, 2014. http://www.nytimes.com/2014/08/05/us/joshu-sasaki-a-zen-master-tarnished-by-abuse-claims-dies-at-107.html?_r=0.

Wagar, Samuel E. C. "Theosophical Socialists in the 1920s Okanagan: Jack Logie's Social Issues Summer Camps." Master's thesis, Burnaby, Simon Fraser University, 2005.

Weiss, Sasha. "A *Haggadah* for the Internet Age." *The New Yorker.* April 6, 2012. http://www.newyorker.com/books/page-turner/a-haggadah-for-the-internet-age.

Wieseltier, Leon. "Comes the Comer." *Jewish Review of Books.* Spring 2012. http://jewishreviewofbooks.com/articles/92/comes-the-comer/?login=1428599493.

------. *Kaddish*. Knopf: New York, 1998.

Wolf, Rabbi Daniel. "*Machshevet Yisrael*—Survival or Endurance?" *ATID* (2008). http://www.atid.org/journal/my/docs/wolf5768.pdf.

Wolfson, Elliot R. "Afterword: To Pray after Praying/To Dance with No Feet." In *Mystical Vertigo*, by Aubrey Glazer, 267-273. Boston: Academic Studies Press, 2014.

------. "Beyond Good and Evil: Hypernomianism, Transmorality, and Kabbalistic Ethics." In *Crossing Boundaries: Essays on the Ethical Status of Mysticism*, edited by G. W. Barnard and J. J. Kripal, 103-156. New York: Seven Bridges Press, 2002.

------. "Beyond Good and Evil: Hypernomian Transmorality and Delimiting the Limit." In *Venturing Beyond: Law and Morality in Kabbalistic Mysticism*, 186-285. Oxford: Oxford University Press, 2006.

------. "Circle in the Square." In *Studies in the Use of Gender in Kabbalistic Symbolism*, 1-48. New York: SUNY Press, 1995.

------. "Divine Suffering and the Hermeneutics of Reading: Philosophical Reflections on Lurianic Mythology." *Suffering Religion* (2002): 101-162.

------. "Judaism and Incarnation: The Imaginal Body of God." In *Christianity in Jewish Terms*, ed. Tikva Simone Frymer-Kensky, 239-253. Boulder, CO: Westview Press, 2000.

------. "New Jerusalem Glowing: Songs and Poems of Leonard Cohen in a Kabbalistic Key." *Kabbalah: Journal for the Study of Jewish Mystical Texts* 15 (2006): 105-153.

------. "Occultation of the Feminine and the Body of Secrecy in Medieval Kabbalah." In *Rending the Veil: Concealment and Secrecy in the History of Religions*, 113-154. New York: Seven Bridges Press, 1999.

------. "Path Beyond the Path: Investiture Speech for the Glazer Chair in Religion." Lecture. Santa Barbara, University of California Santa Barbara, 2015.

------. "The Cut that Binds: Time, Memory, and the Ascetic Impulse." In *God's Voice from the Void: Old and New Studies in Bratslav Hasidism*, edited by Shaul Magid, 3-9. Albany: State University of New York Press, 2002.

------. "Walking as a Sacred Duty: Theological Transformation of Social Reality in Early Hasidism." In *Along the Path: Studies in Kabbalistic Myth*, 89-110. New York: SUNY Press, 1995.

------. *Alef-Mem-Tau*: *Kabbalistic Musings on Time, Truth, and Death*. Berkeley: University of California Press, 2006.

------. *Giving Beyond the Gift: Apophasis and Overcoming Theomania*. New York: Fordham University Press, 2014.

------. *Luminal Darkness: Imaginal Gleanings From Zoharic Literature*. London: Oneworld Publications Limited, 2007.

------. *Through a Speculum that Shines: Vision and Imagination in Medieval Jewish Mysticism*. Princeton, NJ: Princeton University Press, 1994.

------. *Venturing Beyond: Law and Morality in Kabbalistic Mysticism.* Oxford University Press: New York, 2006.

------. *A Dream Interpreted within a Dream: Oneiropoiesis and the Prism of Imagination*. New York: Zone Books, 2011.

Wolfson, Elliot R., and Aaron W. Hughes. *New Directions in Jewish Philosophy*. Bloomington: Indiana University Press, 2009.

Yaari, Abraham. *Bibliography of the Passover Haggadah from the Earliest Printed Edition to 1960: With Twenty-Five Reproductions from Rare Editions and a Facsimile of a Unique Copy of the First Printed Haggadah in the Jewish National and University Library, Jerusalem*. Jerusalem: Bamberger & Wahrman, 1960.

Yaniv, Bracha, Sara Offenberg, Mirjam Rajner, Ilia Rodov, eds. *Ars Judaica: The Bar-Ilan Journal of Jewish Art*. Ramat-Gan: Department of Jewish Art, Bar-Ilan University, 2005.

Young, James E. *The Texture of Memory: Holocaust Memorials and Meaning*. New Haven: Yale University Press, 1993.

Yudolov, Yiz̲ḥak. *'Otz̲ar Ha-Haggadot: Bibliografiah Šel Hagadot Pesaḥ Me-Rešit Ha-Defus Ha-ʿivri ʿad Šenat Tš"k [1960]*. Jerusalem: Magnes Press, 1997.

Zipperstein, Steven J. *Elusive Prophet: Ahad Ha'am and the Origins of Zionism*. Berkeley: University of California Press, 1993.

Žižek, Slavoj. *Absolute Recoil: Towards a New Foundation of Dialectical Materialism*. New York: Verso, 2014.

Zuidervaart, Lambert. "Theodor W. Adorno." *Stanford Encyclopedia of Philosophy*. Last modified October 26, 2015. http://plato.stanford.edu/entries/adorno/.

Index

Index of song titles

CPSIA information can be obtained
at www.ICGtesting.com
Printed in the USA
LVOW13s1752271217
560963LV00002B/175/P